Our Daily Bread

Our

Geoff Mann

Daily Bread

*Wages, Workers, and
the Political Economy
of the American West*

THE UNIVERSITY OF NORTH CAROLINA PRESS
Chapel Hill

© 2007 The University of North Carolina Press
All rights reserved
Manufactured in the United States of America
Designed and typeset in Plantin, Block, and Melior
by Eric M. Brooks

The paper in this book meets the guidelines
for permanence and durability of the Committee
on Production Guidelines for Book Longevity
of the Council on Library Resources.

Library of Congress Cataloging-in-Publication Data
Mann, Geoff.
Our daily bread: wages, workers, and the political
economy of the American west / Geoff Mann.
   p. cm. — (Cultural studies of the United States)
Includes bibliographical references and index.
ISBN 978-0-8078-3134-2 (cloth: alk. paper)
ISBN 978-0-8078-5831-8 (pbk.: alk. paper)
1. Working class — West (U.S.) — History —
20th century. 2. West (U.S.) — Economic policy —
20th century. I. Title.
HD8072.M266   2007
331.2'97809041 — dc22   2007004541

cloth   11 10 09 08 07   5 4 3 2 1
paper   11 10 09 08 07   5 4 3 2 1

For Michelle, my beautiful lady,

and for our crazy boys

Out of burlap sacks, out of bearing butter,

Out of black bean and wet slate bread,

Out of acids of rage, the candor of tar,

Out of creosote, gasoline, drive shafts, wooden dollies,

They Lion grow.

Philip Levine, "They Feed They Lion"

Contents

Preface

In the middle of winter, 1919, a brief news item appeared on page 3 of the *Yreka Journal,* a small-town newspaper in Siskiyou County, California. The county is in the northernmost part of the state, adjacent to Oregon, and since both southern Oregon and northern California were (and are) timber country, there was always a constant flow of people, money, and technology across the state line. The newspaper story, then, came as no great surprise to its readers, even if the jocular tone hinted at more serious movements in the region. Under the heading "I.W.W. Influx Planned," the *Journal* printed the following account of recent events in the nearby mill town of Hornbrook:

> On what appears to be very good authority, it is rumoured that unless their plans are changed a mob of I.W.W.'s now organizing in southern Oregon will shortly invade Northern California. Whether or not these undesirables contemplate creating disturbances of any kind cannot be learned, but Siskiyou peace officers are prepared to receive the gentry properly.
>
> Last week thirty-three members of the "red card brotherhood" dropped off at Hornbrook. Before they had a chance to make themselves very objectionable, however, the bunch was split up into small bunchlets by the officers and sent out of town in box cars. Two unusually stubborn ones, evidently enamoured of Hornbrook, were reluctant to leave. Persuasion—a fourteen or sixteen inch hickory club answers the purpose admirably—led them to a change of convictions and they, too, went away.[1]

If the crude violence of the "peace" officers' attack on the Industrial Workers of the World (IWW) takes some of us aback, the explanation can only be naïveté.[2] It will shock only if we are unaware, or have tried to forget, that this is how "radicals" were treated for much of the twentieth century in North America.[3] In the West and South, an especially vindictive variety of this violence—a mocking, casual tough-guy violence of the kind often reserved for the brutalization of African Americans—seems to have been directed by the state and capital at the Wobblies, as the IWW was more familiarly known. More than the members of perhaps any other labor organization in North American history, Wobblies were beaten, jailed, shot, burned, driven out of town, even dragged from their beds and hung. Indeed, in the not infrequent cases in the South in which the Wobblies were also African American, the cruelty can shock even those who know very well what happened.

This is not a book about the Wobblies—there are enough books on the IWW, and many of them are excellent—but I do hope it goes some way toward an analysis of that constellation of forces that determined the particular viciousness of these responses. For this is a book about the wage, about cracking open the wage relation and bringing to light its internal movements, its cultural and political content. It is not a book about wage determination, about how the rates and scales of payment are set for wage workers, or at least not primarily, although that of course comes up throughout. Instead, it is about the wage as a relation, a hotly contested political site in which quantity is only one of several critical dynamics at play. The Wobblies are important here because they were interested in the wage in a somewhat similar way. Certainly, they struck often, fought for higher wages, even bargained when they had to, but in contrast to virtually all other unions, they were ultimately—and in this they came closer to Marx's Marxism than many others—against the wage.[4] They often chose to fight these battles on the terrain of the length of the working day, but for them, time was a lever in a program of more fundamental change. They did not propose the end of work but the end of the wage.[5] The preamble to the IWW constitution of 1905 reads, "Instead of the conservative motto, 'A fair day's wage for a fair day's work,' we must inscribe on our banner the revolutionary watchword, 'Abolition of the wage system.'"

To explain antipathy for the Wobblies by pointing to the fact that they were socialists, anarchists, communists, dissenters, pacifists, or "Marxists"—which was often the case—surely will not suffice, since it begs the question why any of these groups are targets in the United States in the first place. The real reasons for the level of physical violence directed at the Wobblies are impossible to isolate, but they are certainly caught up in the same energies that suffuse, among other phenomena, the conservative populisms that continue to bubble to the surface in the United States. I think it not unreasonable conjecture to suggest that the Wobblies' stance against the wage—a position they took from within the wage itself—threatened the "natural" white American order as it was (and is) fantasized in the West and that the "unnaturalness" of this radicalism partially legitimated the abuse of those who offended that order. Indeed, the "natural" appears to have been a point of considerable concern for anti-Wobbly forces. Despite the fact that in the West most of these workers were "white," wherever and whenever the beatings, shootings, and forced removals of Wobblies took place, callous American racisms were more or less explicitly evoked over and over. The racial or national origins of the Wobblies—and of the "unskilled," often itinerant workers among whom they found their greatest constituency—were frequently questioned by scholars, employers, and the state, as was their sexuality, intelligence, reliability, and honesty. Here, the echoes of African American history, although rooted of course in dynamics that are not the same as those involving the Wobblies (to put it mildly), are strong (for more on this, see chapter 4).

What matters to me, then, is the way in which the Wobblies' anticapitalism makes the wage—that nexus of workers' time and employers' money they called the "wage system"—the political pivot point in the mode of production. In the temple of capitalism, they claim, the wage is the central pillar. They explicitly reject the idea that the wage is reducible to some politically transparent quantity: it is the wage as relation that matters.

I agree. The wage is indeed perhaps the most important arena in the cultural politics of capitalism. However, as the chapters that follow demonstrate, what my analysis shares with the Wobblies' is somewhat superficial, and I hope to show that there is a great deal more going on in the wage than they acknowledged. As they knew, Karl Marx once called the wage a "golden chain," and it certainly is an essential component in capital's toolkit, but that comes nowhere near exhausting its meaning or power.[6] Not only is the wage much more than an exploitative mechanism shaped by employers to extract value workers produce, but it is also an essential forum in which workers fight it out under capitalism. These fights always have a bearing on the quantitative distribution of income, i.e., wage determination, but they are never fully contained therein. There are always many other things at stake, not the least of which are absolutely crucial categories like race, gender, nation, class, individuality, and freedom (however we might conceive of them), and the list goes on. Sometimes, the wage relation itself is explicitly on the table, but almost all of the time it is not.

This does not mean, however, that at some deeper historical level real concrete relations are not changing; the idea that to "accept" the wage is equivalent to antirevolutionary class reformism is, as I will show, almost always an analytical dead end, to say nothing of its political futility. In fact, I argue that even many of workers' more "conservative" arguments about the wage—"we just need more"—really do put the wage at stake. Yet they do so not by isolating it as the key to the revolutionary motor but rather by uncovering the internal movement and instability that suggest the possibility of the wage's dialectical supersession by forces immanent to the relation itself. In either case, the wage is an equally critical political space in which these struggles happen.

This hints obliquely at another reason this is not a book about the IWW. For it seems to me that North American radicals' ongoing fascination with the Wobblies' often revolutionary "praxis," and the organization's justifiable eminence in the historiography of the continent's left movements, do not persist without cost. On the one hand, it is of course crucial to constantly retell the story of men and women who refused the system, sacrificed for progressive emancipatory causes, fought racial and gender discrimination, and rejected the "naturalness" of liberal individualism and the invisible hand. In the early twenty-first century, such lessons seem as important as ever. On the other hand, there have been millions and millions of non-Wobblies among the North American working class who cannot be written off as "collaborators" or "dupes." Confronted as we are with the weaknesses of "false consciousness" argumentation and the increasingly compelling mobilization of Gramscian analyses of workers' agency in the persistence of capitalism and the wage system, the obsession with "real" radicals can be distracting and unnecessarily disheartening. First, because we miss the subtle politics, the complex and inconsistent give-and-take, and perhaps the microradicalisms that constitute the everyday lives of millions of workers. Second, because we might come to think that without something like the IWW there is no hope. On their own, either one of these possibilities is cause for concern. Together, they are a recipe for political paralysis, the kind of paralysis that leads us to chant in futile unison, "Why don't they act in their interests?" This question has no answer and is either as fruitless, or as prone to totalitarian recruitment, as it has always been.

Consequently, I take seriously the material import of the political economic and ideological frameworks of workers, not because they necessarily have everything figured out but because what they think informs what they do and what they believe, and these are what culture and politics are all about. If the wage relation not only reflects or measures larger social dynamics in quantitative terms but is in fact one of the key sites at which these dynamics are actually produced, then any social science of the wage must adopt this analytical stance. This is not to say that workers are all thinking the same thing, or even that there are consistent patterns. Indeed, their differences are in many ways the subject of this book. Nonetheless, it is to say that if working people are not singing the songs that radical intellectuals wish they were, this should perhaps no longer index a strategic or conceptual flaw in workers' politics but rather a weakness in the theory of exploitation and hegemony. Insofar as critical social science continues to be shaped by programmatic expectations and disappointments, shoehorning working-class political and cultural history into unnecessarily narrow theoretical trajectories and political strategies, it can prove seriously flawed or just plain irrelevant. Beginning with what could be called the immanent wage theories of working-class political economy seems a far wiser, and ultimately more politically effective, analytical choice.

This means that the cases that follow are *historicized*, i.e., I evaluate their political and cultural meanings according to, as far as possible, the sometimes varied conceptual frames and political economic logic of the working people at that time and place. While I do not presume that these people had even close to all the information and power they needed to develop a comprehensive picture of their various contexts, I do presume that the information and power they did have fundamentally affected the course of history, if not always as they chose. The emphasis is on working people's cultural politics and their relationship to the politics of the wage within "actually existing capitalism."[7] Without this perspective, we cannot even begin to understand remarks like that made by the economist Calvin Colton in 1847—that in the United States high wages are "identical with freedom"—nor can we understand, as I will show, that these still contain an essential, if partial, kernel of truth.[8]

The labor historian David Roediger once wrote that his work has been partly motivated by the desire to understand and explain working-class conservatism and racism in the United States.[9] To the extent that he has helped implicate the working class as conscious agents in reactionary politics, he has effectively taken to their logical and occasionally disheartening conclusions E. P. Thompson's original insights regarding workers' historical agency.[10] Although elements of the chapters that follow tell similar tales, I have set out with less interest in culpability and more in what might be called analytical legitimacy. In my opinion it is clear, as Gramsci says, that as conscious and intelligent historical actors workers develop their own "conceptions of the world"—theories of capitalist political economy. The ways in which these differ across time, space, and society are a product of history and culture. Focusing on the wage as a defining element of capitalism and as an important consideration in workers' everyday lives, I attempt to understand the wage as it comes to life in its immanent contradictions, in these immanent theories, and the struggles they inspire.

To pull this off, I have had an enormous amount of help. Indeed, to tell the truth, I find the number of people who have helped me with this book somewhat disturbing; it is enough to make me wonder whether it was me who wrote the damn thing. And that's to say nothing of the fact that some of them helped *a lot*. To Jeff Romm, Louise Fortmann, Dick Walker, and Miriam Wells I owe the kind of long-term, over-and-over thanks that I am not even going to try to manipulate into words. Hopefully they just know what, and how much, I mean.

Since the manuscript, via the excellent advice of Alan Trachtenberg, found its way to Sian Hunter's desk at the University of North Carolina Press, I have been no less lucky. First, because Sian is the best editor/colleague I could have hoped for, and second, because she put the manuscript in the hands of my now no-longer-anonymous readers, James McCarthy and David Roediger. They have read the whole thing more than once and have kindly yet critically contributed so much of what is good in here that I am kind of embarrassed when I think about it. Again, thanks alone seem to fall short. Working with UNC also meant working with Paula Wald and Grace Carino, which was a real pleasure, and the book is better for it, too.

In addition, several people and institutions helped me with the research, talked to me for interviews, and just made all the work that much more interesting. These include the folks at the Weed Historical Lumber Town Museum, Jeff Stansbury, Gene Vrana at the International Longshoreman's and Warehouseman's Union, the staff of the Haynes Foundation in Los Angeles, and the librarians at the Bancroft Library at Berkeley, the Kheel Center at Cornell, and the Norlin Archives at the University of Colorado at Boulder. Three of the chapters here appeared in earlier form as articles: chapter 3 as "What's a Penny Worth? Wages, Prices and the American Working Man," *Ethnography* 6, no. 3 (2005): 315–55; chapter 4 as "Race, Skill and Section in Northern California," *Politics and Society* 30, no. 3 (2002): 465–96; and chapter 5 as "Class Consciousness and Common Property: The International Fishermen and Allied Workers of America," *International Labor and Working Class History*, no. 61 (Spring 2002): 141–60. I extend my thanks to the publishers of these journals, Cambridge University Press and Sage Publications. The beautiful image on the cover is courtesy of the kindness of the Mary Ryan Gallery of New York City and the Estate of Hugo Gellert. I use it with gratitude.

The book was written at four different institutions—the University of California at Berkeley, the University of British Columbia, UC Santa Barbara, and Simon Fraser University—each of which provided (and in the case of SFU, still provides) a very happy home for me and my "progress." The research and writing were supported in various ways by these institutions and made possible with the financial help of the University of California Institute for Labor and Employment, the Doreen Townsend Center for the Humanities at Berkeley, and the Social Sciences and Humanities Research Council of Canada, which funded a postdoctoral fellowship that gave me the great good fortune to work with and get to know Trevor Barnes at the University of British Columbia.

Over the past few years, many others have commented incisively on parts of what follows (with varying degrees of "agreement," to put it euphemistically), and I would like to thank them: BFP folks (Aaron Bobrow-Strain, Joe Bryan, Ben Gardner, Julie Guthman, Jake Kosek, Scott Prudham, Nathan Sayre, and Wendy Wolford), Trevor Barnes, Michelle Bonner, Sharad Chari, Mat Coleman, Jessica Dempsey, Vinay Gidwani, Kevin Gould, Clair Kim, Gillian Mann, Don Mitchell, David Montgomery, Robin Jane Roff, Jenn Sherman, Jen Sokolove, Mary Thomas, Joel Wainwright, Gavin Wright, and the dynamic membership of the Friday Group at Berkeley. The conversation and friendship of two of these people in particular, Jake Kosek and Joel Wainwright, have affected so much of my own thinking that I cannot avoid seeing their influence everywhere. Neither of them will ever take any credit for this book, but if you read anything you think really worth remembering, I will bet you a pint of cranberry juice that it came from them. Also, although I never forced them to go through the manuscript, my all-too-brief stint among the faculty at UC Santa Barbara gave me the chance to hash out many of these ideas with some great people, and I thank Kofi Taha, Mat Mines, and Howie Winant in particular. Each of them made me feel like the questions were important and worth talking about.

The community that filled my home so often during my time at Berkeley, when all of this got its start, remains central to my life and that of my family, despite the unfortunate distances that now separate us all. None of this would have come together without that gang; they were, and in a weird way still are, my home, and I want to take this chance to put down on paper my longing for the time when at any moment they were all next door whenever I needed them—Jeff Romm, Matt and Birg, Brad and Deb, Sanj and Shalini, Mandy and Deb, Heidi and Ken, Phil and Elaine, Zach and Christie, Josh, Steve C., Chris and Anna, Matt and Alex, Ivan and Anne, and Jake and Jules.

On top of all this, I have my awesome parents, Karen and David, my brother Pete, my sister Gill, and Ian, Lois, Andrew, and Sarah. Add the

Bonner clan, and Andrew and Lori to that, and I think it possible that with them at my back I have nothing to fear. Their enthusiasm for this project has never wavered, which is pretty freaking amazing given how much we can argue over politics sometimes.

I like to think that the soundtrack for this book has been provided by Buddy Miller, Mos Def, Townes Van Zandt, and Tin Hat Trio, but often I have to put my ear to the speaker to hear them. In fact, it has been provided by the irrepressible craziness that is Finn and Seamus. I will never know why I ended up so blessed with these boys, our boys. But then again, I suppose that is how blessings are supposed to work. And they are only part of the story. Because calmly watching it all unfold—or, rather, blow up—is my beautiful lady with a wry smile in her eyes. Lucky, lucky me.

1

The Wage, Cultural Politics, & the West

The wage-form thus extinguishes every trace of the division of the working day into necessary labour and surplus labour, into paid labour and unpaid labour. All labour appears as paid labour. . . . We may therefore understand the decisive importance of the transformation of the value and price of labour-power into the form of wages, or into the value and price of labour itself. All the notions of justice held by both the worker and the capitalist, all the mystifications of the capitalist mode of production, all capitalism's illusions about freedom, all the apologetic tricks of vulgar economics, have as their basis the form of appearance discussed above, which makes the actual relation invisible, and indeed presents to the eye the exact opposite of that relation.

Karl Marx, *Capital*, vol. 1 (1867)

The fifth day after my arrival I put on the clothes of a common laborer and went upon the wharves in search of work. On my way down Union Street I saw a large pile of coal in front of the house of Rev. Ephraim Peabody, the Unitarian minister. I went to the kitchen door and asked the privilege of bringing in and putting away this coal. "What will you charge?" said the lady. "I will leave that to you, madam." "You may put it away," she said. I was not long in accomplishing the job, when the dear lady put into my hand *two silver half-dollars*. To understand the emotion which swelled my heart as I clasped this money, realizing that I had no master who could take it from me — *that it was mine* — *that my hands were my own*, and could earn more of the precious coin — one must have been himself in some sense a slave.

Frederick Douglass, *Life and Times of Frederick Douglass* (1881)

Frederick Douglass, the former slave, earned his first silver pieces at the same time Marx was writing *Capital* only an ocean away. Yet he probably would not have recognized himself in its pages. This is not how Marx would have wished it, of course; the jingling of Douglass's wages in his pocket marked at least the beginning of his absorption in capitalist relations, and Marx is the theorist of precisely those relations. But the profoundly different meanings each ascribes to that single dollar are testament to the historical, cultural, and political distance between them.

This distance is not a product of Douglass's naïveté or of Marx's head-in-the-clouds abstraction; Douglass was far from naive, and Marx's head was definitely not in the clouds (or at least not only). The gap is rather due to the fact that both Douglass and Marx stood at the cusp of, and tried to come to grips with, two radically different processes born of one historical dynamic: the expansion of capitalist wage relations and the collapse of older ways of organizing social production and reproduction. To Marx, who rode the tide of European history in many ways despite himself, the freedman's joy in his "freedom" was understandable, if the freedom itself illusory. For Douglass, whose wages signaled an entry of sorts into history, the promise bound up in his earnings at that moment could not be diminished by what was surely, in this instance, a blinkered critique of the wage relation. Anyone telling him then that he had traded the explicit oppression of chattel slavery for the less coercive oppression of wage slavery would most likely have been met with astonishment, scorn, or simply deaf ears.

And rightly so. The Marxian wage fragments the wage earner; Douglass's wage made him whole. For him, it was part of the passage from bondage to freedom, while for Marx it marked the historical transition to proletarian dependence. But it is hard to imagine a dollar more heavily freighted. On that day, Douglass could fairly have said that, for all his efforts to explain the meaning of value, Marx completely missed what a dollar could be worth. The wage, as a social and economic relation, is not an ahistorical pecuniary exchange. Its politics are historically generated and culturally charged.

There is, then, something special about the wage, something beyond even the enormous significance it is fairly granted as the way many of us earn a living—although that is of course part of it. That specialness, or more precisely, some of the important ways that specialness is constituted in and by the working-class politics of the twentieth-century western United States, is what this book is all about. Hopefully, its title means this is no surprise.

Where We Are Going, How We Will Get There, and Some of the Challenges

In the pages that follow, I examine the cultural politics of the wage, with a focus on the twentieth-century western United States. I develop, through detailed histories, a cultural and political economy of the wage that is sensitive not only to narrowly economic dynamics but also to the ways in which the wage is both formed and given meaning by culture and politics and the history in which they are embedded. Along the way, I try to debunk the common assumptions that the wage is merely a passive quantitative measure of larger social relations or that it is an economic terminus, the politically empty outcome of the process of income distribution. My main interest, therefore, is not *how* wages are determined but rather *what* is being determined: what is really at stake in the wage relation. I argue that the wage is not just struggled *over* but is an arena in which working people's culture and politics are negotiated and developed. It is not simply a site of economic conflict over the distribution of income; it is the subject of critical contests in the cultural politics of capitalism. The political "real wage" must be adjusted for both inflation and history.

This first chapter is intended to serve as a broad introduction to the book's main concerns. It gives some substance to the concept of "cultural politics," which I then use to frame the crucial relations between the wage and race, class, and gender in the U.S. West. At the end of the chapter, I discuss the problem of method, through which I try to confront some of the book's inevitable limitations, especially those that inhere in its empirical focus on the "traditional" object of labor studies—the white male worker.

Chapter 2 prepares the theoretical ground in two ways. First, I frame what I call the politics of measure, by which I mean the ways in which workers have refused the strict separation of quantity and quality under capitalism and put the lie to the idea that the wage is an "objective" indicator. I then suggest a broad critique of dominant threads in wage theory—especially from the discipline of economics—and provide the outlines of a theoretical reconstruction that might follow from that supersession of the quality-quantity opposition (the dialectical "sublation" of quantity in quality) that is the object of the politics of measure. Much of the material I engage in the chapter is embedded in long-standing and often complex theoretical debates in political economy and social theory. I try to stay out of most of these "academic" details in the text. However, where more discussion might be of interest (as I hope it will be to some), or where an argument I make touches on important debates that are not of direct relevance, I have given in to the temptation of the endnote. This holds throughout the book, but especially for the section on method that ends this chapter, and for chapter 2, since the first-cut reconstructed wage theory I develop there provides the basis for the account of cultural political dynamics that constitutes the historical and theoretical substance of the rest of the book. These end notes are not essential, but I believe both the chapters and the book are much better with them than without.

Each of chapters 3, 4 and 5 works through a historical thread in western U.S. labor politics, mapping different configurations of social forces that form the wage and give it meaning. The empirical core of each chapter is different. Although California is the predominant setting in all chapters, some dissect federal policy, others revolve around the organization of the labor process in a particular firm. Each examines the cultural politics of the wage, emphasizing its articulation with a particular axis of social stratification. While the project as a whole highlights the ways in which the wage interacts with multiple social formations like race, class, and gender, each chapter focuses specifically on one of these in order to work through the dynamics in detail. For the most part, theoretical foundations for the cultural political formations I develop, and their relations with other scholarly work, are addressed within the frame of the individual chapters.

Chapter 3 describes the wage struggles of oil workers in post–World War II Los Angeles, part of the general labor unrest in the United States that followed V-J Day (Victory in Japan). These workers, members of the Oil Workers International Union, engaged in a lengthy and bitter strike over wage rates in an effort to protect the improved earnings and social status they had obtained during wartime. I show how the conflicts over wage rates—sometimes over seemingly minuscule monetary differences—were not only about the material welfare afforded by wage income but also about claims to the identity of American working men: engaged economic citizens, family breadwinners, and defenders of an idealized U.S. standard of living. I argue that a better understanding of workers' politics is available through an examination of working-class models of political economy. In these models the wage serves as the critical circulatory link in the capitalist economy and thus not only contains but also represents the means to radical and egalitarian change.

Chapter 4 tells the story of African American timber workers in Siskiyou County, in northern California, in the 1920s. The discussion revolves around technical change in the western lumber industry and the use of a massive log skidder—dubbed the "Nigger Killer"—in particular. Placing the labor politics of the region and sector in a national context, I focus on the ways in which skill, as a critical axis of hierarchy embedded in the wage relation, was reconfigured so as to distribute risk and status according to a racial logic. In and through the cultural politics of the wage in Siskiyou, I trace the process of racial subordination, the mechanisms of a local racism, and the simultaneous bounding of blackness and production of whiteness.

Chapter 5 recounts the experiences of the International Fishermen and Allied Workers of America, a Pacific coast fishers' union that existed from the late 1930s to the early 1950s. The chapter describes the emergence of a politically assertive class consciousness among thousands of small-boat fishers in Alaska, Oregon, Washington, and California. These small operators, rejecting the entrepreneurial identity assigned them by the larger capitalist economy of the United States and coercively imposed by the state, used the logic of the wage to claim the class status of workers. Arguing that the spatial and property structure of the fishing industry effectively made them employees, they attempted both to contract collectively with capital (fish processors) and to obtain managerial control of the natural resource upon which they depended.

With some historical and theoretical ingredients ready to hand, in chapter 6 I try to further develop chapter 2's reconstruction of wage theory in light of the previous histories. This leads to a confrontation with a problem whose importance in the cultural politics of capitalism is belied by the lack of attention it has received: the theory of worker interests, some version of which silently underwrites all work on class, the wage, and labor politics. What I propose is a theory of worker interests under capitalism founded in the politics of measure, and I argue that the wage is perhaps the most important arena (though not the only one) in which a working-class politics of measure "fights it out." Insofar as the wage is widely believed to posit and reproduce workers' class-specific "interest" under capitalism—increasing relative or absolute real wages—the cultural politics of the wage produces and articulates the relation between the worker and the mode of production. In the process, it simultaneously constitutes the space and time of class politics itself: the workday, the working life. The capitalist wage thus specifies a workerhood whose "interest" must necessarily be the wage, but the wage is always saturated with so much more. What I call the politics of measure is precisely that effort on the part of workers to articulate an "interest" that is always in formation and in no way given *ex ante*. This is, as much as anything else, the problem of ideology, and in the book's conclusion I attempt to briefly describe some of the possibilities that follow from framing the problem in this manner.

Cultural Politics

An analysis of "cultural politics" links this project with the growing body of literature concerned with the politics of "culture," which "treats culture itself as a site of political struggle."[1] By culture I refer neither to the conventional anthropological notion of a more or less bounded social group nor to the broadly "aesthetic" dimension of social life. Instead, I mean that enormously general category that includes "all aspects of social life from the point of view of their linguistic, symbolic, affective, and embodied norms and practices. Culture includes the background and medium of action, the unconscious habits, desires, meanings, gestures, and so on that people grow into and bring to their interactions."[2]

Culture is thus the totality of the social field that helps us make sense of the world by suggesting categories, temporalities, lenses, and languages that can abet the organization of everyday life. To investigate cultural politics is to examine the politics that constitute, reproduce, challenge, and reconfigure culture so understood. This investigation, however, is far from descriptive but is undertaken from a fundamentally critical position: "to ask what practices, habits, attitudes, comportments, images, symbols, and so on contribute to social domination and group oppression, and to call for collective transformation of such practices."[3] The cultural politics of the wage emphasized here involves the many ways in which the wage as social relation and as pecuniary exchange is shaped by the politics of culture and in turn helps determine the very form and meaning of culture under capitalism. Any reference to cultural politics in what follows should be understood in this light.

Cultural Politics of the Wage

Some of the ways the wage is bound up with race, class, gender, and citizenship are commonly acknowledged, even glaringly obvious. For instance, wage workers are usually considered members of the working class, and there are persistent and widely recognized racial wage differentials (i.e., where white and nonwhite workers do the same work, nonwhites earn less). Yet the workings of capitalism allow for a great deal of flexibility in both the ways the wage can work and the work it does, and other links are less obvious or less the subject of everyday policy discussion. These more complex dynamics are inevitably primarily political—a quality that "common sense" and positivist analyses of the wage either categorically reject or to which they are insensitive—and they are thus, like many things political, the subject of heated, if sporadic, contemporary debate.[4]

To take one of the more prominent issues as an example, some historians argue that there is a fundamental relation between the origins of class and race in the nineteenth-century United States, pointing to the close association of the ideology of free (i.e., wage) labor and emerging notions of "whiteness."[5] Others, like historian Sarah Deutsch, use historical ethnography to map the ways these dynamics play out in particular times and places. Deutsch illuminates a thoroughly white supremacist and ironic relation between wage work and freedom in the southwestern United States, where hired-out wage labor brought dependence, not autonomy, to the Hispanic people of New Mexico. Related studies by Gunther Peck show that for some immigrant workers in the West, to be skilled and waged could mean to be whitened, creating "racial wiggle room" to diminish ethnic difference and associated discrimination.[6]

Such relationships have been examined all over the United States and across the rest of the capitalist world. In virtually every case, the focus is the influence of historically particular national and regional conditions, and the interactions between these scales, in differentiating workers and wage relations. Gavin Wright's study of the evolution of the postbellum economy of the southern United States is a brilliant example. Working with virtually every type of historical evidence one could discover, Wright comes to the compelling conclusion that the region's pre–World War II "backwardness" was principally due to the isolation of southern labor markets and the consequent stagnation of technique, investment, and strictly racialized social relations.[7] In a very different but complementary project, sociologist Richard Biernacki's comprehensive study of the development of labor as a commodity in Britain and Germany shows how differences in culture at the scale of the nation shaped productive relations and labor processes in the two countries from the very beginning of the industrial era. As he remarks, "divergent assumptions led to differences in the definition of wages, the calculation of costs, rights of employment, disciplinary fines, and design of factory buildings."[8] Ronald Dore has done related comparative work on the forces shaping individual and group identity in the culture and politics of work in Japan and Britain.[9] According to the dominant liberal-rational analytical tradition in political economy, not only are these particularities uncommon, but they are simply not supposed to happen.

Parts of this project unfold at the intersection of some of the historical structures that interest these scholars. Product markets, for example, which play such a crucial role in Wright's account, are also important to each of the primarily historical chapters that follow (chapters 3, 4, and 5). The relevance of national labor and economic policies is central to the story told in chapter 5 in particular, as it is in Biernacki's account. Nonetheless, while these more conventional subjects of political economic analysis are threaded continuously into the historical context, since the goal of this book is to understand the cultural politics of the wage, the principal emphases of this book are the axes of stratification I have identified as of primary interest from the outset: race, class, gender, and citizenship. Macrostructural political economic phenomena are examined insofar as they impact the ways in which these more immediate social hierarchies intertwine in, and help produce, the cultural politics of the wage. The analysis of the wage, though, is complicated at its origin because the weave of the web of social relations within which it is politicized is by no means clear. Indeed, the architecture of that web is the topic of energetic debate, especially regarding the relationship between race and class—and this is only further complicated by the diversity of histories brought to bear in any one conversation. The question being asked—even though some think it is unanswerable and are sick of it being asked—is to what degree are race and class autonomous or interdependent, or both? Is one theoretically or experientially primary? Is either epiphenomenal to other social dynamics?

Personally, I think it is essential to continue this conversation. It has a long and fascinating international pedigree, a pedigree that is far from primarily "academic." Its formative participants have almost all been activist intellectuals who have dedicated their lives and work to discovering, teasing apart, or deconstructing the histories of racial and class injustice in the capitalist world economy: writers like W. E. B. Du Bois, C. L. R. James, Oliver Cox, and Frantz Fanon, among many others.[10] The extent to which these axes of exploitation have overlapped, trumped, and destabilized each other was a critical piece of the puzzle for each of them, and it still matters a great deal today. Moreover, even if we might consider the questions ultimately unanswerable, the effort to work toward a response drives some of the most powerful critiques of contemporary social order, an endeavor certainly not less meaningful as time passes. Since the social upheaval of the 1960s, the debate has, perhaps unfortunately, been increasingly dominated by professional academics. Luckily, most have been socially engaged intellectuals from a range of disciplines, individuals whose political commitment to theoretical work is well recognized: seminal early contributions by people like John Rex, Robert Blauner, Stuart Hall, and Michael Reich have been extended and reworked more recently by writers like Ann Laura Stoler, Adolph Reed, Michaela di Leonardo, and Nikhil Singh.[11]

Taken as whole, work on the so-called race-class nexus suggests a wide spectrum of relationships between race and class hierarchies. This is not the place for a full review, but in general it can be said that early contributions tended to lean toward extremes—race is reducible to class (Cox), or vice versa (Fanon)—and that theories have become more nuanced, complicated, and historically sensitive over time.[12] Stuart Hall's famous comment that in Britain "race is the modality in which class is lived" and "is also the medium in which class relations are experienced" provides a ground for the recent and increasingly subtle theorizations of the dialectical relationship of race and class (and of all axes of social stratification).[13] This is the point at which today's most subtle thinkers on race and class, like Paul Gilroy and Thomas Holt, begin.[14] They move beyond the search for a common or dominant structural foundation and focus instead on the historically specific interplay between what Holt calls "a set of linked social relations that are neither wholly determined nor wholly voluntarist."[15]

Why the West?: Cultural Politics and the Wage in the Western United States

Fortunately, some of the most theoretically sophisticated work on these relationships in the past three decades has been done in studies of the western United States. Alexander Saxton, Mario Barrera, Devra Weber, Miriam Wells, and Tomás Almaguer, to name only a few scholars, have each analyzed the historical complexities of these relations, drawing heavily upon the work of theorists like those mentioned above.[16] This empirical work also covers the breadth of theory, ranging from Saxton's class primacy, to Barrera's synthetic "class-differentiated colonial perspective," to Almaguer's contention that race orders the class structure.[17] (It is worth noting that, because of the detailed histories that situate these claims, the arguments for analytical primacy are not as blunt as those made by radical economic theorists like Reich.) Others have described a more dynamic relationship between social structures. The most important point of more recent work is that race is an independent social force, a product of class struggle but also an autonomous constituent thread in the evolution of social stratification. This is certainly not only true of race; Wells, Robert Thomas, and Peck grant citizenship a similar contingent autonomy, and Vicki Ruiz and Deutsch have written about gender in the same vein.[18]

What I think strikes the reader of all of this work so forcefully and repeatedly, however, is how overwhelmingly complicated the race-class-gender "nexus" problem is, even in the most narrowly delimited "real-world" instance. This is surely the reason so many express exasperation with the questions at hand. "Stop asking," they seem to be saying; "it's not helping." Yet the fundamental theoretical, political, and analytical difficulties of relating class, race, gender, and citizenship in the West and elsewhere are left behind, even with considered political purpose, only at our peril, and not only because is it too easy to imagine that a problem left behind has been dealt with adequately (this one has definitely not been). More important, if it is the case, as I believe, that important political problems are by definition not resolvable—in the sense that we might imagine "answers" that provide closure, or some "equilibrium," at which point they will remain static, despite history—then unceasingly raising these kinds of questions is a matter of political responsibility, one that intellectuals are extraordinarily fortunate to be able to take up as part of their everyday work.

In this case, my efforts to examine the cultural politics of the wage in the West are impossible outside such questions, for they give fair warning of the complexities confronting the development of a theoretical account of the wage that attempts to remain open to history while still providing breadth of insight and contemporary political purchase. Each of these cultural and political economic relations, while possessing their own dynamics, remain inextricable from one another and bound up in and constitutive of the wage relation itself.

Still, although history forever challenges theory, it does not render it redundant. Emphasizing contingency and conjuncture—"intersectionality," as it has unfortunately come to be called—describes much but explains little. Ultimately, and usually whether we choose to or not, we necessarily wrestle with larger theoretical questions through history, even if it is always possible to find instances that undermine their explanatory force. My purpose is to embrace the creative intellectual risk taking this involves—to choose to put something important at stake—just as my own political and intellectual heroes (if I may have some), like Du Bois, Rosa Luxemburg, or Eduardo Galeano, have done. Here, my focus is the wage, a "vital category of social life," as David Harvey says, a (perhaps *the*) fundamental capitalist relation.[19] Since the analysis begins and ends with capitalism, class is always in the picture. I do address social hierarchy as a product of what Almaguer (remarking on the relation of race and class) calls "mutually constitutive yet autonomous stratification systems," but whether or not I successfully realize my own hopes to avoid granting class theoretical primacy, I do accord it theoretical centrality.[20] The wage is, first and foremost, a marker of differential relations to the means of production—I believe this is a fundamental premise of all political economy, whether classical, radical, or "new" (i.e., neoliberal)—and class is thus the relation with which all others interact in the chapters that follow. These interactions constitute the histories I recount.

For these histories, as it has for many of those scholars mentioned above, the West provides fertile ground because it unsettles some classical social scientific concepts. In particular, the region's history and political and cultural economy disable models relying on taxonomic social systems in which households fit neatly into two or three classes. Such divisions are blind to the dynamic western mix of large-scale corporate-industrial activity, petty-commodity production, the (more or less coercive) wage labor both employed, and a great deal in between. Indeed, for writers like Saxton, Wells, and Richard Walker, the significance of petty-commodity production in the region by itself demands a fundamental rethinking of the meaning of class and of the relation of class to other social hierarchies, especially race, in the U.S. West. As the discussion of Pacific small-boat fisheries in chapter 5 relates, ambiguous class position is particularly important for an analysis of the wage, for it destabilizes the givenness of the concept as an unproblematic and standardized marker of class position and underscores one of this book's main arguments, i.e., while the wage founds the dominant class relation in capitalism, by no means can it determine the form and content of that relation in history. As I will also keep saying, there is no meaningful limit to the diversity of class politics as they play out on the ground.

The West is also exciting territory for a study in natural resource labor politics and "resource capitalism."[21] In their focus on the regional and local dynamics of the U.S. West, each of the writers mentioned above, as well as each of the chapters that follow, fleshes out the historical particularity of the region, demonstrating its distinctive cultural and political economy of work based in cultural diversity, labor scarcity, export orientation, resource abundance, worker mobility, and radicalism. This is not to say that other regions do not have their own dynamics or do not share some of these qualities. It is to say, however, that the explosive economic development of the West, extraordinary even by the exceptional historical standards of the United States, has helped shape a western labor history and politics within which the interaction of social structures, and the politics of the wage it animates, have particularly fascinating characteristics.

Perhaps most important, since the economic order of the region "is without question a capitalist one," the wage has played a crucial role in the cultural and political economy of the region since it was appropriated by the United States. Carey McWilliams's famous remark about California—where "the lights went on all at once, in a blaze, and they have never been dimmed"—may not be perfectly suited to the rest of the Pacific coast, but the energy and ambition it conjures up aptly describe much of the region's natural resource industrial growth in the twentieth century.[22] In the forests and rivers of the entire Pacific slope, the fervor of productivity and accumulation was little different than in California itself; indeed, it was usually driven by a California that was simultaneously driving much of America.[23]

Moreover, the West is a fascinating arena for a look at the cultural politics of capitalism because the region's development is a product of both the biophysical conditions of resource abundance and social configurations that produced that abundance. What Richard Walker has shown for California from the gold rush on is applicable to the rest of the region in later years: not only have natural resources driven capitalist accumulation and economic growth, but social and cultural relations within western natural resource industries have helped create and maintain the sector's ideological primacy in the imaginative geography of the West.[24] This is no less important for the rest of the United States and much of the world, since the received wisdom concerning the natural resource economy of the West also reproduces the self-consciously rough-edged "natural" Western identity that excuses someone like Clint Eastwood from having to explain what he is doing every time he squints into the sun or spits tobacco juice. The fact that these economies and identities are crucially related gives the West and its history an ideological weight whose import is all the more glaring in an age of self-styled American "cowboy" imperialism.

The dynamics of the histories considered herein are thus partially a product of the physical geography of the region and its relative distance and difference from the rest of the United States, the resource-intensive economic development that has characterized the western experience, and the distinctive social order of worker independence and small property. For instance, chapter 5, on coastwide unionization among fishers, is animated by a particularly western workers' concern for organization across vast spatial and economic expanses, the contradictory experience of being both employer and employee, and resource depletion. Chapter 3, which details the labor struggles of oil workers, is a story about Los Angeles and the United States as a whole, yet it is also about the experience of the resource-industrial working class in the West, its participation in resource abundance, and its conflict with a petro-capitalist bloc whose enormous influence was refracted, and often magnified, by the lens of the distinctive regional oil economy. The story of African American migration to California in chapter 4 begins with labor scarcity and western working-class mobility and its constantly emergent sense of whiteness and freedom from "wage slavery." And precisely because of this western specificity, each of these stories has something to say about the U.S. experience more broadly.

All of which is to say that the wage has a great deal to say about the cultural politics of the West, and the West can tell much about the cultural politics of the wage. The historian Carlos Schwantes has rechristened the West a "wageworkers' frontier," and it is this sense of a regionally distinctive capitalist laboratory that makes the West important for me.[25] I work through the historical cases to illuminate some of the local, cultural, and natural specifics of western capitalism and their extraordinary breadth and differentiation. In turn, I depend upon these histories to reflect light upon the more general diversity of the politics and meanings of the wage and of capitalism as a mode of organizing social labor.

The Problem of Method: White Men and the Dialectic

These more general questions of approach inevitably point to the problem of method, a problem I would like to tackle on two planes. First, as formulated above, the task at hand involves both decomposition and reconstruction. I must crack the wage open, refuse its "obviousnesses," and formulate, from the diverse movements and relations that compose its historical-geographical specificity, other conceptions and analytical possibilities. These are the bare bones of the dialectic, at least that of the Hegelian-Marxian line, and it is just such a dialectical sensibility that I try to bring to bear. But the dialectic being what it is—i.e., difficult, sometimes enormously so—I cannot leave it at that. The term gets thrown around quite often in contemporary social science to describe any to-and-fro determinate relation (A affects B, B affects A, and so on); the "nature-society dialectic" is exemplary. While any commitment to dialectics recognizes that the dialectic is always at work in the world, most of the time there is nothing to my mind properly dialectical about the investigations in question. At the least, to-and-fro, or "mutually constitutive" binary relations, do not define the dialectic and prove very effective at silencing the complicated kinds of questions that are involved in dialectical thinking and analysis. Thus, even though some very helpful explanations of the dialectic are available, a great deal of confusion persists, even among those who would call themselves Marxist. The problem is not merely that there is more than one compelling account of the dialectic or that important areas of disagreement remain. The confusion is with us partly because vagueness is essential to the dialectic and partly because the whole point is that it is not something that can be figured out or defined and then left behind as "done": it is a never-ending process historically *and* analytically.[26] I try to deal with some of this in the paragraphs below.

Second, there is the pressing issue of white masculinity, which shapes the book in several ways. I bring this up at this point because I would like to position it as a primarily methodological problem (which means it is always theoretical too). Certainly—and this is not my main point—one of the ways white masculinity matters here is that I am white and male, although to say so at this point is almost certainly a "meaningless piety." I neither disown nor neutralize my (privileged) position by acknowledging it, and I do not try to do so. The most one can do is to "sound its precariousness," recognizing that doing so does not somehow make the narrative transparent. I place myself in the text, hopefully subtly, and the conversation can begin there.[27] Another methodological concern with white masculinity arises concerning "data." It is certain that the histories I tell here, each of which is relatively fragmentary and "forgotten," would have been all the more so if the protagonists had not been white men; this, however, is not my main point either.

Rather, what I mean when I posit white men as a methodological problem consists in the bland fact that the historical substance of the book is largely a history of white male workers in a quintessentially masculinist space—western natural resource production. This tangles up with the two difficulties I outlined above, certainly, but the more important implication is the obvious one of "generality." To what extent can I make claims about "workers," the "working class," and the wage relation based on three detailed histories of white American men working in the U.S. West in the twentieth century? To be honest, I do not think that leaving this question unanswered should indicate that the content or argument of this book is irrelevant beyond the experience of white men. Indeed, the book uses these particular histories as a lens on questions that are of enormous import for many different groups and people, and I hope that readers find the analytical and political possibilities the argument opens up readily evident.[28] Nevertheless, pride and hope aside, the question asks itself and merits a response. First, because a similar question asks itself of many books, not just this one, so confronting it might have some wider utility. Second, trying to come to grips with the thorniness of the issue will only make whatever significance my claims might have more apparent.

So: to what extent can I make claims about "workers," the "working class," and the wage relation based on three detailed histories of white American men working in the U.S. West in the twentieth century? Not surprisingly, I do not have an easy response; but I do have a somewhat more complicated one. I take up the complexities of the idea of the "working class" in more detail in the chapters that follow. As far as the West is concerned, I have argued above for its fertility for this kind of study, especially to the extent that capitalist social relations are of interest, as they are here. But it is also worth noting, as each of the histories suggests, that the very idea of the West is also entirely complicit in white male Americanness, even (partially) constitutive of it. The U.S. West is perhaps *the* white male geographic imaginary, at least in North America. White American men in the West serve as symbolic concentrations of themselves, condensed masculinity: the lone cowboy, the burly logger, the weary fisherman, the stump farmer hacking his land from the woods with rough-hewn tools. (Not incidentally, to the extent that any real people fleshed out these ideal types, more often than not they were wage workers, contrary to the myths of yeomanry.) Books and more books have been written about this raced and gendered dynamic, covering popular culture, intellectual history, labor politics, and more, and the point seems to me irrefutable.[29]

These figures—whose appeal, like Paul Bunyan's, lies partly in their nostalgic aura, since we know they are no longer out there (if they ever were)—are central to any understanding of contemporary American cultural politics, and they are absolutely crucial to the stories told here. In many instances, these are white men self-consciously acting out white masculinity, quite frequently troubled by the fact that the set seems to have changed and the script no longer makes as much sense. Indeed, in the case of the Los Angeles oil workers (chapter 3), these gender-normative scripts are not implicit but exhibited as evidence for all to see. My objective is to bring a critical interpretive eye to these histories, to think through the significance of these ideological dynamics for cultural and political economy as ways of understanding the world. The critique of a culturally specific white masculinity in a world in which it is hegemonic can never be entirely provincial. Moreover, the manner in which I dig my way into these histories is meaningful, I believe, far beyond the particular sphere of white male workers.[30]

This is where the dialectic comes in. For in bringing what I am calling a dialectical sensibility to these histories, I set the wage in motion (to use the Hegelian phrasing to which Marx turns again and again), or, more accurately, I try to capture some of its qualities as it exists already in motion.[31] In other words, my objective is to describe the dialectical movement that unfolds in the wage relation, motion driven by the contradictions, oppositions, and historical dynamics immanent to it. I say dialectical sensibility—not method or approach—because this constant motion and constitutive particularity are *in the world*. Movement is not a disturbance of "natural," otherwise stable equilibria but is inherent in the material and symbolic order; the dialectic, in its most fundamental form, merely describes this movement.[32] Even more important, recognizing this—that "reality is not, it becomes," as Lukács said—demands a historical analysis that tries to both understand and convey this fleet-footed evanescence.[33] A dialectical sensibility, then, does not settle. It refuses, as often as possible, to allow concepts to rest. It attempts, always, to "refine, segment, split and recombine any general category," tracing historical movements that "differentiate in the very moment that they reveal hidden connections."[34] The problem is partly to identify generalities but always to grasp that they are not themes (universals), of which specifics (particulars) are variations. Rather, they are common elements among the many specific determinations. To imagine that each historical case is a variation on a theme is to smuggle in "inviolable natural laws," which is definitively antidialectical.

I realize that to claim that the dialectic is not about "natural law" is to contradict the commonplace that Marx's theory of history, greatly indebted but in no way identical to Hegel's dialectic, is "teleological," that everything is fatalistically worked out in advance by the logic of the economic "base."[35] There is, as one can imagine, an immense literature on this, and every possible argumentative claim has been staked. My own position in this minefield—that to think of Marx as a seer is a major misconception and that the accusation of "economic determinism" is gross oversimplification at the very least—is based in Marx's texts (and in Hegel's, to a lesser extent) and in the work of people like Theodor Adorno, Diane Elson, Stuart Hall, Fredric Jameson, and Moishe Postone. Each of them has demonstrated convincingly that Marx must be read as a much more "open" thinker than endless uninspired high school social studies interpretations of the *Manifesto of the Communist Party* suggest.[36] Even without delving into their reasoning, however, a straightforward refutation of this misunderstanding is provided by the several occasions in his work when Marx writes of the future, at which points he does not say what shape it will take, only that it will be different and that it has the potential to be radically so.[37] Exceptions to this can be found in the *Manifesto*, but to pin a fatalistic teleology on Marx based on the vision of historical change laid out there requires substantial decontextualization. It is called a "manifesto" for a reason; we cannot let its incisiveness cloud the fact that, although it is full of analytical gems, throughout it runs a very pragmatic thread. Without reducing the *Manifesto* to political rhetoric, it is nonetheless warranted to point out, for example, that when a candidate stands at the podium and pronounces "Our platform is what the people want, and they will bring us into office to make it so," that is not teleology or prophecy; it is performative rhetoric—it seeks to produce what it purports to describe. Indeed, even in the case of the *Manifesto*, "iron necessity" must be read carefully: if everything were predetermined, "Workers of All Countries, Unite!" would have been a newspaper headline, not a rallying cry.

Moreover, finding Marx the prophet becomes even more difficult if one sticks to his major mature writings, the *Grundrisse*, the *Contribution to the Critique of Political Economy*, and the three volumes of *Capital*. Postone argues brilliantly that the problem lies in a fundamental misreading of these works by "traditional Marxism." They do not constitute, as is usually believed, a "critique of capitalism from the standpoint of labor" but, rather, a "critique of labor in capitalism": "the labor which constitutes value should not be identified with labor as it may exist transhistorically."[38] Although Marx does discuss "laws of motion," he is very clear that they are not "natural" or "universal" but historically specific, not to mention tendential. His point, in fact, as Lukács saw perhaps better than anyone, is that history is *not* destiny, that capitalism, despite what the "bourgeois economists" say, is neither a natural outcome nor a stable climax state. Dialectic is not determinism but "history at its least automatic."[39] We must *act*.

Properly dialectical thought or analysis, then, must begin with what Marx called the "definite," i.e., the concrete, particular world. In every case, there are myriad particular determinations with which all of us have to wrestle if we are to be able to understand the motion that constitutes the processes of "reality." We do so through a process of what Marx called "real abstraction": we work out categories through which to think. But it is essential to remember that a general category, like "production in general," is only a "rational abstraction in so far as it really brings out and fixes the common element and thus saves us repetition." The general has no concrete life outside the particular. From this view, there exists nothing like a Platonic form, only "a certain social body, a social subject." "Whenever we speak of production, then, what is meant is always production at a definite stage of social development—production by social individuals." These productions, and their constitutive moments (production, distribution, exchange, and consumption), constitute, as "distinctions within a unity," an unfolding historical "totality" which is by its very nature the ungraspable "outside."[40]

To "operate" dialectical thought, if you will, is to dig into the concrete soil from which abstract thought emerges and situate that soil in its dynamic landscape. This means always historicizing both the categories and their thinkers—"the one absolute and we may even say 'transhistorical' imperative of all dialectical thought"—denying them any ahistorical rigidity.[41] Jameson calls this "thought to the second power": approaching the category and its social origin as of the same cloth, reconceptualizing contradiction by moving to a "higher level," one closer to the whole, in which what seemed incommensurable can now be seen to be inseparable.[42] In other words, the category, like the wage, is "returned" to its thinking source, and the concrete life of the thinker is seen as part of the category itself. This is not closure, of course, but a step toward knowledge.

This is what I try to do by bringing a dialectical sensibility to the wage. I work from the concrete, detailed histories presented in chapters 3, 4, and 5 and "refine, segment, split" the wage in each case in an attempt to uncover its inner complexities, contradictions, antinomies: as the contrast between Marx and Douglass shows so plainly, the concrete historical wage is always about the unresolvable conjuncture of freedom and unfreedom, quality and quantity, conservative security and utopian hope. To take as much of this into account as possible requires a methodological commitment to take seriously the categories and "theories" of the wage articulated by workers, so as to identify the meanings and conflicts within the wage as a concrete relation. Again, it is not that these theories are "correct" or comprehensive—as we will see, sometimes they are built on racial or gender logics that are not only politically pernicious but quasi-mythical—but that they matter, they shape cultural and political life. Consequently, I historicize these categories and conceptions, and the workers who thought through them, to understand the ways in which these immanent contradictions are part of a collective whole that is capitalist social relations as they operate in the world. This process sets the stage for a dialectical "reconstruction" of the wage (beginning with chapter 2 and continuing with chapters 6 and 7), which I hope is incisive and compelling while no less open to the very same dialectical historicization than the immanent political economies I describe here. By setting the wage in motion, or capturing the wage already in movement, as an uneven and antagonistic sphere of political process, I hope to illuminate the diverse possibilities in its content and form. By approaching the wage as a "vital category" of thought and life under capitalism—one with a wide range of particular thinkers—I "lift the lid" on what turns out to be a brim-full boiling pot, not an empty jar.

The fact that these possibilities do not always turn out to be democratic, emancipatory, or inclusive brings us back to white masculinity as methodological concern. For in the face of white male power, my pointed recruitment of the dialectic represents an effort to do two things at once: first, to uncover, as much as possible, theoretical points of purchase for the analysis of capitalism wherever and whenever; second, to constantly underscore the specificity of the histories of the heterogeneous white-male-worker geographies of the West. This is a dialectical effort to simultaneously historicize and theorize. It involves searching the concrete for movement that has the potential to burst its historical bounds—the energy of what, in the next chapter, I call the politics of measure—while remembering that there are no movements that are not both part of the whole and immanent, saturated by their time and place. Thus the specifics of white western masculinity matter enormously here, and the relative privilege and often brutal histories that constitute these specifics are flagged throughout. However, they do not matter in an "exceptional" way, but in the way that the specifics always matter.

The principle of quantity, of difference
which is not determined by the notion, and
the principle of equality, of abstract, lifeless
unity, are incapable of dealing with that
sheer restlessness of life and its absolute
and inherent process of differentiation.
  G. W. F. Hegel, *The Phenomenology
  of Mind* (1807)

2

Against Equilibrium
The Politics of Measure

In trying to prepare the ground for an analysis of the cultural politics of
the wage, I have continually run up against an old challenge: confronting the relation between quantity and quality. It is true that investigations
of the quantity of quality are common—subjective ordinal ranking, for
example, or composite indexes of "well-being"—but such efforts are not
really interested in the relation between quality and quantity or in its social
meaning. They are, rather, an extension of quantification into the qualitative; indeed, they are usually straightforward attempts to make qualitative
(usually a code for "subjective") experience calculable. In contrast, coping
with what Antonio Gramsci might call the organic and conjunctural relations of quantity (how much) and quality (meaning) is far more important,
I think, if far more complex. Outside the discipline of philosophy, where
the problem of "number" has occupied thinkers at least since Aristotle,
one could draw a very small circle around attempts to contend with the
quality of quantity. At the most basic level, this is what I am trying to do.

In everyday terms the definition of the wage is simple: a payment to
an individual for a unit of work. The earnings from that payment are an
important measure of the wage earner's well-being because they provide
the means through which he or she purchases consumption goods. This
definition is reinforced by the common understanding of labor politics as
consisting primarily of the contest between employers and employees over
rates of pay and related nonwage material benefits like health insurance,
compensation, pensions, and so on. Most wage theories begin with this everyday definition and attempt to explain how the wage rate is determined.
They vary widely in the significance they accord nonmarket factors, but

there is little concern for anything other than quantitative characteristics. The implicit assumption is, as Georg Simmel writes of money in general, "its quantity is its only important determination as far as we are concerned. With reference to money, we do not ask what and how, but how much . . . *its quality consists exclusively in its quantity*."[1]

But this formulation does not exhaust the content of the wage; its quality is *not* solely its quantity. Rather, the wage is also a social relation within which workers are employed, one that includes the institutional structures of production, the labor process, struggle over the distribution of income, consumption, and labor reproduction. Wage rates are a crucial aspect of the wage's materiality, but they are neither the only nor the necessarily predominant one.

Since most wage theory begins with the assumption that the wage is identical with the wage rate — an assumption I challenge in what follows — analyses of wage determination virtually always focus on the quantity question ("how much?") to the neglect of the quality question ("what exactly is being determined?"). Consequently, most theories are not so much dismissive of the idea of a cultural politics of the wage as definitionally incapable of contending with it. Pointing to this gap in the conceptual apparatus is not new, and critical economists have made similar accusations for decades. The California economist and bureaucrat Carleton Parker remarked in 1918 that economics examined no part of the "wage relationship" in a way that could help explain the "distressing and complex" labor unrest of his day. Reflecting on the analytical inadequacy of wage theory, he wrote: "Human nature riots today through our economic structure with ridicule and destruction, and we economists look on helpless and aghast."[2] In 1956, the economist Kurt Rothschild argued that since "the wage problem touches the most vital interests of people and social groups, there will be few human activities that have not some bearing on such a wider theory of wages."[3] More recently, Stephen Marglin, in a magnificent reassessment of economic theory, explicitly acknowledges the inevitable limits of theories of income distribution and economic growth that elide the social meaning of the wage. "In societies like ours, one's work and pay play an important role in the very definition of self. To offer to work for less than the going wage is necessarily to lower one's self-image."[4]

These interventions have not been completely in vain. Orthodox wage theory has developed a great deal since Parker's time, although some continue to adhere to the narrow perspective he attacked. In addition, more recent approaches, or less orthodox approaches Parker was willing to take seriously, have contributed significantly to a theoretical move away from narrow market determinism to more political and historical conceptions of the wage. These offer explanations of how the wage functions and changes over time and how it is related to larger political spheres.

Still, the wage rate continues to be regarded as the key datum. That is, the wage is seen solely as an output, a quantitative measure of income on the left-hand side of the political economic equation; as an economist might write it, wages are a function of politics and the market. There is an important grain of truth in this, but it is only one grain among several. For according to this perspective, the wage is purely *reflective* of the broader sphere of culture and political economy. Even in the most "sociological" wage theories, it remains nothing more than the exchange value of the return to labor determined by the market, with a social "qualification" added by the recognition that market-distributive value is partially determined—in its quantity—by culture and politics.[5] Thus, the wage is understood as the result of politics but as itself politically empty, a pecuniary indicator of determinant relations.

This book argues for a very different understanding. My goal is to use history to show how this relation works, to examine the wage as politically *productive*. The wage is not merely a quantitative reflection or indicator of relative power in or beyond the labor market; nor is it representative of workers' marginal productivity or "human capital." Any of that may sometimes, momentarily, be true of the wage *rate*. But the wage is a crucial site of the cultural politics of capitalism, a dynamic and indeterminate (or "overdetermined") forum in which the cultural and political economy of capitalism is produced. As such, it is somewhat like the commodity market as analyzed by Marx: not a mechanical and rational outcome of some human necessity playing itself out in the world but instead a cloudy, complex, and historically specific sphere in which that human "necessity" (along with other human phenomena, like class, race, gender, and relative social power) is partially created. The wage produces the politics of social difference at least as much as, and probably far more than, it reflects it. It is not an empty indicator of bargaining power but a simmering pot of the material and symbolic stuff that makes up lived time and space.

In other words, the wage deserves the inordinate political and theoretical attention it has received (especially in economics and political economy), but it deserves this attention as much or more for reasons that are rarely examined. Indeed, those reasons might go some way toward abetting the ongoing project of breaking down the distinctly unhelpful separation of political and theoretical attention. Of course, this division is partly the product of such restricted disciplinary range: those knowledges that unreflectively hold "number" as the object of theoretical attention are also those that work hardest at excising social "content" and most vigorously deny their own embeddedness. The somewhat surprising disciplinary fraternity of economics and traditional musicology in this effort is testament to the fact that it is not confined to those people usually called "scientists."[6]

All of which is to say that the wage is special in contemporary capitalism because its signal importance is formally inevitable and substantially indeterminate. In other words, it describes an open, dialectical relation, one in which no universal content, or predictable "equilibrium" end point, can be anticipated. The meaning of the wage consequently has several facets and is open to both empiricist "common sense" and more dialectical "unveilings." It is simultaneously the form in which many of us obtain money—thereby stipulating our participation in the capitalist dynamic and the quantitative limits to that participation—and the content of a working-class cultural politics whose object is not, as is commonly assumed, merely the transcendence of those pecuniary limits. The working-class politics of the wage is, rather, an immanent critique of the capitalist social order; indeed, it usually suggests nothing less than the transcendence of the very idea of a capitalist politics of quantity. Although wage struggles are always clearly about competing distributive claims (to money), and the powers that inhere to those who get their hands on money, in the final instance, these are of partial importance. Demands for higher wages are of course crucial, but they are neither entirely "about" quantity nor a neutral instrumental means of realizing relative success in other so-called noneconomic spheres of social life.

Instead, wage demands are more appropriately understood as one of the forms cultural politics must take in a mode of production whose syntax makes it impossible to put together an intelligible sentence that is not based on the opposition of quantity and quality, economy and politics. The culture and politics of the wage as articulated by workers' struggles are thus more than the quality of quantity or the quantity of quality, i.e., more is better, better is more. They are, in a far more radical way, constituted by an ironic effort to transgress the binary, to reject the idea that there is not something more important that must be said, some fundamentally political predication that quality and quantity ultimately share.[7]

That effort has certainly not been consistent, internally coherent, or homogeneous, even in one place or time. It has been produced in conjunction with a diversity of ideological forms—citizenship, religious affiliation, and race are some of the more common—and has by no means always been an inclusive, democratic, or hopeful endeavor. Nonetheless, our assessments of the more or less exploitative nature of the wage relation and our normative judgments of the "justice" of a cultural politics of the wage can lead us to miss wage workers' persistent struggles to identify and invigorate a politics in an arena that is supposed to be strictly "economic."

Avoiding this is no simple feat, since struggles over the wage compel workers to grasp the wage by its political handle, its *quality*, a handle capitalism literally cannot see. And when workers and their organizations, clutching the wage by this handle, then hold it up as evidence of injustice, exploitation, or unfreedom, it seems, through the lens of the market, that they are merely hand waving. It appears they actually do not have a hold of the wage: they do not really "get it," they do not understand that their purchase on the system is illusory, even infantile. It seems that it is not really the wage they are brandishing, that they have confused it with some other, usually "normative," claim that actually has nothing to do with exchange, nothing to do with the mechanics of supply and demand. And the power of that market lens is such that workers, like everyone else, often believe this too, and in the evanescent movement of the quantity-quality dialectic, solid quality again appears to melt into air.

One of the more insistent arguments of this book is that the problems with this market lens do not consist only in that it is out of focus or misdirected: in fact, it operates like a spectroscope in reverse, systematically flattening social life, making concrete relations, relations with historical "volume," appear without depth, merely two-dimensional. In capitalism (as Marx says) the wage is not merely an exchange value. It really is the wage that is at issue here (not merely some qualitative claim made in its quantitative name), and the struggle over the fundamental political predication I mentioned above is the struggle over what it is that articulates both aspects of the wage, its use values and exchange values, to constitute the lived wage relation as a whole.

This is not to say that working-class wage politics are or should be uninterested in exchange value. Wage-as-price is an essential category to the dynamics considered here. It is to say, however, that an emphasis on exchange is never separate from "qualitative" concerns, and the wage is thus a much more comprehensive, explicitly political and cultural category when mobilized by wage earners than by wage payers. Part of the problem, of course, is that the meaning of the wage for capitalism is one-sided by definition. If Simmel is wrong, if the wage has a quality that consists in something other than its quantity, then it is very different from the wage as it is usually understood. Indeed, if the wage has a quality (use value) and a quantity (exchange value), the definition of the wage as merely the price of labor or labor-power does not actually make much sense at all. What is the quality or use value of a price? In the attempt to shift the terrain of the wage struggle beyond that of the market—which almost every wage struggle involves—the working-class politics of the wage actually challenges the very meaning of the object of that politics. Granted a central place in politics under capitalism, the wage is paradoxically rendered less fixed, more open, and far more complicated. This indeterminacy presents possibilities and problems for all concerned—not just capitalists.

A Politics of Measure

The question of what it is that predicates both quality and quantity, and thus what renders the wage both quantitatively and qualitatively indeterminate, is, I think, essentially one of value. And we all know how messy that is. Still, tackling value, or at least some of its historically specific manifestations, is one of the goals of this book, and one of the arguments I will make repeatedly is that the cultural politics of the wage is simultaneously particular and fluid. In the forms of value that find expression in the fullness of the wage relation in the times and places considered here—class solidarity, white privilege, masculine autonomy—one can see this embeddedness and instability (both of which take historically specific forms themselves). What these—and all—expressions of value share, however, is their irreducibly political and historical character. Value is not beyond politics and history; it is the product of politics and history.[8]

So, while I want to make every effort to avoid unnecessary forays into high theory, and the bibliographic contests that usually ensue, I do want to introduce an idea of Hegel's that I think is helpful at this point. In the *Logic*, Hegel confronts the problem of quality and quantity, which he calls "sub-categories of Being," and their relation to each other. Although his discussion has many important subtleties, for present purposes his account of the two subcategories is reasonably close to "everyday" notions. Quality is "determinate Being," the "unmediated" "character or mode" of what "simply *is*." Quantity is "pure being," being that is "indifferent" to the character of what is; it reaches its "perfect mode" in number, and its "determinate mode" in "quantum (how much)."[9]

Anyone familiar with Hegel's work, however, will note that with quality and quantity we remain one short of a triad. Hegel often works in conceptual trios, and this one is completed by "measure," "the qualitative quantum . . . where quality and quantity are one."[10] With the concept of measure, Hegel tries to come to grips with the fact that often quantity has a particular (i.e., determinate) quality and vice versa. There are quantities that mark a radical qualitative transition, in which "a seemingly innocent change of quantity acts as a kind of snare, to catch hold of the quality."

His most straightforward example is the changes marked by 0 and 100 degrees Celsius, points at which water, having changed very little, if at all, in the "measureless" distance between, becomes all of a sudden something completely different—ice or steam.[11]

Hegel goes on to suggest that measure, "which appears alternately as a mere change in quantity, and then as a sudden revulsion of quantity into quality, may be envisaged under the figure of a nodal (knotted) line." The metaphor of a knotted line—which I find quite suggestive and will lean on occasionally in the pages ahead—is borrowed from astronomy and refers to the point in the observable orbit of any celestial body at which it intersects the ecliptic (the path of the Sun across the stars as it appears to those of us here on Earth). The knot, or node, is a point belonging to both orbits, no less essential to either for that fact. According to Hegel, measure, the unity of quality and quantity metaphorized by these celestial knots, "forms the essential structure" of "existences in Nature."[12]

It is worth noting that by calling out Hegelian concepts here I am not appropriating them to an analytical mode that is properly Hegelian. Although Hegel is of course important to the dialectical sensibility I discussed in the previous chapter, I do not intend to place the concept of measure in some more totalizing Hegelian teleology (to the extent that teleology is what gets cast as Hegelian these days). Indeed, for Hegel the concept of measure is only a moment in Being, the first of three subdivisions of logic (the others are Essence and Notion), and has nothing like the political significance I accord it here. Rather, my use of Hegelian measure is more morphological than anything else, an attempt to cope with the concrete ground shared by quantity and quality. And, hopefully, the connections between this conception of measure and the politics of the wage as presented here are fairly clear. What I am suggesting, with the idea of a cultural politics of the wage that challenges the quality-quantity opposition—a cultural struggle to formulate an intelligible political statement according to capitalism's syntax of calculability—is a "politics of measure," a politics of the fullness of the unity of quality and quantity. This involves not only contest and negotiation over the "knots," the points—like 0 and 100—at which the two evidently coincide. It is not merely a politics "about" measure but also, and crucially, a politicization of measure itself, the articulation and assertion of measure in the realm of the apparently "measureless" range between and beyond the knots. The politics of measure is in effect constituted by the persistent effort to articulate the unity of quality and quantity, to tie knots in the slippery thread of value.[13]

This idea of measure is also important to keep in mind throughout what follows because it corrects a common misconception that is symptomatic of what I believe to be a broader misinterpretation of Marx's analysis of capitalism and historical change. The unparalleled importance of Hegel's *Logic* to Marx's method is well documented.[14] Still, Marx's insistence on the primacy of production, and his claim that social relations are specific to the mode of production, are often criticized as baldly economistic, i.e., "quantitative." But Marx's theory of historical movement, whatever other flaws it may have, is much better understood as a theory of measure; for him the coerced and vigilant opposition of quality and quantity, use value and exchange value, politics and economy, was a product of capitalism, not some natural condition. Identifying the possibility of getting beyond it—beyond even the idea of "labor" in capitalism—is one of his most important, but least understood, contributions.[15]

So, value is a knotted thread. What I am calling the politics of measure is the unending effort to tie the knots and see that they hold. These knots are definitely not "equilibria," stable points to which the quality-quantity relation "returns." On the contrary, they are points of purchase, the moments in which, along the slippery and unremarkable thread of "pure" quantity, politics produces the very spaces and times of value in which this "purity" is troubled, tangled up with the world. And although these dynamics are particularly significant wherever and whenever money plays a formative role, I think it is no accident that the wage is perhaps the most important site.

Determination and Indeterminacy: Exorcising Equilibrium

If the above holds, the following critique must, if briefly, map some of the principal coordinates of the economic literature on the wage that are not dealt with elsewhere in the book and that presently constitute the vast majority of scholarly work on the wage. Indeed, a comparable review of noneconomic literature would be almost impossible because that literature basically does not exist. My objective is to turn a critical but open eye to the main strands of wage theory in a manner that addresses the way in which they might hinder or contribute to the development of a cultural politics of the wage and to identify potential points of departure. The grain of the analysis is necessarily coarse, but my method is to sift methodically and progressively through the dominant concepts and the relations between them so that, without losing sight of their particular analytical possibilities, we can move beyond them to develop the rudiments of an approach adequate to a cultural politics of the wage.

The rest of this chapter suggests a rough map of "economic" wage theory, which I divide into four schools, lumped into two broad groups:

first, neoclassical, Keynesian, and institutional, and second, classical-Marxian. With this map laid out on the table, I then try to illuminate, in a dialectical fashion, the immanent contradictions that push strictly "economic" analysis beyond its own borders.[16] I attempt this through a reading of Piero Sraffa—an economist who is frequently dubbed, depending upon the commitments of the interpreter, the heir of either Marx, Ricardo, or both—that seeks economic analysis's limits not at its "edges" but at its core. It will come as no surprise that the discussion is selective, but my analysis follows a primary critical thread through the material: I try to show the varying degrees to which the theories suggest that the wage is structurally determined by equilibrium in the labor market or related spheres, i.e., in a political economic balance point in the relationship of workers and employers. As one might guess, it turns out that they differ greatly on the extent to which such an equilibrium can have any analytical meaning, and if so, the degree to which it is stable in time and space.

I have organized the discussion of each "school" in order of the decreasing meaningfulness of the idea of equilibrium and an increasing anticipation of quantitative *and* qualitative indeterminacy in the wage. It bears emphasis that the indeterminacy in which I am interested is a persistent, structural characteristic of the wage relation, not a hypothesized empirical moment of "disequilibrium" leading to or straying from stability at a larger temporal or spatial scale. Indeed, as I will try to show along the way, an understanding of the ways the wage can work is severely constrained by the myth of equilibrium. This holds not only in the face of those few diehards who continue to argue for the relevance of strict market clearing and dream of perfect information and the end of political "meddling" in the market. It also holds for social scientific equilibrium modeling in general, which is beholden to what is no less than a normative faith in the ontological and epistemological priority of stability, fixity, clarity, and universality.

I recognize that this seems an extreme position. But the "naturalness" of stability is a radically conservative cultural norm. Social science that analyzes the unending variability, dynamism, and heterogeneity of the concrete world of, say, work or exchange, with the idea that variation, movement, or "disequilibrium" represents a straying from some natural state of being, however temporary, is asserting this "fact," not showing it. Indeed, it produces a social state that is, ironically, not really "social," if the social always drags the political along with it. The extremity of the Milton Friedman–esque market-clearing model is only the most glaring example of an approach to social relations that imagines that there is something other than history happening, a something that posits the value or meaning observable phenomena "should" have, were it not for all the things that made them otherwise.

Yet the "otherwise" is all there ever is. We are the otherwise. Equilibrium is a depoliticizing myth, one that attributes to quantity an ontological independence whose political origins are energetically effaced. When we are told we have realized one of these special moments—a "natural" rate of inflation, an equilibrium unemployment rate—not only does it never seem to last very long (this is attributed to longer-term movement around a posited intertemporal equilibrium point), but the fact that our everyday lives might have had something to do with it, lives we have no choice but to live in some way or other, is vigorously removed from the equation. Equilibrium in these approaches is the economy stripped of politics, the world without thought; indeed, it is precisely the immunity from politics (or at least political change) that sanctifies these loci as equilibria in the first place.

That said, and since I have explicitly described this as a cultural political ambition, one may expect me to begin a critique of wage theory with the dismissal of mainstream (i.e., orthodox or neoclassical) economics so common to cultural studies and critical social science more generally. "It's all positivist rationalization," I have been told. "*Homo economicus* is a myth that no longer needs debunking," and more words to that effect. I have refused such advice for at least two reasons. First, a critical reconstruction of wage theory demands a critique of extant wage theory. To skim over neoclassical economics' analytical and political insights in a cultural political critique of "economic" categories would be like listening to a military march with the drums muted: while some elements of the instrumentation might be clearer, the theoretical and ideological "rhythm" would appear much less powerful and much less structured than it in fact is. Radical political and cultural economy thus has an obligation to take orthodox economics seriously, especially when attempting to remap terrain that has long been ceded to it. Unless one buys the claim that the wage has some ahistorical essence existing beyond discourse, power, and epistemology—unlikely among those most opposed to neoclassical analysis—it seems clear that the wage in the capitalist United States is as much a product of that analysis as anything else. Like many other critical economic concepts—saving and investment are two more excellent examples—the wage has been the territory of economics long enough to be fundamentally altered by its dominance; we need to undo this blinkered read of things "economic," but if we do not attempt to understand orthodox economics, we will not understand the wage and its cultural politics.[17]

Second, contrary to the implicit assumption of much critical cultural and political economy, while neoclassical economics is certainly a species endemic to modern capitalism, like all species, it is related to others, past and present. The Marxian tools used (often loosely) by many "radical" critics of contemporary capitalist politics and culture—concepts like mode of production, exploitation, the reserve army of labor, and even class—are by no means unproblematically operated in a deconstruction of orthodox economic theories and methods. The radical and neoclassical traditions share a great deal of common analytical ground. The assumption of straightforward individual self-ownership is one of the more unsettling examples, as the philosopher Jerry Cohen has pointed out, but it cannot be forgotten that self-interested rational action arguably underwrites some elements of Marx's theory of social change in a fashion not entirely different from the role it plays in today's positivist orthodoxy.[18]

Moreover, neoclassical and neo-Keynesian wage theories are very important to what follows, not only because of the more limited insights upon which one might draw but even more because of their significant historical-ideological force. In the most fundamental ideological way, they shape the language, strategies, and goals of the working-class politics of the capitalist wage in the twentieth-century United States. They provide, and then buttress, the words and concepts that workers struggle to make sense of, appropriate, and sometimes challenge and delegitimize. The goal here is thus not to develop a better theory of wage determination but to do something completely different (something dialectical), in which hegemonic wage theories and their political valences are themselves historicized and made part of the problem of the wage itself.

The progressive embrace of indeterminacy parallels the introduction and recognition of a politics of the wage. By thinking through existing wage theory, we will be left with a limited political theory of the wage, at which point we will have the opportunity to extend this theory's politics, and to add culture to the mix, so as to confront the cultural politics of the wage that animate the chapters that follow.

With all this in mind, then, it is probably not surprising that even within existing wage theory the object of explanation is not consistent. It turns out that, for methodological, political, and analytical reasons, what wage theory theorizes is not the same in all cases. Strictly "economic" wage theories, the neoclassical and neo-Keynesian varieties of which dominate contemporary scholarly and public policy wage analysis, are an exercise in the systematic specification of the factors influencing wage *determination*. Contrary to some caricatures, this does not necessarily boil down to a series of more or less mathematically complex optimization problems. Labor economists, for example, have developed a suite of quasi-sociological concepts—like higher-than-expected "efficiency wages" that attract and keep good workers—in an attempt to confront the observable diversity of wage outcomes.[19]

Nonetheless, what is important here is that what is being explained is not actually the wage, either as social relation or even as simple pecuniary exchange. The object of explanation is rather the quantitative magnitude of the wage: neoclassical economists are usually interested in the (microeconomic) determination of the wage *rate* (the amount of money paid the worker per unit of time or effort, say, $10.00); Keynesians are most concerned with the (macroeconomic) determination of the wage *share* (the proportion of revenue that goes toward wage payment, say, 31 percent).[20] The wage itself—the human relation that can unfold only across time and space as part of uneven and heterogeneous capitalist labor relations—is not unpacked or illuminated; it is bracketed. To say that this theorizes the wage is like saying that ecological models of the factors contributing to tree growth (rate or level) or forest stand size (share) suggest a theory of the tree. If it is argued that economic wage theory is not intended to address these phenomena, then it is no disparagement to say that it utterly fails to do so.

Acknowledging this, however, does not mean that either the ecological or economic variety of these formal efforts is fruitless or futile. Neither does recognizing that both are extremely limited empiricist representations of social or environmental dynamics—dynamics that are unquestioningly naturalized a priori—necessarily lead us to ask for some sort of fundamental ontology of the wage or the tree (although I think that in the case of the wage, at least, this would be extremely helpful). Rather, a historicist theory of the wage might be more akin to a biogeographic theory of patch dynamics. Why does the wage (or forest) look and work the way it does, and not otherwise? Why the wage (or trees) here and now, and not other relations and processes (or vegetation types)? How do the existing empirical conditions shape the range of possibilities for constituent actors like workers (or species)? How would these actors be different if things had been otherwise? And perhaps most crucial to a theory of the historical fact of the wage—and here we must step beyond what is probably an already strained metaphor—what does the wage *mean* to wage earners, and how does this vary across time and space? Does the wage define the worker as worker? If so, what if the wage is not "natural" and productive relations could be otherwise? Would "worker" being a meaningful category at all?

These questions are at the heart of this book, but existing wage theory lacks the vocabulary and syntax to ask them, limitations that in turn shape

how the wage is talked about—and in many ways more important, how
it is not talked about—in capitalist society. This chapter works through
theories of wage determination, hopefully in an engaging way, to politicize
them, to unearth some of the politics buried in them, to explain them while
demonstrating their limitations. The goal is to get us to the point where we
might be able to put together an intelligent question about the *meaning* of
the wage, a question that not only recognizes its own embeddedness in
history but asks beyond the workplace and beyond determination. Here, I
divide existing work into two rough categories: first, the range of theories
of wage determination that have operated in the mainstream of the discipline of economics in the twentieth century, the neoclassical, Keynesian,
and institutional approaches; second, a range of more "classical" wage
theories in the work of David Ricardo, Karl Marx, and Piero Sraffa.

Neoclassical, Keynesian, and
Institutional Theories of the Wage

Contemporary economic theories in these schools are founded upon a
set of assumptions about market function, access to information, and preference formation that undergird the belief that, in the absence of interven-
tion, factor and goods markets will be "perfect," i.e., prices will equilibrate to a level at which there will be a buyer and a seller for all products
and at which all available resources (including labor) will be fully utilized.
Their significant differences arise less from varied theoretical commitment to these conditions than from the mode through which they believe
such forces work themselves out in concrete social life. Many neoclassical economists acknowledge that markets rarely, if ever, clear in practice,
and Keynesians argue that they never will; institutionalists are even more
skeptical.

But predicting disequilibrium conditions is not the same as rejecting
equilibrium. All three approaches frame wage analysis, and economic
phenomena more broadly, by comparing empirical data with a posited
norm of cleared markets and full transparency.[21] So, even though orthodox economics now tries to deal with obstacles to market clearing,
its entire analytical apparatus is predicated on the assumption that these
"impediments" prevent what would otherwise be the universal realization
of equilibrium. Keynesians anticipate permanent unemployment under
capitalism, but this empirically supportable claim is drawn from a model
of human relations that is still beholden to a structuralist faith in the "scissors" of supply and demand. Indeed, Keynesian economics is in many
ways just a theory of nonclearing dynamic equilibrium; the scissors leave

behind some scraps (unemployed capital and labor), but they work in an essentially neoclassical way. The problem is capitalism's imperfections, i.e., the extent to which it is not working the way it could or would if perfect. And if institutionalists always expect historical specificity to matter, they nonetheless read it as a force that buffers us from what would be, in the absence of the social, a universal, ahistorical stability—a current running beneath history, as it were. In each case, individual actors (or households) are assumed to maximize utility (i.e., income) within defined constraints by consuming some combination of leisure and goods according to exogenously determined preferences. As with the neoclassical approach, the metaphysical power of equilibrium is presumed by naturalizing and universalizing a social psychology—that of the English shopkeeper, Marx joked—in which the choice to enter the labor market and work for the market-determined wage (by definition a function of skill and technology) is based entirely in a utilitarian calculus of the benefits of doing so.[22] Wage earning is one means to an optimizing end; in itself, the wage has no particular social or cultural qualities relevant to economic decision making. The difference between neoclassical, Keynesian, and institutionalist theories is just the difference in the difficulty assumed to inhere in this calculation in practice.

That said, this is certainly not the place for a lengthy critique of contemporary economics and its highly formalized methods. I want only to highlight a couple of critical limitations common to these approaches, limitations that shape their analytical capacity to deal with indeterminacy, history, and ultimately politics and culture. The first of these is scalar and historical, the second epistemological. In both cases, neoclassical approaches represent the more inflexible theoretical position, and Keynesianism and institutionalism mark a progression in openness while nevertheless retaining at least some commitment to the underlying methodological individualism and theory of history (or lack thereof) that dominate the diversity of conventional economic thinking on the wage.

The temporal and spatial scale of neoclassical economics is the instant, an instant realized in consumption. The unit of analysis is the disembedded individual, who acts in the world by realizing the utility inherent in whatever his or her preferences (subject to certain constraints) lead him or her to choose to do. The time is the now, and the space is the personal. Consequently, wages are a relatively simple problem—at least in theory. As the British economist John Hicks remarks in a seminal early statement of neoclassical wage theory, "[t]he theory of the determination of wages in a free market is simply a special case of the general theory of value. Wages are the price of labour; and thus, in the absence of control, they are determined, like all prices, by supply and demand."[23] He goes on to acknowledge the complications that may obstruct market clearing in the "real world," but he concludes with a reaffirmation of faith in the Invisible Hand's price mechanism.[24]

Although neoclassical economics at its most rigid accepts Hicks's statement without qualification, a great deal of theoretical work done since Hicks's time complicates this story, and not just at the margins of the discipline. Persistent earnings inequality, wage rigidity, and unemployment have long stumped unadorned neoclassical wage theories; indeed, nearly seventy-five years ago these problems constituted a large part of the motivation for the approach outlined in Keynes's *General Theory*. Nobel Prize–winning economists like George Akerlof, Joseph Stiglitz, and Robert Solow have all struggled to specify the source and quantitative significance of impediments to the smooth functioning of labor and other markets.[25] Akerlof tries to redescribe the wage as a "gift"; Stiglitz helped found an entire subdiscipline, the "economics of information," that illuminates the importance and unevenness of information in any transaction; and Solow has argued that since labor markets are "social institutions"—because the commodities have minds of their own—they function differently than other commodity or factor markets: "One important difference between the labor market and the market for fish is that the performance of the worker depends on the price paid for her services. . . . Because the wage rate enters the story in this double role, as a productive factor as well as a simple cost, it is not available *simply* to balance supply and demand in the usual efficient way. It cannot perform both functions perfectly. It is precisely the character of the labor market as a social institution that makes it generate an inefficiently low level of employment."[26]

Yet even here, despite Solow's admission that "phenomena like persistent unemployment and sticky wages . . . embarrass the simple supply-and-demand model," the focus on quantity blinds economists to the social content of the wage relation.[27] This is neoclassical economics at its most "anthropological," yet history is still absent, politics is nowhere to be found, and the realm of the social or cultural is reduced to calculating individuals privately and rationally assessing themselves as commodities.[28] Even in Akerlof's theory of gift exchange, unlike that of the anthropologists from whom he borrows the idea, there is no politics.[29] Worker organization for a higher wage is ignored in favor of depoliticized and unquestioned norms of "fairness," which affect the interpersonal relationship between the individual worker and the employer—an argument that has been recently reworked as a "morale theory of wage rigidity" or a "choice theoretic theory of mood."[30]

The Keynesian wage is a different beast, if not as different as might first appear. The evident contrasts are due to Keynesians' embrace of imperfections (i.e., human beings) and a consequent rejection of the neoclassical notion of an objectively determined production function—a mode of economic organization in which the price mechanism allows for the efficient allocation of factors of production.[31] Instead, it emphasizes subjective propensities to save, invest, and consume. It also rejects the neoclassical idea that money is a "mere unit of account." Rather, according to Keynesians, money enjoys a "liquidity premium": in contrast to fixed capital, say, its ready convertibility makes it a preferred asset, at least partly because "it is of the essence [of capitalism] that wages are fixed in money terms, and real wages are determined by adjustments in the price level."[32] As a consequence, money is a material influence on the economy, subjectively valued relative to other commodities.

In the Keynesian model, demand for capital investment is cast in the central regulatory role in the economy. (Keynes famously described investment demand as a function of capitalists' "animal spirits"; Joan Robinson restates this more rigorously as "the propensity to accumulate.")[33] Profits are thus a function of the "psychology of the businessman," and wages are not determined by equilibrium in the labor market but "residually: the output left over after capitalists' appetites are satisfied is available to workers as wage goods."[34] This means that, in contrast to what economic orthodoxy teaches us to expect, supply and demand will not push wages down, even in the absence of regulatory interventions like minimum wage laws. It is people, not fetishized "market forces," that make wages "sticky" (unlikely to drop with market shifts). Because money matters to people in a special way—they are not interested in being paid in corn—it is not the nominal or money wage that adjusts; it is rather the real wage that moves to clear the wage goods market.[35]

The implication for workers is clear. Because forces beyond their control determine the organization of production and the social wage in capitalist economies, they are forced into a distributive struggle over money wages alone, with real wages basically fixed, or only temporarily distorted, in any one period. Keynes attributed this misdirected effort to "money illusion," the propensity to forget that it is not the numbers on the coins and bills but money's real value, its purchasing power, that matters. But since the aggregate real wage is determined outside the labor market or other institutions over which workers may have influence, i.e., by capital and the state, working-class politics inevitably revolves around the relative distribution of wage incomes among different groups of workers, not between workers and capitalists.[36] The upshot is that workers are naive, basically passive subjects of history. In Marglin's apt summary of the Keynesian position, "class interests may be opposed, but the class struggle is long since over."[37]

"Money illusion" is basically a discredited idea, especially if one looks beyond the very short term. The powerlessness argument—workers are not foolish, just too weak to resist—is, however, considerably more plausible, even if the class struggle is not actually over.[38] Indeed, I think it is only with plugged ears and closed eyes that one could refuse to deal theoretically with the essentially defensive posture of working-class political economy under capitalism. Nevertheless, the radical fruit of Keynes's strictly liberal macroeconomic seed—fruit that workers, unions, and critics of all stripes were quick to pick, or at least to demand—grows at precisely this point in the mode of production. According to this view of the world, the success of working-class wage struggles, based in particular upon the social unacceptability of wage cuts, is important not only for working-class welfare but for the health of capitalism as a whole. Since economic cycles strike worker-*consumers*, reducing the demand that maintains capitalists' animal spirits, the logical policy response is to stimulate incomes.[39] As Adam Przeworski puts it, Keynesianism "suddenly granted a universalistic status to the interests of workers.... The significance of increasing wages changed from being viewed as an impediment to national economic development to its stimulus. Short-term particularistic interests of workers could now be held to coincide with the long-term interest of society as a whole."[40]

The practical implications of Keynesian wage theory thus became wedded to a social democratic political program that had little to do with the broader macroeconomic model (and analytical lineage) in which it was embedded. The prodigal "Left-Keynesianism" born of this marriage—Keynes was certainly not a "lefty"—meshed well with the politics of "purchasing power" so influential throughout North America and western Europe during and after the Great Depression.[41]

Of course, the weight of these ideas did not disappear with the 1930s or the end of World War II. For radical economists, however, the problem presented by populist high-wage consumption politics was the extent to which they actually reinforced the class stratification and exploitation to which they imagined themselves in opposition. According to the regulation school's influential elaboration of Gramsci's concept of Fordism—drawing inspiration from Louis Althusser's (still) controversial reading of Gramsci in the late 1960s and early 1970s—the power of capitalism is in no way unveiled but is rather further obscured by the politics of purchasing power.[42] According to the regulationists, the Fordist "mode of regulation" evolved in the mid-twentieth century as an intensive, state-sponsored class compromise in the interests of capitalist accumulation. As formulated most famously by the economist Michel Aglietta, the regulatory regime consisted of "institutionalized economic struggle in the form of collective bargaining" and a "social consumption norm"—and the high wages this required—which together served as "an articulation between process of production and mode of consumption."[43]

There is much to admire in the regulationists' account, and despite some powerful critiques, it has been worked out in fascinating detail in the past twenty years, especially by a few brilliant and creative economic geographers.[44] The explicit attention to ideology is of course a radical and essential contribution to the problem of the wage under capitalism. Nonetheless, while the politics so important to the approach has helped denaturalize capitalist class relations in a rigorous way, the economic analysis on which it rests is in effect a rehashed Keynesianism that cannot take us much further than Keynes himself. The foundations of Keynesianism—capitalist animal spirits, short-term money illusion, a rigidly macrostructural vision, and homogeneous working subjects—are all there in full bloom. Indeed, Aglietta follows Keynes much more (and Gramsci much less) than he would like to admit. He implicitly assumes both working-class powerlessness in the reproduction of Fordist social relations and a dynamic equilibrium (albeit with unemployment) that relies on a renamed Keynesian real wage stability he calls the maintenance of a "reference wage."[45]

For Keynesianism is in no way a "disequilibrium" theory, even though it sowed the seeds of more critical economics, moving wage theory (among other things) away from the quasi-perfect equilibrium determination presented by orthodox economics. It is, rather, a dynamic equilibrium theory that does not require full employment. In it, workers are passively playing someone else's game, even if the rules are more affected by their collective economic disfranchisement. The introduction of working-class resistance in the form of wage stickiness is of course a crucial lesson for any cultural politics of the wage, and it shall not be forgotten in what follows, but it is coupled with an assumption of worker naïveté and almost total powerlessness that is fundamentally untenable in the face of working-class history. Still, Keynes hinted that the wage, at least as an exchange relation, might work the way it does at least partly because of worker politics. There are people here, people who matter.

It is here, perhaps, that it is best to introduce the institutionalism that became so crucial to American economics during and after World War II. Institutionalism, which found some of its most articulate advocates in prominent labor economists like John Dunlop and Clark Kerr, falls somewhere near Keynesianism in its approach to the wage, but it uses what one might call a more historicist route to a nearby destination. Indeed, at first glance, it may appear that institutionalists begin their analysis where Keynes left off—with market imperfections, sticky wages, and persistent unemployment. Yet the microeconomic interests of these war-era economists, many of whom were directly involved in policy development, made Keynesianism an incomplete and often unwieldy tool kit. To confront the evident diversity of economic relations in a nation as large as the United States, institutionalists instead went about draping a relatively vague socioeconomic geography over analytical contours provided by orthodox supply-and-demand theory. They situated economic processes within social relations, saw custom or norms at work in economic decision making, and were consequently only loosely committed to neoclassical theoretical conclusions, more flexible when history demanded it.[46] All institutionalists—and there is a full range, from liberal to radical—start here.[47]

Thus, while the tendency toward market clearing is assumed to *underlie* social relations of production, distribution, and consumption, institutionalists expect real labor markets to be differentiated by space, skill, occupation, and industry and subject to institutional barriers to capital and labor mobility. Indeed, in the postwar heyday of "modern welfare capitalism" during which they wrote, firm-specific labor markets were common (so-called internal labor markets), and wages were determined by organizational mechanisms that might be only indirectly linked to external goods or factor markets.[48] Institutionalists thus rejected fundamental tenets of both neoclassical and Keynesian economics. They showed that there is no reason to expect the wage to be even partially determined by workers' marginal productivities (as neoclassicists would have it), and they explained why other markets will not necessarily move so that the wage determined marginal productivity (as Keynesianism implies). Instead, while either is theoretically possible, the wage any worker actually receives is determined by the particular characteristics of the relevant labor market, and labor markets are sufficiently isolated by institutional factors that wages can differ dramatically.[49] Some institutionalists even went as far as admitting that stopping at institutions still might not cut the analytical mustard; as Kerr himself said, "the interrelatedness of wage rates may be traced to more political, ethical, or operational than to labor market considerations."[50]

The result is an explicitly historicist theory of wage determination in which the specifics of the "wage bargain" dominate. Union wage theory—an idea incompatible with the homogenized, ahistorical worker of neoclassicism and of the *General Theory*—is therefore crucial to institutionalism. Even in the simple act of establishing labor market boundaries, worker organization has a fundamental influence on the wage.[51] In other words, markets usually do not clear, wage rates are not strictly determined, and all one has to do is look around to see why this is the case.[52] This emphasis on custom, tradition, and the social differentiation of labor markets prepared the soil for later, more critical approaches to structural wage inequality and discrimination.[53] Concepts derived from institutionalism like "noncompeting groups" and "segmented labor markets," among others, provided some of the more fruitful openings for the (belated) introduction of race and gender to economic analysis.[54]

Although institutionalists rarely addressed issues like class, race, and gender explicitly, their framework helped economists confront undeniable social facts that were virtually impossible to deal with using disciplinary tools.[55] Even the most blinkered and cursory examination of work in the United States finds that opportunity and access are not evenly distributed along any of these axes of social differentiation, and the institutionalist approach helped critics explain how these social divisions can have an immense impact on labor market and wage outcomes.[56]

The radical possibilities here have been welcomed by critical economists, especially in the United States. David Gordon, Richard Edwards, and Michael Reich, the three scholars most responsible for the development of a Marxist institutionalism often called "segmented labor market theory," put it as follows:

> By turning attention to the manifold "imperfections" in labor markets, the institutionalist tradition has advanced our understanding of the sources of objective differences among workers' experiences in production. . . . The institutionalists also correctly highlight the cooperative aspects of union-management relations in the post–World War II era. However, we also think that the institutional school fails to analyze adequately the determinants of skills, customs, traditions, and rules in the workplace; does not locate the contours of unionism and labor market structure in a sufficient theory of capitalist development; and goes too far in stressing the durability of the postwar labor-capital accord. . . . [W]e propose an alternative working hypothesis: The disunity of the US working class persists in large part as a result of objective divisions among workers in their production experiences.[57]

In other words, wages are neither precisely determined by market forces (neoclassical) nor necessarily bound to a fixed real value (Keynesian); they are a reflection of political negotiation and struggle. The problem, however, is that this negotiation and struggle are analytically limited to the workplace. Of course, Gordon, Edwards, and Reich do not dismiss the relevance of broader temporal, cultural, and geographic context, but they effectively homogenize it, so that an examination of labor politics anywhere in the United States can begin from the same set of historical and theoretical postulates. Acknowledging the social importance of phenomena like racism and gender discrimination, they nonetheless find their determinants on the shop floor.[58] Workers' lives outside work—regional, racial, and family politics, for example—appear as an outcome of this struggle, not a causal factor.

Relative to the notion of cultural politics introduced earlier, of course, this is an excessively narrow idea of politics and culture; in fact, it is in many ways merely a "left" variation on the orthodox economism that reduces politics to economics. A cultural politics of the wage, in contrast, must move both beyond "mere" wage *determination* and beyond the workplace. Production will inevitably be a focus, but it cannot be the sole point of origin of struggles or the only social arena in which they resonate. If that were so, then wage theory, along with the wage, would come to rest at a politically bounded social equilibrium determined from nine to five. History and everyday life demonstrate that this is not so.

Classical Wage Theory: David Ricardo and Karl Marx

In the first of two well-known attacks on Marxian economic theory, Paul Samuelson—perhaps the most influential neoclassical economist of the twentieth century—claimed Marxian wage theory is based upon a "grandiose simplification of the economic system." This simplification is accepted because it is "the very model in which improvement of labor's share of the total income would be easiest. . . . The later neoclassical economists would consider this as the extreme case of a marginal product curve for labor that is infinitely steep over a wide range: confront so steep a curve with a coinciding infinitely-steep supply curve of labor, and you have indeed created an indeterminate equilibrium wage with all the scope for collective bargaining and class power struggles that you could want."[59]

The power of Samuelson's critique is certainly debatable (i.e., who is the author of the grandiose simplification here?), but his mockery does identify the heart of Marxian wage theory: there is no labor market equilibrium in the neoclassical sense. The concept is incommensurable with Marxian analysis, in which "supply and demand regulate nothing but the temporary *fluctuations* of market prices."[60] The real concern of wage theory is the class struggle as it is embedded in the particular histories of capitalist development—a conception in such sharp contrast with the neoclassical view that Samuelson, analyzing it through his naturalized market lens, could make no sense of it.

Yet even if Samuelson had been interested in reading more, he would have been somewhat disappointed, since Marx's wage theory has received less attention than almost any other aspect of his critique of political economy. Perhaps this is partly because, on the surface at least, it is pretty straightforward and does not appear to need much in the way of elaboration. Marx, following David Ricardo, begins by recognizing a clear social division between the people who own and control the means of production, such as machinery and land, and those who do not and are therefore forced to seek employment to earn a living.[61] This is what Marx means when he says that the wage is "presupposed" by capitalism, its level determined by "the price of the necessary means of subsistence."[62]

This is also why Marxian and Ricardian conceptions of the wage are often described as "subsistence wage" theories. As David Harvey says, "nothing could be further from the truth," but much of what has been written about Marxian and Ricardian wage theory—even by "sympathetic" economists—is nevertheless dismissive because the historical facts of rising real wages under capitalism so blatantly contradict any "increasing immiseration" thesis.[63] Indeed, so many readers misread "subsistence wages" that the concept still deserves clarification.[64] That the "subsistence wage" is belied by the "facts" of history is of course true, but the claim that Marx or Ricardo did not see this is totally disarmed as soon as one bothers to read either of them (especially Marx) on the subject. For, among other more complex theoretical and historical reasons for rejecting the idea of a minimum-for-survival wage (some of which I discuss below), Marx points out numerous times in his published work that any idea of "subsistence" is always socially, not physiologically, defined: it "diverges from this physical minimum; it differs according to climate and the level of social development; it depends not only on physical needs but also on historically developed social needs."[65] Ricardo makes the same point in very clear language.[66] (The term "subsistence" is in fact sufficiently misleading that Stephen Marglin has proposed "conventional wage" as an alternative, a bit of advice I will follow.)[67]

The meaning of the theory of the conventional wage for an understanding of the politics of the wage partly depends upon the classical distinction I mentioned earlier between the wage share and the wage rate (this distinction, it will be remembered, was also important to Keynes). Although the theory of the conventional wage is commonly believed to apply to the wage earned by individual workers, i.e., the wage rate, Marx was explicit in his application of the concept to the working class as a whole, i.e., the wage share of total income: "This minimum wage, like the determination of the price of commodities in general by cost of production, does not hold good for the single individual, but only for the race. Individual workers, indeed, millions of workers, do not receive enough to be able to exist and to propagate themselves; but the wages of the whole working class adjust themselves, within the limits of their fluctuations, to this minimum."[68] The Ricardian-Marxian conventional wage consequently functions as both floor and ceiling, determining a functionally constant, if historically specific, aggregate wage share—what Marx called the "social wage."[69]

Marx's appropriation of Ricardian ideas is famously selective. Moreover, when he did get his hands on Ricardo, he often reworked him so that only the terminology remained the same—the theory of value, for example, looks very different in Marx than it does in Ricardo. To Marx, these reconfigurations were absolutely necessary. To adopt Ricardo's ideas uncritically would be to maintain an implicit faith in the universal, natural status of capitalism as a climactic developmental achievement.[70] Thus, while Ricardo clearly saw that subsistence was not a physiological threshold, he forecast stagnant wages and an increasingly supine working class à la Keynes. But according to Marx, not only is subsistence never a merely physiological category, but accumulation in the context of a conventional wage share and class struggle creates a *rising* real wage rate, within the bounds of which "an immense scale of variations is possible."[71] Both these assertions have been borne out historically: real wages have risen under capitalism, especially in expansionary times and regions like the twentieth-century western United States, and wages vary enormously, even within restricted times and spaces; the idea that Marx would have "denied" this is absurd—he *anticipated* it.

Of course, Marxian wage theory is not primarily anticipatory but critical. It distinguishes itself from other approaches by analyzing the wage not only as a quantity, like the wage share or the wage rate, but as a social power relation between capital and labor as classes, and between workers and employers as individuals and small groups. Thus, although the rising real wage, as a function of accumulation and of workers' efforts to share in it through class struggle and shop-floor politics, may sound a hopeful note for the plight of workers under capitalism, the story does not end on a cheery refrain. For Marx, "a rise in the price of labour, as a consequence of the accumulation of capital, only means in fact that the length and weight of the golden chain the wage-labourer has already forged for himself allow it to be loosened somewhat."[72]

Marxians argue that the wage is a monetary compensation for the sale of labor-*power*, the commodity form of the worker's capacity to work.[73]

The wage is not equivalent to the value of the labor performed (the contribution of the worker to the product) but to the price of labor-power as commodity.[74] Consequently, it is less than the price the capitalist receives for the sale of the product and "masks the difference between abstract human labor as the substance of value and the value of labor power," for "even surplus labor, or unpaid labor, appears as paid."[75] Marxian theory thus stands out against other approaches in postulating an ideological or legitimating role for the wage. It is a "mystification of the capitalist mode of production" that blinds the worker to his or her exploitation by obscuring the extraction of surplus value that helps constitute the capitalist mode of production.[76]

This wage theory has been widely applied, in descriptive accounts of the ways in which exploitation works, in segmented labor market models, and in synthetic attempts to use the analytical tools of neoclassical economics to illuminate the microeconomic details of differential relations to the means of production. It plays a key role in Antonio Gramsci's discussion of the "Fordist ideology of high wages" as the means through which workers' consent is essentially purchased by capital.[77] It is the basis of Michel Aglietta's claim that "the reproduction of the wage relation is the kernel of the law of capital accumulation," and it has become a staple axiom of the radical labor studies literature.[78] Michael Burawoy, for example, shows how the evolution of shop-floor culture abets the wage's task of mystification.[79] Richard Edwards, Michael Reich, and Mario Barrera have each demonstrated the ways in which social difference impinges upon the wage relation, both qualitatively and quantitatively.[80] Samuel Bowles and Herbert Gintis have used it to develop an extensive critique of neoclassical behavioral assumptions using both sociological analysis and formal economic models.[81]

This work has gone a long way toward introducing politics to wage analysis.[82] Yet the most influential of these interpretations of Marxian wage theory continue to work from two premises that must be abandoned if history is to be adequately explained. The first is the ahistorical assertion that, from a discursive or ideological perspective, the wage is the tool of capital alone. The second is a tacit but persistent faith in the existence, somewhere, of an equilibrium that is analytically relevant to the theory of the wage. These premises operate independently, and some writers eschew one or the other, but rarely both.

First, according to an orthodox Marxist "logic"—a potentially problematic concept in and of itself—the politics of the wage is presumed to be reducible to a single core function: the legitimation of exploitative capitalist relations of production. Although this onetime article of faith is rarely articulated today, it still occasionally leads to arguments (often based on a selective reading of Lukács) about workers' false consciousness, through which they are duped into perpetuating their own misery.[83] However, contemporary Marxist theory, in the fertile ground turned by Gramsci, recognizes that these mystifications cannot be maintained by capital alone. Active consent from workers, who must be persuaded of the benefits of the wage relation, is also a part of the story. In these explanations, workers recognize their oppression but are nonetheless partners in a "Faustian bargain" with bosses. The message implicit in the work of Stanley Aronowitz, for example, runs through much recent Marxian critique of the wage: workers act against their own "interests" (for a variety of reasons) and accept the exploitative status quo.[84] In fact, much of radical political economy from the 1960s to the 1980s can be read (ironically) as arguing that at least while capitalism remains the dominant mode of production, Keynes fairly got it right: the working class has indeed basically been fooled and is mostly fighting over capitalist scraps.[85]

The more sophisticated Marxian treatments of the wage, like those of Bob Rowthorn, Paul Willis, and G. A. Cohen, tease apart the ways in which the workings of capitalism have been challenged and reconfigured in part by workers' historical and political agency, to show that they are not fooled and are capable of measured judgment.[86] These analyses reject the true-false consciousness dualism, arguing, as Stuart Hall says, that "the relations in which people exist are the 'real relations' which the categories and concepts they use help them to grasp and articulate in thought."[87] Interestingly, though, the wage theory that drops out of these critical and complex insights is remarkably similar to that proposed by institutional economists. Since the politics of the wage is a capitalist politics of legitimation, when the wage is no longer an effective legitimator, it is no longer a significant political site. Politics thus comes to subsume the cultural, but the wage as a political arena is dismissed. It becomes just what it is in Kerr's imperfect labor markets, the quantitative outcome of the struggle over the distribution of income. The wage is again instrumentalized as income qua welfare. It is not where politics happens but a pecuniary measure or outcome of those relations.

Even though the concept of equilibrium is mostly foreign to Marx's own work, Marxian wage theory's second limiting premise is an unquestioned assumption that a theory of equilibrium is essential to wage formation in the labor market. Neo-Marxian economists like Roemer and Bowles, who use formalist neoclassical methods, adhere rigidly to this article of faith.[88] But as the histories I recount in the next three chapters show (and as Marx says), wage rates have no straightforward market-determined level;

they vary enormously and are always influenced by the agency of workers, capitalists, and the state. Indeed, determination in the "purely" economic sense is impossible, for it posits a wage outside lived history, a wage that must somehow exist "in general," apart from its particular instantiation. This is not merely a technical issue, in that it violates the fundamental premises of the materialist dialectic; it seems to me untenable on even the most momentary reflection.[89] Even a relatively stable phenomenon like the conventional wage is not an equilibrium in the economic sense of a stable point to which a system will settle following disturbance. Rather, the conventional wage is the product of ongoing political negotiation between wage earners and employers, in conversation with the state; it must be actively maintained, not passively allowed to "balance."

Nonetheless, intoxicating notions of formal equilibria (however "dynamic") have gradually become analytical premises common throughout economic analysis, from Marshall to Keynes to Akerlof to Roemer.[90] Even though the class antagonism at the heart of Marxian analysis represents a fundamental challenge to the metaphysics of supply-demand models, many Marxists seem unable to restrain themselves from seeking—and thus, of course, discovering—"natural" points of economic stability, even if merely momentary. Yet even at a strictly theoretical level, ignoring history entirely, these postulated equilibria are conceivable only if actors have (a) generalizable and identifiable "interests" and (b) socially consistent modes of action for realizing those interests (or coming as close to realizing them as possible). In contemporary Marxian economic theory, "[d]epartures of the real wage from equilibrium—as a result, for example, of price inflation—are assumed to be temporary: unless there are shifts in class power, class struggle is equilibrating."[91]

From a class analytical perspective, at least, many Marxists might be expected to agree with the claim that actors have generalizable and identifiable interests; there is considerably less consensus on whether there are socially consistent modes of action for realizing them.[92] (In fact, I will argue in chapter 6 that the commonsense idea of interests represents a significant barrier to understanding the wage and working-class politics.) The result is that, against the historical specificity that is the very foundation of the Marxian critique of capitalism, equilibrium stows away in the analysis in the name of an ahistorical, and ultimately unsubstantiated, faith in "science," a narrow and antidialectical method in the form of a "reproducible solution," the functional outcome of rational interests and their rational pursuit: an antipolitics.[93]

This is, I believe, an extremely unfortunate development, analytically and politically. For this anticipated stability is inseparable from a theory of clearing labor markets in which supply is exogenous, a proposition that goes against the very basis of Marxian theory, standing as it does in blatant contradiction to a recognition of the "reserve army of the unemployed." The reserve army is the context in which all of this inevitably takes place, at both global and local scales and everything in between; it is all the workers without work, the incessant disciplinary pressure on the wage and all those earning one. It is nothing other than "endogenous" labor supply—the reserve army is not "outside" the labor market; it is "inside" it in the most fundamental, structural ways.[94] As a result, the imputation of equilibria in Marxian wage theory inserts prescriptive and normative conceptions of workers' and employers' interests—i.e., "workers are assumed to maximize X according to Y constraints"—and fabricates a stability in labor market outcomes that essentially dismisses a priori unanticipated, misunderstood, or novel political and cultural dynamics, including those relevant to the wage.

Together, these premises—the politics of the wage is a politics of capitalist legitimation, and equilibrium analysis—hobble a wage theory that is in many other ways supremely sensitive to politics. To move beyond wage determination to the cultural politics of the wage, it is necessary to expand this notion of politics and eschew expectations of equilibrium. Contending with the histories of the wage in the following chapters demands a recognition that the wage is not some empty end product of everyday interactions in the labor market and the workplace; it is, at least in part, where workers' and employers' politics and culture happen. It is animated by labor as well as by capital, neither solely on capitalist terms, nor in predictable ways. It is not only the bosses whose interests are developed and pursued with the wage, or even within capitalism. Positioning the wage on both sides of the equation, if you will, as both determined by and determining the workings of culture and politics, frees social analysis from the blinkered constraints of equilibrium and from a one-dimensional understanding of the wage as an employers' tool wielded against a duped or powerless working class.

A Way beyond Determinacy?: Piero Sraffa

The Cambridge economist Piero Sraffa leads us some way toward the reconstructive work we need to do. Sraffa was a classical economist born (thankfully) too late: he completed Ricardo's attempt to construct a standard measure of value and described the economic impacts of Marx's economic model of "equal organic composition of capital."[95] He was also, however, among the most trenchant critics of his two nineteenth-century predecessors. He dealt what some consider the deathblow to the dominant interpretation of the famous labor theory of value (prices are proportional to embodied labor values) so critical to both Ricardo and Marx, showing that it holds only when profits are zero.[96]

To anyone who has been exposed to Sraffa's work, it may be surprising to find it the basis for a cultural and political approach to the wage. He is certainly enigmatic: a member of Keynes's powerful "circle," he nevertheless always stood outside the Cambridge school in important ways. A retiring and somewhat introverted specialist, Sraffa was credited by Wittgenstein for the epiphany that led him to renounce his early work and develop the more "anthropological" account in the *Philosophical Investigations*. And, even though Sraffa published only a handful of articles and one longer essay, his stature among "heterodox" economists is almost unrivaled.

By himself Sraffa cannot take one very far beyond the limits of formal economic analysis. His major contribution to the literature — *The Production of Commodities by Means of Commodities* (1960) — consists of a technical, terse, and abstract hundred-page essay. He offers no empirical analysis, and he addresses very few of the larger implications of his conclusions in any depth. This is left to the reader. Nevertheless, what may appear as only an echo of the classical emphasis on a material basis for value in fact hints at how much is missing from an account of wages, profits, and prices that glosses over politics. Sraffa bluntly points beyond the system of production, positing (if not showing) the social forces at work in the economy that must inform a theory of the wage, or of profits, or of price.

Sraffa's crucial step, for present purposes, is the rejection of the classical assumption that the conventional wage is given in any particular historical moment, determined by some combination of biological necessity and social custom.[97] While this is of course in the spirit of Marx's account, if not that of many "Marxists," there is a possibility of breach here that takes the critique closer to a cultural politics of the wage and away from the self-imposed constraints of Marxian wage theory, without demanding that its critical conception of wage politics be abandoned.

The exact content of Sraffa's contribution to economic theory is debated, but at a minimum it includes a fundamental challenge to the existence of the neoclassical production function (the basis of the supply curve). By extension, it rejects the idea that price is demand-determined (a position that prompted Samuelson to label Sraffa's price theory "one-legged") and thus fundamentally undermines marginalist theory in general.[98] Sraffa offers the challenge by demonstrating the logical implausibility of the neoclassical claim that by organizing production according to consumer preferences, market prices determine the distribution of income among wages, profits, and rent (on land). Instead, he shows that relative prices depend upon distribution. Indeed, they cannot be known until either wages or profits are exogenously given.[99] Admittedly, this is novel only insofar as it constitutes a rigorous "proof" of Ricardian-Marxian distribution theory.[100] But Ricardo and Marx believed that since the wage reflects a socially determined "subsistence," it must be independently determined outside the system.[101] In contrast, Sraffa argued for an acknowledgment of what he called a "more appropriate, if unconventional, interpretation of the wage": "We have up to this point regarded wages as consisting of the necessary subsistence of the workers and thus entering the system on the same footing as the fuel for engines or the feed for cattle. We must now take into account the other aspect of wages since, besides the ever-present element of subsistence, they may include a share of the surplus product."[102] Thus, it is profit, not wages, that is exogenous. Sraffa never takes the discussion very far himself; he only suggests that the rate of profit is "susceptible of being determined outside the system of production, in particular by the level of money rates of interest," i.e., by central bank or state fiat.[103]

Maurice Dobb, another eminent Cambridge economist and a colleague of Sraffa's, points out that the Ricardian-Marxian theory of the "conventional wage" clearly represents a critical move in the analysis of the politics of the wage, redrawing "the boundaries of economics as a subject . . . so as to include social, and moreover institutional and historically-relative, changing and changeable, conditions that were excluded from Economics as viewed in the post-Jevonian tradition."[104] On at least two trajectories, then, Sraffa takes us in the directions we need to go, although in doing so he simultaneously acknowledges his own explanatory limits.

First, dismissing subsistence constraints upon the wage (as rate and as share), he introduces a much greater degree of indeterminacy to the quantitative question of wage determination than his nineteenth-century forefathers tolerated. Marx recognized that wages varied widely, but he refused to blur the lines of his distributional categories, i.e., constant capital, variable capital, and surplus value. Yet if profits are exogenously given—in other words, determined by relations outside the "economy" as it is conventionally circumscribed (a position that resonates with a Marxian approach)—then the wage acquires what Sraffa calls a "definite meaning." Its "definite meaning" is absolutely *not* a "definite value" or "definite rate" but is rather a dependence on the rate of profit and prices that provides a powerful explanation for the articulation of workers' culture and politics in terms of, and from within, the wage relation.[105] Indeed, it is important to note that the explanatory potential this opens up is as useful to ideological analysis in the spirit of Gramsci as it is to the more "behavioral" frame to which Sraffa was most likely referring.

Second, "as soon as the possibility of variations in the division of the product is admitted," the politically charged labor markets, nonequilibrium wages, class struggle, and social hierarchy that constitute everyday social life in and out of the modern workplace make sense not only empirically but theoretically.[106] The politics of the wage are no longer those of capital alone.

Together, and situated in a broader Marxian analytic, these ideas help us shine some light on those aspects of concrete historical wage struggles that are effaced by the flattening reverse spectroscope of orthodox wage analysis and the faith, however repressed, in ahistorical equilibria. In this new light, in which the wage is an absolutely critical political arena in which working people act in and on capitalism, these struggles regain their political "volume" and become full social spaces in which a great deal more is going on than the quantitative resolution of exogenous power differentials or the conflict of distributional "interests." Rather, in the depth of these histories, the meaning of the wage relation is challenged from within that relation itself, and the opposition between quantity and quality that capitalism posits, and struggles to maintain, is subject to the dialectical movement that gives meaning to the politics of measure. As we will see, the cultural political dynamics that saturate everyday life under capitalism do not *impinge* upon the wage but *constitute* it.

Why was the extra penny so important to
the Union? It will take ten years to make up
the loss of one month's work, at the rate of
a penny an hour.

    Arthur Ross, *Trade Union Wage Policy*
    (1948)

Union men and women will fight for a nickel
an hour more. Millions have trudged the picket
lines since the war ended to safeguard the
American standard of living.

    International Oil Worker, 25 March 1946

3

What's a Penny Worth?

Wages, Prices, & the American Working Man

Wage negotiation is penny politics. At the bargaining table, quality and
quantity—use value and exchange value—are hard to distinguish. Indeed, as the labor economist Arthur Ross points out in this chapter's first
epigraph, there are many cases where the fight for "more" in wages means
"less" in income. Yet there is nothing in this framing that is logically incompatible with a universalizing "rational optimization," however "irrational" any particular decision set might appear to the outside observer. Perhaps, we might say, the more-less contradiction lies in something as simple
as a poorly estimated discount rate or a misinterpretation of workers' time
horizon relative to that of capital. Maybe they value future income more
than anticipated? Maybe the duration or period of political relevance is
longer than previously thought? Alternatively, we might smooth out these
seemingly bumpy "irrationalities" by telling ourselves that, surely, if they
obtained less income holding out for one more penny, then they must have
obtained "more" of something else. In rational choice theory, the stuff of
this "more" is commonly glossed as "utility," the desire for which is presumed to constitute the individually particular motor for human history.
According to this logic, the quantity at issue—utility—can come in many
culturally and politically valuable qualities: security, dignity, autonomy,
citizenship, identity, and political power, to name a few.

    To refuse this logic is not to eschew the pecuniary quantities in which
these struggles get framed; nor does it mean refusing the responsibility to

take the difference between ninety-nine cents and a dollar seriously. But it is crucial to acknowledge that utilitarianism reduces quality to flavor, and politics to accumulation. The behavioral analyses that fall out of rational choice thinking are constructed through questions to which the answers are already known and always the same. In the case of wage negotiation, they avoid entirely the more vexing question of what is actually at stake. What if it is not merely something *more* that workers want but something *different*? Why put so much store in a nickel or a penny? Taking the "extra penny" seriously means trying to understand the specific quality, the historical particularity—the political possibility—of *this* penny: not one penny among any of the other ninety-nine but this one, the one-hundredth penny, fought for at this time in this place by these people.

In terms of a politics of measure, the extra penny Ross is wondering about is not identical with or substitutable for any other. If it were, we would be in the "measureless," the space of mere quantitative change. Rather, in its historical-geographic specificity, the extra penny marks a cultural political threshold, beyond which the world is not merely quantitatively bigger (although it may be that too) but qualitatively different. Measure, as I hope is becoming clear, is precisely this node or knot that constitutes the space in which value is politicized, and the politics of measure consists in not only the struggles in that space but also the struggle to produce those spaces, to tie knots in the thread of value where there had previously been only slippery measurelessness.

This chapter is in some ways an extended response to Ross's question—why was the extra penny so important?—through a discussion of one union local's efforts to tie such a knot, to make the wage the political site at which the post–World War II United States might be articulated with its democratic promise (a promise that was in no way open to all, as we shall see). Through the lens of a history of Local #1-128, Oil Workers International Union (OWIU), Los Angeles petroleum refinery workers who took part in the great wave of strikes immediately following World War II, I describe the political and cultural economy of wage determination as a "moral economics" of everyday life in the emergent postwar United States. I am specifically concerned with the ways in which, in the months immediately following the war, Local 128's wage conflicts served as a means to specify and reproduce a particular normative model of the "American working man": a politically engaged (white) male worker, sufficiently well compensated to provide for the security and future of a "traditional" nuclear family.[1] This model developed in response to changing conceptions of economic citizenship and family/gender roles, social structures that had been radically challenged by the political economy of depression and war.[2]

The chapter focuses on the experience of workers in L.A., but given the intensity and complexity of wage struggles all over the United States in the wake of the war, it is inevitably also about nationwide union wage politics. I consequently move back and forth between the specific experiences of Local 128 and the OWIU's national organization (the "International"). These shifts are necessary because the history of the local is in important ways special and unexceptional; it is an especially interesting instance of national dynamics as they played out through the particularities of L.A. Both the region's specificity and its generality, its "American-ness," matter a great deal.

The analysis centers on the heated wage-price politics of the first months of peace, approximately August 1945 to August 1947. First, I show how, during this period, oil workers strove to retain and augment control over central elements of everyday life through a particular construction of the relationship between wages and prices. I argue that conflicts over real and money wage rates were the central means through which male workers constructed a moral economy in the postwar United States. As such, these conflicts were critical forms through which they pressed alternative social and political economic agenda and through which they actively participated in the national political economy. This is why the "extra penny" was so important.

Second, against much radical labor history and political economy, I argue that to read mere self-interest, corporatism, apathy, or "false consciousness" in unions' wage demands is to miss the *politically* transformative potential of American workers' struggle over the return to labor: the politics of measure unfolding to return quality to quantity and overcome its limits. The well-rehearsed argument that, after World War II, the labor movement acquiesced to capital, that the rank and file's revolutionary "nature" was betrayed by its leaders' essentially nontransformative income and security agenda, elides because it cannot explain the fact that many union members saw the "Great Accord" of high Fordism not only as a major victory but as a victory won through struggle, not surrender.[3]

This chapter, then, is based in oil workers' wage-price politics as they were articulated by the workers themselves from within the wage relation. I show how the wage, as both exchange relation and social relation, reflects extant social and political economic conflict and at the same time fundamentally shapes that conflict. The wage is often the lens through which working people in the United States view the broader political economy, and the political and cultural power that unions have invested in the wage is testament to its crucial role in the political economy of the working class. Insofar as the postwar moment contained the seeds of changes both long sought and dreaded by male oil workers, the wage served as an instrument in their efforts to control these transformations and as a measure of them.

Such an orientation toward the wage does not necessarily entail working-class "deradicalization"—a process that must be historically identified rather than assumed—even if some memory of militant glory days is historically warranted (and often it is not). Rather, it seems to me that the arrogation of political economic intelligence, implicit in the unreflective ease with which intellectuals use this term, only pushes the working class and radical scholars further apart. This abets powerful reactionary political strategies and ideologies; political "experts" both left and right tell workers their politics are nonrevolutionary, but only the Right seems to trust their judgment. We must remember that "[o]rganized workers do not have to climb barricades every time capitalism experiences a crisis, but this implies little about their 'militancy.'"[4]

This persistent political problem is the background against which the chapter develops. The discussion is founded upon a historical ethnography that feeds on the many disciplines that constitute what is presently called "working-class studies." Although I am uncomfortable with the term for the distance it seems to build into the author-subject relation, the work of geographers, historians, sociologists, and others with which the field is associated provides much of the essay's scholarly terrain.[5] The arguments I make regarding the complexities of working-class agency, and its geographic and historical specificity, are based on the words and actions of working men on their own terms. What I piece together from the historical record accords with the work of "new" labor geographers like Andrew Herod, emphasizing workers' agency in both the resistance to and persistence of capitalism. In a loose sense, I propose an ideological and political economic analogue to Herod's "labor's spatial fix." Where Herod is concerned with "thinking about how the social actions of workers relate to their desire to implement in the physical landscape their own spatial visions of a geography of capitalism which is enabling of their own self-reproduction and social survival," I focus on the ways the wage becomes a dynamic arena in which these same desires are projected onto the ideological and political economic landscape.[6] Insofar as wage struggles help shape intra- and interclass relations, they partially determine the very form of capitalism, including the means through which it persists. Working-class studies, as I hope the following discussion demonstrates, should be Herod's "labor geography" writ large: it must examine specific capitalisms as the product not of simple class dominance but of actual and ongoing historical struggles.

The discussion is organized into five sections. In the first, I briefly describe the L.A. oil industry at the end of World War II and flesh out labor's postwar politics of "take-home pay." The second section examines the politics of price in the immediate postwar period, linking it, through the wage, to organized workers' struggle to describe an "American standard of living." The third discusses what it was to be an American working man in the emerging postwar world. I show how arguments concerning real wage rates were part of workers' simultaneous attempts to define a more egalitarian Americanism and protect the privileged economic role of the male in the household. In the fourth, I describe contractual mechanisms oil workers tried to insert into the wage relation to achieve some of their goals. In the last section I consider the politics of the wage, and the relation between the economic and the political, in light of this history.

L.A. Oil Workers and the Politics of "Take-Home Pay" at War's End

The struggles over the distribution of income immediately following World War II challenge any notion of the wage as a politically empty measure of relative bargaining power. The legacy of wartime social consolidation demonstrates the degree to which politics infused every dimension of wage negotiation. For, while much of the success of U.S. war mobilization was due to the "social patriotic ethos" that was the "quasi-official ideology of the World War Two home front," this ethos did not simply reproduce the presumed lack of class consciousness that made the United States "exceptional."[7] The successes of coordinated war production testify to the sweep of production workers' ideological enlistment in the war effort. At the same time, these ideological and material processes fostered an American egalitarianism that highlighted class inequalities and politicized interclass income differentials. Working people were told they were the "Arsenal of Democracy," and many took it to heart, demanding a political economic citizenship commensurate with their productive contribution.[8]

Through what labor historian Nelson Lichtenstein calls a "mobilization dialectic," workers' political economic enfranchisement thus simultaneously facilitated labor's cooperation and destabilized axes of conventional social stratification, ideologically extending productive American economic citizenship to labor's rank and file.[9] American workers who recognized these discursive developments for what they were—state-legitimated steps toward progressive political goals—wanted to help win the war and improve their lot in a more just America. The ways in which income distribution apparently shifted in workers' favor during the war—diminished income inequality, higher wages, and controlled consumer prices—reinforced this development. "Wages represented more than money to most workers. The level of reimbursement symbolized a worker's social worth."[10] In fact, wages were both symbol and measure of America and American democracy.[11]

Los Angeles was known throughout the early twentieth century as the "city of the open shop," but World War II reinvigorated organized labor in L.A., and the OWIU was a prime beneficiary.[12] Local 128 grew from 2,426 members in June 1938 to 6,912 in September 1945, becoming the OWIU's largest local, and its increasing confidence in its security and power reflected this growth.[13] In 1944, following what one member called "a year of unparalleled success in the organization of the oil industry," membership grew by more than one-third. At war's end, members said "the feeling [was] good in Local #128," which was "in a sounder position than ever before." One month before V-J Day (14 August 1945), rank-and-file representatives to the district council declared that "#128 has its house in order" and the postwar era promised "more unity than ever before."[14]

These reconfigurations were all the more radical in L.A., particularly in the oil industry.[15] Oil was perhaps the greatest single factor in the form and prosperity of the metropolitan region's development, and from the 1890s until at least the 1950s, L.A. can be accurately called an "oil town."[16] As the *Los Angeles Times* remarked after World War II, "Our economy here is built on oil."[17] Petroleum's importance to L.A. meant unionization in oil fundamentally influenced how these politicized notions of worker citizenship resonated throughout the region.

This unity was perhaps more readily achieved because L.A.'s approximately fifteen thousand oil workers were almost exclusively white men. They and their families lived in "suburban industrial clusters" developed near refinery sites like Brea, Long Beach, San Pedro, Whittier, Fullerton, El Segundo, and Torrance.[18] They enjoyed relatively high wages and benefits, stable internal labor markets, long periods of employment, and historically discriminatory labor practices that prevented nonwhites and women from entering the workforce in significant numbers.[19]

Yet uncertainty loomed on the horizon, even for relatively privileged workers. The city's wealth and population exploded during the war. Between 1941 and January 1945, the U.S. government contracted sixty billion dollars in war production in the L.A. industrial area alone.[20] From 1940 to V-J Day, L.A. received more than half of California's 1.5 million new workers.[21] Between 1940 and its October 1943 peak, L.A. manufacturing employment increased by 293,000, or almost 200 percent.[22] Shipbuilding and aircraft construction, "war baby" industries providing much of the employment growth, concentrated in L.A. and accounted for 70 percent of California manufacturing jobs by 1945.[23] Coordinated resource utilization and market controls enabled unprecedented levels of industrial production. Incomes and profits rose markedly, and unemployment was extraordinarily low.

The end of war production was thus a frightening prospect. Many expected the bubble to burst spectacularly, unemployment, inflation, and coordination problems throwing the entire nation into a recessionary spiral matching that in the early 1930s: drastically curtailed government spending, reduced working hours, plummeting production and profits.[24] If price controls were relaxed or removed, prices of goods and services artificially suppressed since 1942 would skyrocket. Massive unemployment would greet military personnel reentering a labor market already glutted by displaced war workers, devastating aggregate demand. And, as the state whose economy was most completely organized toward war production, California would be hit particularly hard, L.A. receiving the worst.[25]

In light of these possibilities, unions mobilized to protect the political economic gains they obtained during wartime. In a bitter reversal, the decades-long struggles to secure the eight-hour day—the "sanctity" of which workers emphasized to show how twelve-hour days were proof of their extraordinary commitment to the war effort—seemed to come back to life as a tool of capital, and the end of the war forced workers into a historically exceptional effort to fight the *reduction* of the working day.[26] The longer-term contradictions implicit in that position led unions, especially in core industries like steel, rubber, automotive, and oil, to defend the maintenance of "take-home pay." With the rest of organized labor, the OWIU argued that substantial "wage adjustments" would be necessary as soon as the war ended to make up in hourly rates what would be lost in weekly earnings as a result of reduced hours.[27] Such "adjustments" were necessary to maintain workers' purchasing power to mitigate economic collapse: "[A] 30% slash in earnings means 30% less for the butcher, the baker and the candlestick maker . . . a 30% slash in the earnings of industrial workers shrinks the farmers' market by exactly that amount."[28]

For several reasons, the OWIU entered this fray with exceptional energy. First, the petroleum industry assumed enormous importance during the war. Maximum production in the fields and refineries was essential to the prosecution of the war effort. This meant not only the expansion of an already politically powerful industry but also growing union membership and legitimate claims on the part of oil workers to a central role in the production of "Victory Juice."[29] Second, in contrast to war industries like shipbuilding, petroleum markets were not expected to collapse with the end of the war, as domestic demand rose steeply with increased consumer spending and the end of government rationing.[30] Third, by V-J Day, petroleum refinery employees were the best-paid manufacturing workers in the United States, in both hourly wages and weekly earnings.[31] Workweeks of forty-eight to fifty-two hours were standard throughout the industry, and the anticipated postwar decrease in hours (to forty), especially in light of high relative wages, was of particular concern to the OWIU. Local 128 shared all these national-level concerns. In addition, it recognized the enormous local political and economic significance of union consolidation at this critical moment. Los Angeles unions campaigned under the banner "Finish the Job—Organize L.A.," since the histories of L.A. and its oil industry highlighted the exceptional opportunity the moment seemed to present.[32]

"The Arithmetic of the Future":
Wages, Prices, and Purchasing Power

The Strike of 1945

Although the national reconversion recession was less dramatic than some predicted, L.A. experienced "one of the most severe economic depressions in its entire history."[33] As soon as the war ended, weekly earnings and hourly wages fell across all sectors, and both regional unemployment rates and consumer price indexes rose rapidly in absolute terms and relative to other parts of the United States.[34] Manufacturing was hit especially hard, as statewide employment fell by nearly half, from an October 1943 peak of 1,145,000 to 600,000 in November 1945.[35]

Local 128 felt the impact of these changes immediately. The shorter workweek in L.A. refineries lowered real earnings by 12.5 percent in the eight weeks between V-J Day and the middle of October.[36] Moreover, local members claimed their real hourly wages had fallen during the war. According to OWIU calculations, the local cost of living increased 43.5 percent between 1941 and 1945, while wages rose only 20 percent.[37] With postwar inflation, workers' incomes were sure to be even more drastically devalued.

In mid-September, International president O. A. Knight (a member of Local 128) told a special meeting of L.A. refinery workers that "the Union is attempting to maintain a stable economy and a decent standard of living, by maintaining at least the present rate of pay." Given industry opposition, he said, "economic warfare is here until some serious problems are solved." The OWIU issued a strike call on 17 September but put it on hold when some companies and the federal government expressed some willingness to bargain. On 25 September 1945, six weeks into peacetime, the OWIU executive met with representatives of eleven oil companies. The union pressed for a 30 percent "wage adjustment" to maintain wartime take-home pay, in line with the famous "52–40 or Fight" program of the Congress of Industrial Organizations (CIO), which called for fifty-two hours' pay for forty hours' work. Industry, under significant public and government pressure, allowed that reduced hours and earnings were a concern and made counteroffers.[38] In L.A., these ranged between 12 and 15 percent.[39]

Local 128 rejected these compromises. By the summer of 1945, local leadership believed the union had "tremendous economic power to support the justified demands of labor" and the local had, as member R. E. Warren put it, "more unity now than ever before."[40] Prospects for a strike looked good. Although, as one member remarked, it needed to be "conducted in a manner that will not unnecessarily inconvenience the public," price controls meant a postwar strike would not necessarily increase consumer costs and provoke public opposition.[41]

After last-minute negotiations organized by the secretary of labor failed, Local 128 went out on 2 October. Two days later, however, under the authority of the War Powers Act, President Truman directed the navy to seize and operate all struck refineries in the "national interest." The following day, Knight telegrammed the secretary of Local 128, asking all workers to return to the refineries and bargaining tables and urging full cooperation with the government.[42]

The OWIU's temporarily aborted wage militancy marked the beginning of a strike wave that eventually put more than six hundred thousand workers on picket lines across the country. The federal government's efforts to coordinate industrial reconversion through labor-management cooperation fell apart at a national meeting of union and corporate leadership in the late fall.[43] By the end of 1945, major strikes over take-home pay were under way in the auto, steel, rubber, and mining industries. At the end of November, with oil negotiations stalled and the strike proving symbolically critical to the government's reconversion efforts, Secretary of Labor L. B. Schwellenbach created a panel "representing the public interest which shall investigate the labor dispute relating to the wages which should be paid on the resumption of a 40-hour week in the seized [petroleum] plants and facilities."[44]

The Oil Panel had a shaky start. Its authority was unclear, and oil companies mocked it as a "kangaroo court." Many major employers declined to attend the hearings. Those that did send representatives argued that the union's demands were "exorbitant and unjustified," that the panel was incapable of making the necessary decisions, and that the only "valid ground for a wage increase" was the gap between cost-of-living increases and changes in earnings. The OWIU, however, took seriously the opportunity to state its case to the government and the public. It gathered extensive statistics to defend its demands and published a pamphlet that was sent to "all member of Congress, ranking government officials and public leaders."[45] The basis of this defense was the centrality of high wages to the American economy and way of life:

> In placing our case before you, we do so firmly in the opinion that the oil workers' fight to preserve their living standards is a matter of concern to all Americans because it affects the key problem of our times—that of maintaining full employment through adequate purchasing power. . . . Oil workers do not propose to see their living standards slashed in such a fashion by the richest industry in America. In taking this stand they are fighting selfishly for their families. In a larger sense they are fighting for the American standard of living itself—the pride of our nation and the envy of the world.[46]

The union argued that its demands were not only fair and necessary but also, contrary to industry claims, completely feasible. The union held that oil companies would have no difficulty absorbing the wage adjustment: "Because labor costs of refining are only 6.5 percent of operating costs, the prospective savings in (a) overtime, (b) taxes, and (c) through higher productivity will offset the increase in labor cost resulting from the wage increase." Moreover, the "financial position of the companies is so strong as to make unnecessary any price increase."[47]

In an industrialized economy like that of the United States, petroleum is as explosive politically as chemically. Oil is an essential input in virtually all industrial production, and oil workers hardly exaggerated when they called it the "black blood" of the economy.[48] Higher oil prices are interpreted as a threat to the national economy and to the "American way of life." Insofar as petroleum is produced domestically, this threat is internal, even traitorous. Negotiating wage increases in the oil industry is consequently a daunting task.

Accordingly, maintaining take-home pay without raising consumer costs was critical to oil workers' wage objectives, and disabling worker attempts to influence product markets was equally critical to industry. Given oil's significance to the war effort and postwar reconversion and growth, sectoral and general price increases that could be attributed to union wage demands were politically disastrous for the OWIU and the rest of the labor movement.

Nowhere was this truer than in L.A., where an oil strike "hit at the very vitals of the livelihood of the Pacific Coast." The *Los Angeles Times* later remarked, "[W]e do not have the alternate fuel, coal, on which the East can rely"; an oil shutdown threatened the region with "paralysis," and a 1946 economic survey of the region concluded that the "future of the petroleum industry is vitally important to the economic welfare of Los Angeles."[49]

The members of Local 128 attempted to mitigate public opposition and counter antilabor media in several ways. First, they reiterated the OWIU argument that a "wage adjustment" was not a raise. As Elro Brown, representing Local 128 in negotiations with Union Oil, put it to management, "We were not figuring this as a wage increase but only trying to maintain a fair take home pay." Second, with the public and management they pressed the claim that industry could easily afford the changes. Third, they proposed to ration gasoline in the event of a strike in a manner that disrupted consumers as little as possible.[50]

According to industry and the *Times*, however, price controls made any pay raise above 15 percent unworkable. In strike negotiations, management representatives contested union estimates of price increases and highlighted the need to "satisfy their stock holders." They ran advertisements in local newspapers warning "hopping mad" consumers of rising gas and fuel oil prices. The *Times* wholly supported management, arguing that the brunt of wage demands would not be borne by industry alone but would be "of the type that hits John Q. Public in his pocketbook." Union rationing schedules had "all the earmarks of Communist origin, since it would be a first step in a 'proletarian dictatorship.'"[51]

Industry's strategy was effective with the public, but the vestiges of the New Deal and war mobilization state were sympathetic to union arguments, at least at the end of 1945. When, to the evident dismay of other oil companies, Sinclair Oil agreed to an hourly increase of 18 percent in late December, the Oil Panel's arbitration role was made redundant. The deal broke the deadlock between the OWIU and management, and the panel merely generalized its terms across the industry. The most significant dimension of the panel's decision, therefore, was its decision concerning the legitimacy of a compensatory price increase, which was denied. This represented as important a victory for the union as the wage increase; wage demands were embedded in a militant wage-price politics founded upon consumption as much as production.

The American Standard of Living

Some radical critics, especially those associated with the regulation school, see this "commonsense" Keynesian attachment to "purchasing power" as the integral element in the Fordist "management of the production of wage-labour." They argue that the articulation of production and consumption creates the conditions for a "canalization of the class struggle" through institutions like collective bargaining, a process conducive to rapid and stable economic growth, but one that leaves "the field free for a ferocious intensification of capitalist labour discipline in production."[52]

Unions like the OWIU saw it very differently.[53] "Purchasing power" was based on what United Automobile Workers' (UAW) president Walter Reuther called "the arithmetic of the future."[54] It politicized the wage as the central institution of the American economy, the circulatory link between production and consumption. Moreover, workers' dual identity as producers and consumers provided a macroeconomic foundation for their ideological and political economic claims. High wages were a central pillar of workers' political and cultural norms, materially beneficial, and a sound economic policy objective. The OWIU claimed that unions' wage demands "have safeguarded and strengthened the very foundations of American civilization. They have strengthened the schools, the churches, the hospitals, the libraries. They have made it possible for the merchant to make a living. They have safeguarded American prosperity."[55]

To oil workers, then, maintaining take-home pay did not entail trading acquiescence for income. On the contrary, Local 128 declared the OWIU "the most progressive and democratic of all the great American trade unions" and held that the content of American-ness was at stake. Wage demands were a means to "restore the cut in purchasing power which refinery workers will suffer as overtime hours of work are eliminated. It is but a partial step in the struggle to win the American Standard of Living." The OWIU claimed to have "chosen now to fight out the issue of *prosperity vs. depression*," which was "determined not by cloudy generalizations and pious hopes, but by the size of America's pay envelopes." Local 128 unanimously resolved that "all unbiased surveys show that industry can pay the full take-home-pay and still maintain their pre-war rate of profit," for "every day the employers in the oil industry are salting away moneys from their latest commodity increases which rightfully belong to the workers."[56]

These are fundamental claims about the meaning of the wage for the distribution of income and the capacity of working men to fulfill family obligations and enjoy some long-term control over domestic life. They invigorated contract negotiations and OWIU internal communications throughout the postwar era. For instance, bargaining with Union Oil in 1945, negotiator Elro Brown drew on these "justifiable" expectations to explain Local 128's wage demands. He told company representatives that it takes "the whole of a man's wages to live" and asked "if they felt that a laboring man was not entitled to lay away a little money for contingencies or did they feel the men were like their machinery to get what they could out of them and then scrap them and get new men." Industry's demands, oil workers claimed, were based upon a "medieval economic notion" that clearly meant "another catastrophe duplicating the early 1930s, with breadlines, Hoovervilles, and veterans selling apples to those citizens lucky enough to have a nickel to spare." The wage struggle was the working man's fight to save "American civilization."[57]

Oil Men and American Working Men

Men Earn, Women Spend

Everyday life for working-class families in L.A., and throughout the United States, was transformed by depression and then by war. Economic crisis and wartime labor shortages allowed women to enter the workforce in unprecedented numbers, despite union opposition to recognizing women's full membership. Even in households in which the male was not enlisted, women's contribution to family earnings grew dramatically. In the face of these changes, unions like the OWIU found themselves in a tricky position. While a pluralized economic citizenship resonated with oil workers' political programs, and membership concerns encouraged organizing new workers, the economic enfranchisement of millions of women workers challenged the sanctity of male workers' "family wage."[58]

This represented a radical change in the oil industry. Workers' pride in the manliness of their work is a constant throughout OWIU records and the literature on oil work.[59] Not only was masculinity materially important in the ways that workers interacted with one another, but it underwrote the very ethos of oil work. "Oil men," as both workers and management proudly called themselves, considered the industry the toughest and most important—the most American—in the world. They appropriated the tradition of western field workers, who were "the supermen of Industry; men without peer in the fields of rugged individualism and pioneering. The Oil Worker is more responsible for the progress made in the Twentieth Century than any other worker. Take away this worker and all Industry stops." These men, for whom "danger and the risk to life and limb only create a greater pride," are "willing to face any number of hardships"; they exemplify the "spirit . . . so typical of many early Americans."[60]

Consequently, women's employment in L.A. refineries, beginning in late 1942, and workers' wives' employment in other war industries, flew in the face of tradition and discourse in an industry a Standard Oil of California advertisement called "almost as masculine as the army." In meetings during the war, male members—women were not members of decision-making or negotiation committees—reluctantly acknowledged that employing women in the refineries was "inevitable," "the only solution for the continuance of operations on a war time basis." If not undertaken voluntarily, they knew it would be federally imposed.[61]

Opposition to women in the refineries, and a general lack of union concern for their interests, are therefore hardly surprising. Local 128 formally defended the claims of women workers who were discriminated against or harassed during the war or laid off at its end, but these grievances were rarely pursued. Instead, women's interests were often seen as inimical to unionism—and to the economic citizenship it embodied—at least as they were articulated in the workplace. For instance, women complaining of harassment by foremen at Shell Chemical in Torrance were urged by their union brothers to "cooperat[e] with their stewards" or accused of being "agitators."[62] This process of marginalization, though counter to workplace solidarity, represented the extent to which the shop-floor presence of women undermined the centrality of the American working man to the oil industry and to American-ness more broadly. The war had destabilized domestic gender roles—male breadwinner, female homemaker—but postwar prosperity presented an opportunity to reestablish it. Wage-earning women did not fit labor's political vision; rather, they were temporarily performing the jobs, and earning the wages, of men who would return to work after the war.[63]

The fight for take-home pay was thus described as a kind of David-and-Goliath standoff: union men fighting for an American standard of living, protecting their families from menacing economic change while their wives and children watched from behind the picket fence. Victory in the conflict over wages meant "more milk for the kids, better clothes for the little woman, a better home for the whole family."[64]

These idealized gender roles helped constitute oil workers' ideological and political commitments, union organization and strategic discourse. They were not so much foundational as part of the very aggregate that cemented the foundation per se. Less committed union members were labeled "weak sisters"; men joked about the rising prices of women's clothing; organizers were reminded, "[D]on't neglect the little woman when you're talking unionism to her husband."[65] Of course, these sentiments were not exceptional among males of all class positions at the time. Indeed, the ubiquitous contemporary "ideal of masculinity," unattached as it is to any particular social or political formation, is a product of the particular "fears and hopes of modern society."[66] Its discursive "polyvalence" helped make sense of oil workers' superficially paradoxical efforts to reconstruct a "traditional" patriarchal domestic order while radically reconfiguring U.S. class relations. Masculinism could justify "the most progressive and democratic of all the great American trade unions" fighting to keep women at home.

In this context, the wage could hardly be more politically significant.[67] When the OWIU declared the wage the "principal issue before the American people," it referred directly to the "problem" working women presented both to the recovery of the patriarchal private sphere and to the functioning of the postwar productive citizenship that would constitute the public sphere. For oil workers, take-home pay was the material link between the two spheres. First, decreased earnings threatened men's "family wage" because it was that much harder for a single worker to support a family, which diminished the political economic and social status of all American working men and their families. Women would be "forced" to work, or workers' families would have to accept a lower standard of living. Second, at the household scale, lost purchasing power was framed as a direct capitalist attack on the housewife (figure 1). Inflation, or wage rates that rose more slowly than prices, weakened a woman's ability to take care of her husband and children according to "minimum American standards" of "health and decency."[68] Moreover, it demeaned male workers and the ideal of masculinity itself.

This analysis was based upon a model of the family unit in which men-producers and women-consumers were bound together by the economic fabric of the wage. The OWIU took the desirability of this "natural" division of labor to be so uncontroversial after the war that the union founded all of its wage claims in an arithmetic that plainly assumed the "national welfare" was best served by a society composed of families dependent on a single male wage earner.[69] In this normative household economy, gender was partly defined by specific and exclusive domains of economic knowledge: men know wages, women know prices. Women kept the books, did the budgeting and shopping, and experienced inflation firsthand. During the strike of 1945, the *International Oil Worker* quoted the wife of a union member: "Every woman with a family knows that on an average pay-check of about $65.00 a week it's pretty hard to raise three or four children right," and an OWIU pamphlet suggested rising prices were something "which every workingman's wife knows only too well."[70] The liberal political weekly *The Nation* spoke in similar terms to its (presumably male)

THE VILLAIN STILL PURSUED HER

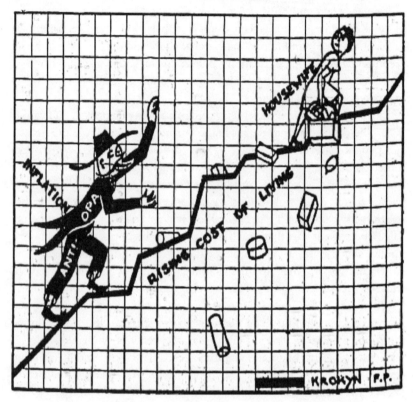

FIGURE 1. *"The Villain Still Pursued Her."* (International Oil Worker, *August 1945*)

readership: "His wife spent 45 per cent of the family income on food. One might think from this that . . . workers indulged themselves by catering to a cultivated palate, but in point of fact the money they spent on food averaged a little more than 30 cents a meal a person. If you don't know what that means, ask your wife."[71]

Despite these acknowledgments of women's particular economic expertise, oil workers nevertheless described women's "spender" role as a contradiction, both aspects of which reinforced their wage demands. On the one hand, wives were careful consumers managing the household. On the other hand, happy wives required luxuries, especially clothes. Women's tendencies to consume unnecessarily justified both higher wages and male breadwinners' role as the household's political agent. Workers spoke of having to "foot the bill" for women's expensive "little ensembles," of women spending carelessly, as if unaware of the value of money.[72] Cartoons depicted women rummaging through their husbands' pockets while the husbands implored them to "leave a buck for PAC [Political Action Committee]."[73] Men understood how hard they had worked for their dollar and what active economic citizenship entailed.

Price Controls and the Protection of the American Working Man

Under an administered price structure, these challenges to class and gender structures influenced the politics of price and income distribution in unprecedented ways, pushing wages to the forefront of postwar ideological conflict. With the establishment of the Office of Price Administration (OPA) and the National War Labor Board (WLB) in 1942, wages and prices of essential goods were determined by federal agencies. Workers thus entered the postwar era with an economic agenda buttressed on the one side by a new politics of productive citizenship and on the other by regulated markets. Struggles over wages and prices—the arena of the first test of this newly powerful vision of industrial belonging—easily became struggles over the "American way of life" that workers had helped preserve:

> Underpinning the entire structure of American civilization and culture is this business of good wages. That's the business of unionism. It certainly isn't the employer's business. His business is to make money —dividends for stockholders and for salaries for the top executives. But somebody has to worry about the bedrock of the American standard of living. To the glory of the American labor movement it can be said that the Oil Workers Intl. Union—CIO and the other unions have done a top-notch job in defending and advancing wage scales. As a result, America has the highest standard of living in the world.[74]

The OWIU's response to the WLB and OPA was relatively consistent with that of the rest of organized labor: grudging cooperation with the former and enthusiastic support for the latter. The chief complaints regarding the WLB targeted the inequalities of administered "sacrifice" for the cause: its detailed administration of industrial relations, which, in combination with the "no-strike" pledge and the wage ceilings set by the "Little Steel" formula of July 1942, rendered the collective bargaining process useless and froze unfair pay differentials as if prewar inequalities were unworthy of redress. Local 128 frequently went before the regional WLB to protest "gross inequities" in companies' wage structures, to object to the establishment of classifications "obsolete and detrimental to many workers in the production department," or to help press for increasing the ceilings of those wages that had "a bearing on rates paid our workers."[75]

In contrast, OPA was enormously popular with unions and the public, demonstrating the breadth of consensus on organized labor's analysis of inflation as a product of capitalists' administered scarcity. To consumers, the agency presented the opportunity to keep prices, as President Knight said, at a "proper level" and "to prevent this gouging of the American public that is going on in practically every store and in practically every other establishment of the nation, where they have anything to sell."[76] In addition, according to male oil workers, OPA not only protected their status as breadwinners but also lessened the unfair burden rising prices placed on their wives.

A significant part of OPA's appeal was its capacity to administer real wages and its symbolic challenge to the price mechanism as the principal organizational force in the American political economy. In real income terms, the agency not only provided consumers with price stability and some assurance of "equal sacrifice" during the war; it also suggested a means through which to retain labor's improved political economic position afterward by politicizing the labor and product markets.[77] With the end of hostilities, and the consequent end of the "no-strike" pledge, regulation persisted in petroleum markets, while it relaxed in labor relations.[78] With production, distribution, and pricing still heavily regulated by OPA and the Petroleum Administration for War (PAW), the war's "wage and price controls" had the truly radical potential to become simply "price controls" in the postwar era. For many oil workers, this promised the protection of real wages and the family security and industrial citizenship that constituted them. By these standards, opposition to OPA was not only antiworker but antifamily and anti-American. It denied the justice of income redistribution and belied the promise of the war years.[79]

Wage-Price Politics and Collective Bargaining

Although organized labor's efforts to save price controls ultimately failed, oil workers did press for contractual mechanisms that supported the same male-centered, class egalitarian political economic vision. In negotiations, neither the International nor Local 128 relied upon interindustry comparison to justify wage claims. Instead, in light of reduced real wages and increased corporate revenues, they focused on the gulf between the socioeconomic and political security of capital and that of labor, aggressively pursuing a variety of equalizing arrangements that would ensure what Local 128 representative Elro Brown called plainly "a just share of profits" and price stability with or without OPA.[80] These overlay, and were partly legitimized by, a push to reduce wage dispersion within the local that also reflected the wage-price politics of the American working man. These efforts modulated the relationship among oil workers, and between the OWIU and management.

Largely owing to WLB policies, the wage structure of U.S. industry narrowed dramatically during the war. Increasingly regulated production motivated a detailed coordination of labor relations and the labor process. Establishing wage brackets within the constraints imposed by Little Steel and the ideology of equal sacrifice, the board's decisions cumulatively diminished interindustry wage differentials and decreased occupational and skill wage gaps.[81] In the oil industry, and especially in L.A., this trend was even more pronounced, as Local 128 bargained to reduce intralocal wage dispersion further. Although the goal was higher wages, oil workers used wage negotiation as a site to build intralocal solidarity, demanding wage schedules that would have particularly equalizing outcomes. In combination with the WLB, these efforts created a wage distribution across L.A. oil workers, the narrowest in the country prior to the war, that was even further compressed during and after.[82] Booming membership during this period is at least partial testament to how attractive a commitment to industrial egalitarianism was to L.A. workers.

For example, although the effort failed, they demanded equal money raises for all workers, regardless of occupation, since these would "spread greater benefits in the lower paid classifications, where it is most needed." If this effort had been successful, the raises would have reduced overall wage inequality by granting a higher proportionate increase to the lower waged. Industry was well aware of the organizational power of this strategy. Percentage increases augment wage inequality, and in front of the Oil Panel corporate representatives insisted that only a percentage-based wage increase would be acceptable — this despite the fact that the structure of such an agreement has no inherent financial advantage.[83] Part of the local's arguments for reducing wage differentials drew on long-standing worker-based arguments concerning the relationship between the disagreeableness of a job and wages. In contrast to the conventional "rules" of capitalist labor markets, according to which the "dirtier" or more unskilled jobs are generally less well paid, union members asserted that economic rationality demanded that the less appealing the job, the higher its wage rate should be.[84] In negotiations with Shell in 1945, for instance, Local 128 representatives claimed that productivity was in many cases an unjust wage determinant, that a "disagreeable job warrants more money."

Similarly, in meetings with Union Oil Company, they demanded wage increases because particular tasks were "more hazardous" to "physical fitness" and "personal feelings."[85]

The solidaristic orientation of oil workers and the degree of organizational unity that it helped foment in Local 128 were exceptional, especially in L.A. They were also remarkable given the large, and relatively high waged, craft component of the refinery workforce the local had to convince not to join American Federation of Labor (AFL) unions like the Pipefitters or the Operating Engineers. But they were undoubtedly effective. As a local member commented one month before the war ended: "[F]actionalism is practically nonexistent."[86] This relative political harmony functioned as a backdrop for Local 128's efforts to institute three strategic labor-management equalizing mechanisms, each of which worked at a different scale: shift differentials to assert some control of the workday; contractual cost-of-living adjustments to protect workers from economic shocks; and regional and national long-term security protections to maintain labor's improved political and economic position after the war.

The first of these strategic equalizing mechanisms took the form of demands for some control of the working day in Local 128 refineries. Because of capital costs, petroleum refineries run almost constantly, and three shifts are necessary in any twenty-four-hour period. Workers generally rotated through day, evening, and graveyard shifts and were paid the same for each. While acknowledging and welcoming the constant demand for oil, oil workers resisted the way in which this scheduling disrupted their nonwork lives and demanded some compensation for its inconveniences. As the war came to an end, they began pressing for progressive shift differentials—the more nonstandard the shift hours, the higher the wage. Like the postwar wage adjustments, differentials were also demanded on money terms. Local representatives argued they were justified because "rotating shifts are especially deleterious to employees," since "on rotation work an employee never becomes adjusted to a regular cycle of living."[87]

Industry rejected these claims, asserting that shift bonuses were built into the existing wage structure. But Local 128 argued that shift differentials were a matter of "social justice," for they allowed a worker to maintain what negotiators described as a "regular" home life, thereby preserving his health and productivity.[88] The WLB agreed, granting Torrance oil workers the first shift differentials in California, but it was not until the negotiations that ended the strike of 1945 that Local 128 contracted with industry for four- and six-cent differentials for evening and graveyard shifts. As further testament to the political economic significance of small amounts of money, the union granted these payroll adjustments enormous symbolic weight. The *International Oil Worker* reported that they were no less than part of an effort to "safeguard and strengthen the very foundations of American civilization."[89]

Second, workers and management debated union contracts with "escalator clauses" that tied wage increases to changes in the cost of living.[90] Although, on the surface, these appear to benefit union members by buffering them from postwar economic volatility, they were by no means immediately welcomed. Like other unions, Local 128 was skeptical of the "cost of living bonus" offered by the oil companies, which many workers believed "merely serve[d] to freeze the level of real wages, thus depriving wage earners from such other benefits to which they may be entitled because of technological development or because of an expanding economy." Moreover, escalator clauses seemed to close the door on large-scale changes in the distribution of income. At the peak of their organizational power, the local chose to "neither accept or reject" such proposals, which they deemed "a clever move by the companies to forestall and delay actual negotiations for substantial wage increases."[91]

Local 128's eventual acceptance of indexed wages in 1946—the first such agreement in the United States—was predicated on the future openness of the collective bargaining process, so that escalator clauses would not merely fix a "reference wage" to which workers were forever bound.[92] Keynesian real wage inflexibility may eventually have borne out, as Aglietta argues, but in the immediate postwar years many workers and affiliated organizations—including "radicals" like the Socialist Workers' Party—believed that the collective bargaining process could still be structured in their favor. When the OWIU signed indexed contracts to end the postwar strike, the union proudly proclaimed: "From now on the union—not the monopoly—sets the wage pattern in oil."[93] Just as CIO national president Philip Murray later laid out in the *CIO Reemployment Plan* of 1947, escalator clauses provided an "inflation barrier," a wage floor supported by labor's resistance to real wage erosion.[94]

Of course, the spread of cost-of-living arrangements may have created inflationary pressures by contributing to the rigidity of the wage structure over time, and by abetting the influence of worker-worker comparison in wage bargaining. Indeed, some economists have pointed to the increasing inflexibility of the postwar industrial wage structure as the origin of both rapid and "creeping" inflation.[95] But oil workers did not describe these adjustment mechanisms as important because they maintained their relative position at the top of the wage hierarchy. Instead, they agreed to them because they believed they would protect workers against inflation's redistribution of income from wages to profits while unions continued to negotiate for real wage gains. In light of labor's theory of inflation, this made good sense; if rising prices were the result of capitalist greed, then inflationary indexing prevented workers from losing ground while negotiations were ongoing. In fact, indexing might even suppress inflation by reducing capitalists' incentive to raise prices, since they would be forced to pay the price almost immediately.

The third, and most ambitious, mechanism was Local 128's participation in the OWIU's wider national campaigns to protect and extend workers' postwar political and economic security. Los Angeles oil workers also undertook loosely organized efforts to maintain and strengthen what legitimacy labor had recently achieved in the region. Both were explicitly driven by the vision of industrial masculinity that underwrote the wage-price politics of the American working man.

At the bargaining table, Local 128 argued over profits and workers' just claims to them as American working men. Minutes of negotiations, union meetings, and OWIU literature all echo members' belief in the importance of the "American standard of living," "American wages," and the critical role of working-class purchasing power in the maintenance of democracy. These statements echo the OWIU's national political campaigns after the war, which, like those of other CIO unions, emphasized the need to move from labor's position of strength to a fully articulated, "Fordist" American democracy: "The jungle of industrial relations has been cleared out. A man knows his way around now. If there is injustice—then there are ways provided by the union contract to protect a man's rights on the job. We are industrial citizens—not serfs of an absolute monarch."[96]

Outside of attempts to reinforce price controls and defeat Taft-Hartley, these programs generally sought to establish a guaranteed annual wage and ensure full male employment. Guaranteed income programs were justified by the same claims used in wage bargaining. First, they would maintain the purchasing power that supported the economy, protecting not only oil workers but all Americans from the "potentiality of the chaos and economic waste and of the spiritual costs of 'boom and bust.'"[97] Second, they would "prevent embarrassment" by enabling a working man to provide for his family "year-round" (figure 2). Full employment would serve the same purposes. According to the logic of purchasing power, it would increase consumer spending and ensure the economic security of American families and the American way of life. As the OWIU claimed, "Joe Worker is just an American trying to make an honest living, educate his children and own his home. He believes he has a right to a living and a right to have something to say about his job. If he didn't feel that way about it, he wouldn't be an American."[98]

The Old Fashioned BELT

designed for Seasonal
TIGHTENING

or

GUARANTEED SUPPORT
for Year-round Wear

for the
ACTIVE
MAN

**PREVENT
EMBARRASSMENT**

**IMPROVE
CIRCULATION**

GUARANTEED

ANNUAL WAGE

UNION
MADE

Local 128 participated in these campaigns in L.A. and donated funds to the OWIU Political Action Committee, which worked out of Washington, D.C., and International headquarters in Denver. Its contributions exceeded all others, and not simply out of organizational duty; the politics of these campaigns were a part of everyday discussion. At weekly local and district meetings, members frequently spoke to one another of the enormous ideological and political economic stakes in the struggles. Statements from rank-and-members like "the future of American democracy is in our hands" and "we must keep our contracts and maintain our basic agreements so that we won't let the service men down that expect to take their rightful place in industry when they return" were not uncommon or disingenuous.[99]

The larger efforts also took on special importance in L.A. Since political power in the hands of organized labor was historically unprecedented, Local 128 was eager both to keep up the fight and to win public support. This required constant organizational vigilance in the face of industry and media opposition, and ongoing public relations efforts to defend union demands and dissociate the local from communism.

Most opposition took the form of blaming labor for postwar inflation. The OWIU, because of oil's significance for reconversion, was a prime target. As the *Los Angeles Times* remarked at the beginning of the 1945 strike, "This is not a fight of sweated labor against injustices—it is a rank attempt to strike at vulnerable points on the industrial front and to force acceptance of the demands by paralyzing the national economy. The oil industry is a vital target because its shutdown threatens the nation's transportation facilities. . . . With the nation sitting on a pile of inflation dynamite and with the crying need for speed in the reconversion program, it is no time for union labor or any other group to be playing with fire."[100]

Oil companies, berating OPA and "labor racketeers," also accused the OWIU of actually fomenting inflation: "[S]trikers can't have their fattened pay envelopes and their low prices for gasoline and oil." Moreover, OWIU price control demands were economically disastrous, underwritten by plans for a "proletarian dictatorship" that had "all the earmarks of Communism."[101]

In what one member described as the "vicious" collective bargaining conditions that characterized the L.A. oil industry, Local 128 understood that if the union was to maintain its political presence, it had to deflect these accusations. In the face of a regional "coalition of companies" and a historically unsympathetic polity, rising prices and "un-Americanism" together sounded a death knell. In response, the local declared itself "bitterly opposed to communism and all other subversive ideologies" and denounced the Communist Party as "despicable and ugly." Members threw themselves energetically into local working-class life and politics: they joined community groups that fought rent increases and pressed for the construction of affordable housing and child-care centers; they worked to influence the composition of the L.A. Harbor Commission; they even bought a church for the membership.[102]

In addition, they entered municipal and state political battles. Along with the rest of the state CIO, they rallied behind the McMillan State Full Employment bill ("Little Murray"), a California parallel to the federal Full

Employment ("Murray") bill. They demanded the termination of the California State Reconstruction and Reemployment Commission (CSRRC), the state reconversion agency, whose Oil and Gas Committee had no labor members. They backed progressive candidates like Congressman Clyde Doyle and Mayor Fletcher Bowron and opposed Bowron's friend Earl Warren's governorship. While each of these efforts had immediate political goals, in aggregate they represented an attempt to protect oil unionism in a metropolis on a path back toward hostility to organized labor.[103]

This project ultimately failed. By late 1946, OPA closed its doors, hopes for a full employment program were disappointed by empty legislation, and corporate taxes were drastically reduced. The working class responded by abstaining during the 1946 elections, which only abetted the political reversals that culminated in Taft-Hartley—an act the California CIO called "the first step toward fascism in the United States"—and its severe restriction of labor's legitimacy and radical depoliticization of collective bargaining.[104] With the end of price controls, the OWIU lost a valuable public relations and organizing tool, and after a 1948 California strike was crushed by a well-organized oil industry enjoying popular support because of gasoline shortages and rising prices, Local 128 membership fell through the floor. The local, and the International, fared even worse than most of a labor movement substantially weakened in an increasingly reactionary political climate.

Conclusion: The American Man and the Meaning of the Wage

The *International Oil Worker* printed this little poem the day Congress passed Taft-Hartley (over Truman's veto):

My pocketbook is empty,
My heart is filled with pain;
Prices still are mounting,
But my wages are the same.[105]

The poem suggests an important conjuncture. For, while the labor press's headlines screamed opposition to "Tough-Hitler (Pardon Us, Taft-Hartley)," the wage was not forgotten for a moment, not even in the shadow of a "fascist" "slave bill."[106] In the face of one of the most severe political tests of organized labor in U.S. history, the wage remained central not only because of its significance for economic welfare but also because it is a site of vast political possibility. The experience of Local 128 bears this out.

There is nonetheless a thread running through some radical scholarship (and virtually all mainstream economics) that paradoxically theorizes the economic and the political as experientially separable, even mutually exclusive. In this work, the economic is fundamentally prepolitical; it can produce political subjectivity, but it is itself politically empty. Nicos Poulantzas, for example, in a discussion of working-class action when confronted with the beginnings of "fascisization," claims that "in the complex articulation of economic and political struggles, it is the economic that progressively assumes the dominant role." He regrets this "defensive" turn away from the "correct path" of "political class struggle."[107] More recently, Mike Davis finds the "central dilemma" of American labor history in the "paradoxical disparities between economic militancy and political passivity, individual awareness and collective lack of confidence."[108] Although Davis's ultimately very convincing argument is that this opposition is less paradoxical in view of the constant and often brutal repression of working-class political activity in the United States, the opposition itself obscures the essential unity of the political and economic agency of many U.S. workers and their organizations. Moreover, it thoroughly depoliticizes the program of social change that helped motivate wage struggles like those of Local 128 after the war.

Certainly, the experiences I have examined do not entail direct challenges to the structure of the capitalist employment relation. Indeed, my account may seem to accord with the "American exceptionalism" consensus that oil workers, and by extension American workers, were in fact not motivated by class politics. Even worse, it may be read as a defense of dominant political economic organization. But this is not my message. Rather, these and other conflicts over the wage in no way signal the eclipse of the political by the economic. In fact, my hope is to show how fundamentally political wage struggles are: for the OWIU the wage was at the center of class struggle not only because it represented the material stakes but because it helped carve out the very political terrain upon which class relations were dynamically realized. In capitalism, class struggle makes sense only when we know what the wage means at a particular time and place.

In the wage readjustment process that followed the war, oil workers tried to realize their political goals through the very strategies that Davis calls "economic militancy." The realization of the Americanism promised by the war in the form of a more equal distribution of income, protection of the "traditional" family economy, and full enfranchisement of the working class, although clearly political and cultural objectives, were understood as most readily achievable through "economic" struggle. The separation of politics and economics, in this instance at least, is artificial, for political transformation originates in many places. The OWIU's struggle over the return to labor and the apportionment of the "extra penny" are only politically passive if seen from a perspective outside workers' "pay-day to payday" everyday life and apart from the (sometimes very "con-servative") values at the core of their experiences. This is not to say that U.S. workers were, and are, essentially reactionary. Rather, the point is that economic militancy on the part of the working class in the United States, especially in the face of corporate power like that in the oil industry, is in fact political militancy.[109]

Recognizing the political militancy of postwar wage struggles helps make sense of much of the content of working-class politics as the Cold War began, and it forces us to revise some elements of the standard radical account of the "Great Accord." First, as the history of Local 128 demon-strates, the politics of the wage is thoroughly masculinist. This is in itself unremarkable, or at least unsurprising, but the "economic militancy" of working-class men this political position entails makes a great deal more sense if we see it as one part in a larger vision of the economic citizenship of the American working man. The "family wage" makes the economic very political. Moreover, the very stakes in the postwar U.S. class struggle, on this front at least, fundamentally gendered its form. The politics of the wage not only reinforced "traditional" domestic roles but was a product of them, so much so that the conflict between unions and management was as much about class—the solidarity of American working men—as it was between classes.

Second, we need to shelve the homogenizing theme of most work on the U.S. working class. Writing on the "Treaty of Detroit"—the 1950 agreement between the UAW and General Motors—Davis remarks: "On the one side, the contract conceded the permanence of union representa-tion and provided for the periodic increase of wages and benefits tied to productivity growth. On the other, the contract—by affirming the in-violability of managerial prerogatives, by relinquishing worker protection against technological change, and by ensnaring grievance procedure in the bureaucratic maze—also liquidated that concern for rank-and-file power in the immediate labor process that had been the central axis of the origi-nal 1933–37 upsurge in auto and other mass production industries."[110]

The brilliance of Davis's historical vision notwithstanding, I believe this interpretation misses a critical dimension of working-class politics in the United States: how much the pecuniary details of these develop-ments matter, and how even minute differences—the "extra penny" or "nickel more"—are often not only of economic but cultural and politi-cal significance. Against a decontextualized ascription of the politics of the proletariat—which, in Przeworski's words, "has the consistency of rings of water"—the members of Local 128 demand an analysis of political agency and ideology as they are fully incorporated into modern U.S. industrialism, substantially shaped by fine-grained pecuniary variations within a wage labor experience that is often mistakenly written off as essentially the same for all.[111]

By theoretically lumping the experience of workers who fight for, and perhaps earn, a "nickel more" with those who do not or cannot, differences that matter enormously to the working subjects themselves are diminished or erased. The histories of Local 128, and of countless other unions, demonstrate how much this impoverishes a theoretical account of the critical threads in the social fabric of capitalism and limits our understanding of labor politics. If a four-cent shift differential can be construed as part of an effort to rescue "American civilization," this is surely a politics of measure; it demands a finer-grained examination of "proletarian" political economy.

Third, the politics of the wage and the American working man as laid out in this chapter also helps us understand the rise of anticommunism in the postwar labor movement, even if it cannot diminish our regret. The centrality of the wage to the ideological formation of the postwar working class underscores the political pragmatism of anticommunism in the face of larger objectives. The CIO leadership's anticommunism, which eventually led to the expulsion of eleven progressive unions in 1949 and 1950, is often understood as part of that leadership's acquiescence to capital (read "sell-out").[112] But it is perhaps better explained by the difficulties facing the American working man's wage politics after Taft-Hartley. As Harvey Levenstein writes, "Communist opposition to the government's foreign policy threatened to turn the CIO into the core of an opposition political movement that would be strong enough to spread disquiet in Washington but weak enough to invite massive retaliation by a government armed with extensive formal and informal power."[113]

This approach to what Stuart Hall calls the "practical ideologies" of working-class American men explains the anticommunism of Local 128 in a compelling manner: if revolutionary political programs were incidental to the core of Local 128's politics, then repudiating them does not mean "selling out"; it means making a strategic decision.[114] Indeed, if the hard-fought wage struggles of 1945 to 1950 helped shape the Treaty of Detroit as the victory it clearly appeared to be to many working people, it seems like a smart political choice. This is no "aberration" in a "naturally" radical working-class politics. In fact, although it is only conjecture, I believe that organized labor would have fought tooth and nail against any attempt to keep women in the workforce on a large scale, for that would have struck at the very foundation of its politics.

What this highlights, I believe—to echo the implicit and empathetic lesson in Davis's work—is that radical scholarship need constantly remind itself of the fact that workers, and those wishing to work, do not always think the way that theory or abstract programmatic political intelligence would anticipate. People make collective and individual decisions according to the limits of everyday and extraordinary constraints, not all of which will appear politically transformative from an outsider's perspective. But they often work for change in ways perceived possible, and this often takes place through something as fundamental to the persistence of capitalism as the wage. Recognizing and respecting the political agency in that are the first steps in sensitive social science and in breaking down the conceptual barriers between culture, politics, and economy. The goal is not to catalog passivity but to destabilize disparity and underwrite possibility.

But a worker can be described as skilled if
he produces the thing as it ought to be, and
if, in his subjective actions, he encounters
no resistance to the end he is pursuing.
  G. W. F. Hegel, *The Philosophy of Right*
  (1821)

What's in a Day's Wage?
Raced Work & the Social Production of Skill

The story of Local 128 touched no more than briefly upon the details of
what work is, either as the set of more or less technologically mediated individual and collective tasks that together constitute the labor process or as
that set of human mental and physical capacities that are given life by what
in the Marxian literature is called human labor-power. In this chapter, I try
to come to grips with exactly these issues by thinking through the politics
of the wage as it is worked through the concept of skill—that relational but
"commonsense" quality of human work for which, accounted for in hours
or days, the wage is payment.

  This common sense, so crucial to mainstream economic theory, says
that the wage rate is a positive function of the quality and scarcity of different kinds of labor-power, i.e., workers' skills. But skill is often amorphous
and contingent. It is by no means easily definable and is subject to radical
change over time. Cultural politics—of race and gender in particular—is
also critical to the definition of the qualitative evaluation of worker characteristics and identities, or skills. In this, at least, Hegel's remark in this
chapter's epigraph is wrong: the category of skill is not solely determined
by the "subjective" resistance to realizing the ends of one's labor; there
are indeed significant social constraints determining the meaning of skill
as it accords legitimacy to the worker-as-object. The cultural politics of
skill, i.e., the struggle over the ways in which these constraints function, is
consequently always also about the wage insofar as it is oriented around
relative status inside and outside the workplace. The politics of measure,
then, as it operates in and on the wage, is always partially constitutive of
skill and implicated in the organization and maintenance of labor process,
workplace hierarchy, and the social division of labor more broadly.

  In this chapter, I try to bring out these dynamics through an examination of what is, on the face of it, a fairly straightforward claim by white western male workers to the higher wages and status that come with skill. I want to suggest that even in a situation in which relative wage rates — i.e., quantity — are the focus of workers' attention, there is much more going on. Even in the transparency of racialized wage differentials, or in the explicit terminological manipulation that goes into the effort to classify some as skilled (high wage) and other as unskilled (low wage), there pulses a politics of measure that is acting on the dialectical movements of history, unfolding and reconstructing the content and form of everyday categories, like the wage, that we use to understand the world.

The "Nigger-Killer" of Siskiyou County

I would like to start this account of race, class, and skill with an otherwise innocuous item in the collections of a small museum in Siskiyou County, California, the very county anticipating an "invasion" by the Industrial Workers of the World that I mentioned in the preface. The item is a photograph of a massive Lidgerwood skidder — the "Titanic" — and someone in the 1920s wrote these words on the back of the photo: "At the time this [the skidder] was first set up, Long-Bell [Lumber Company] imported negroes from their southern operations. Local lumberjacks objected to the negroes, and there was an average of one negro killed each week in the woods by being caught in the bight of a line. The skidder consequently became known as the 'Nigger-Killer.'"[1]

But hold on a minute. African American lumber workers in the West? "Imported" black southerners in northern California? These facts fit neither the received history of the rural West nor especially that of its forest industry. Moreover, beyond these challenges to the presumably verifiable historical record, other, more troubling problems loom. Who were the workers, and how did this situation come about? How can we account for a "Nigger-Killer" in northern California timber country in the 1920s? And, it might be necessary to add, what role, if any, does the wage play in this?

What follows is a confrontation with these questions, a process that leads from the "facts" of the archives, to a "detour" through the racialized historical political economy of skill in the United States, and on, finally, to the wage and its meaning. The story unfolds for the most part in Weed, California, between 1920 and 1925. By piecing together the stories of the African American workers who came to Weed and trying to understand some of the texture of their daily lives, I hope to reassemble one all-but-forgotten history of African American forest workers in the West (there are others) and to examine the process and content of racism and racial ideology as they can play out in the cultural politics of the wage.

Let me begin, however, with the Titanic. The function and mechanics of the killing machine itself were straightforward. A skidder is used in logging operations to cable-haul felled timber to a point at which it can be transported to mill by train, truck, or river. The Titanic was a hulking, black and silver contraption, its size matched by its enormous power. Huge steam boilers—and the fifteen-foot-diameter drums for which they generated pressure—ran its length, and a complex, seemingly arbitrary maze of piping caged large portions of its sides. Set up on wooden blocks and fastened to the thin forest soil by anchors called "tailholts," it looked something akin to a steam locomotive, with an additional tower from which cables spread out like a spider web.

Men called "chokers" looped the far ends of these cables around felled logs, and the Titanic reeled them in, dragging or swinging the timber to the loading site. The operation was rarely smooth and always dangerous. Sometimes, the log would catch on uneven terrain or slash (fallen brush and trees left on the logged landscape), and when the obstacle gave in to the skidder's tension, a log weighing tons would shoot into the air or across the ground. Other times, a cable would snap, or a choke would not hold, and the line would snap back like a two-inch-thick wire whip. Occasionally, the haul would simply roll over or tumble down a hill, a massive, one-unit avalanche. In any event, men were often crushed, maimed, and killed by errant logs and lines. There are many stories of workers being cut in half by a recoiling cable; indeed, skidding is still dangerous, and choke setting remains one of the most dangerous jobs in the twenty-first-century forest industry.

Notwithstanding these dangers and their materialization, accounting for the "Nigger-Killer" of northern California clearly demands far more than a consideration of mechanical design and worker safety. Neither is it a simple matter of uncovering a ruthless economic rationality, through which heterogeneous labor was efficiently allocated to minimize costs. Instead, it requires an explicitly historical approach to the people, place, and time, interweaving several threads in labor history in both the South and the West within the frame of capitalist wage labor. The political economic and social context within which the Titanic was operated was both particular to Weed and a product of the rapidly changing U.S. West. This context was constituted by workers with individual and collective histories, who nevertheless related to one another in ways that were conditioned by the place and time and by the dynamic historical and regional structures in which they lived and worked. These workers performed various jobs according to a division of labor that was controlled and reproduced in the daily relations between groups of workers and between management and the workforce. All these details are important, as is understanding the means through which these relationships were legitimated and maintained by a cultural politics of wage labor in which measure, the supersession or overcoming of the quantity-quality opposition, was color-coded.

In addition, the centrality of the material conditions of work, and of the relations between workers and the tools of their trade, is glaringly evident in the story that animates this chapter (in some contrast to chapter 3). What is a job like? What does performing it entail? Some jobs are physically demanding, others relatively easy on the body. Some require considerable occupation-specific training, whereas others are learned quickly; some demand a great deal of agility or technical knowledge (or both), others less. Some jobs are dangerous, dirty, hot. Many occupations are "traditional," others somewhat new. A few are highly coveted, many actively avoided. There are some theories that attempt to explain some of these differences, but they rarely do more than specify the relations that ahistorical "rational expectations" suggest ought to hold. As soon as culture, politics, and geography are dialectically reinserted—or better, as soon as we remember that they are necessarily always there, as the discussion of method in chapter 1 explained—dominant behavioral explanations are usually forced to bend and twist so much that they become virtually unrecognizable.

To take an extremely influential example: economic theories of "capital-skill complementarity," "incentive alignment," and "efficiency wages" all predict that capital-intensive technical change will lead to the recruitment of better-paid, more skilled workers.[2] These predictions are belied by the history recounted in what follows. In the course of this chapter, orthodox economic explanations of the relation between the wage, skill, and technical change are forced to relinquish their most fundamental premises when confronted with a historically specific racial logic. The everyday details of work—the past and present characteristics of a job, both "subjective" and "objective"—matter precisely because they can help us understand how work and social status are related in a particular context. More to the point for present purposes, they can help explain why disagreeable, dangerous, undesirable jobs—the jobs African Americans have almost always had in the United States—are also virtually always considered "unskilled." These are essential steps toward any explanation of why we find southern African Americans dying while working dangerous low-wage jobs on a high-technology (for the time) skidder in the woods of the Pacific coast.

I focus upon skill, technical change, the relationship between capital and labor, and the racism of workers and management, emphasizing the historically specific conception of the relationship between skill and race within the cultural politics of the wage. I argue that they are, in fact, not easily disentangled, each dynamically shaping and shaped by the other. Not only is race reproduced by skill-based occupational hierarchies, as can be read from much of the literature on segmented labor markets, but fluid determinations of skill that partly constitute the wage relation can reproduce racial difference.[3]

This argument is partly an extension of labor-process scholars' studies of socially defined "enclaves of production." Robert Thomas's work on the California lettuce industry shows how certain tasks are made into "men's work" and "women's work" through social, institutional (recruiting processes and networks), and monetary (low-wage rigidity) mechanisms. A "test of skill" becomes a "test of manhood," the two concepts incomprehensible outside each other.[4] The chapter follows this logic but extends it beyond Thomas's framework to a discussion of the complex geography of the formation of these processes. It demonstrates how jobs can be politically (i.e., labeled or defined as) "skilled" or "deskilled," sometimes regardless of former status, because of who does the work. This is especially so when the tasks are performed by a group composed of new participants in the regional labor market or when the tasks in question are new components of the labor process (or both). Jobs can be defined as unskilled either because they are the province of "inferior" workers or to ensure that "undesirable" tasks are performed by "undesirable" people, regardless of their abilities or experience: "strategies through which workers seek to limit competition with respect to their employers and other workers" can take the form of acquisition and ascription.[5]

This entanglement can not only help explain how the "Nigger-Killer" came to be the terrible *social* force it was but can also provide fruitful material for a reconsideration of skill and race, two of the more "common-sense" concepts in the realms of cultural politics and of work. The tale of African American lumber workers in Weed demonstrates the subtle but important ways in which the wage has often served as a site at which skill and race are given concrete, if not always fixed, meaning. This happens according to both locally specific and larger structural conditions, and, to the extent to which it is governed by the semantic politics of "definition," it shows how the wage can function to define the relationship between skill and race—black workers are unskilled workers, therefore there are black wages—and how it can partially define the ways in which technical change is confronted by workers and employers. In situations like that of Weed's mill workers, the cultural politics of the wage were in large part focused on the malleability of skill and race in the workplace and community. It did not matter that many African American workers did the same jobs in the South that were considered skilled in the West. Their arrival began a racialized process at the local level through which workers and tasks were reconceptualized as skilled or unskilled. The content of the wage relation in Weed therefore demands a rethinking of any "objective" understandings of either skill or race, since each emerges as a dimension of workers' broader politics of measure.

Supporting these claims means drawing on a varied literature, which is reflected in the organization of the following discussion. I begin with a historical account of African Americans in Weed in the early 1920s that centers on the workers, their employer (Long-Bell Lumber Company), and the structure, labor, and race relations of the U.S. lumber industry after World War I. This brings into focus the specter of the South and southern labor as it haunted western timber workers and northern California. After laying this historical groundwork, I consider the particular legacy of the South in U.S. industrial development and labor politics that informed popular western perceptions of the southern specter. I historicize the regionally particular relation between skill and race and argue that a flexibly racist determination of the meaning of skill abetted the subordination of racialized workers in the face of radical economic change, as it continues to do today. At the end of the chapter I return to the Lidgerwood skidder in light of Weed's African American histories in an attempt to understand the production of a "Nigger-Killer" in northern California timber country, a historical development that appears unlikely only because we have been unlikely to look for it.

African American Lumber Workers in Northern California

In April 1923, a train carrying W. E. B. Du Bois on a West Coast speaking tour ran through Weed. Du Bois did not disembark. Presumably he was unaware that Weed contained one of the largest African American communities in the rural West, one whose members constituted a substantial portion of the Weed Lumber Company's labor force. A very small black population had been in Weed and nearby McCloud since 1917, recruited from the South by labor agents. The vast majority of local black workers, however, came to Siskiyou County, the heart of the timber-rich region near the California-Oregon border, after 1920.[6]

They came one of two ways. One group undertook punctuated and varied migrations from the South; some came by way of Oklahoma, others via southern California, some directly from Alabama or Arkansas. A second group of workers consisted of those who came directly from DeRidder and Longville, Louisiana, in 1921 and 1922, their transportation costs advanced by the majority shareholder in the Weed Lumber Company, the Long-Bell Lumber Company of Kansas City. These last were joined by friends and relatives who followed them to Weed over the next few years. By the mid-1920s, there were one thousand African Americans in Weed, a town of just over six thousand.[7]

The local timber mill dominated the community to which they migrated. Founded by Maine lumberman Abner Weed in 1901, the town was almost wholly owned by his company. And it evolved as a company town in the paternal tradition: Weed Lumber owned the company store, banks, hotels, clubs and other social venues, churches, housing, and the town land. By 1907, Weed Lumber was one of the largest producers in California, thanks in large part to an array of wealthy investors that included prominent San Francisco bankers along with players like Long-Bell. When Long-Bell eventually acquired majority ownership in 1916, it maintained not only the name of its subsidiary but also the company town structure, with which it had extensive experience in the South.[8]

Like many isolated lumber towns in the West, Weed was a rough place in the 1910s and 1920s. The population was predominantly male, and much of it was highly mobile, only seasonally resident. If contemporary newspaper reports provide an accurate picture, shootings, stabbings, fights, and summary assertions of more or less violent corporate authority were common. A thriving red-light district in adjacent Shastina, a town not owned by the company, attracted workers from both Weed and the outlying logging camps. Temporary communities composed of migrant workers filled what were commonly known as the "Jungles" at the edge of town.[9] Local law enforcement exercised a perfunctory company-sponsored frontier justice with impunity.

Racism was of course a powerful organizational force in Weed. From the arrival of the first nonwhite workers around 1910, Weed Lumber coordinated a strict residential and occupational segregation in Weed. Italians—masons who came to construct the mill's power plant and then stayed on for mill jobs—were housed in the parts of town designated A, B, and C Camps. Greeks, who also came for millwork between 1910 and 1912, lived in D Camp. Mexican workers also lived in D Camp and in railway cars on the tracks running between A Camp and B Camp. Stringtown and Rabbit Flat were reserved for "white" mill workers. As one longtime Long-Bell employee recalls, these rigid divisions were further elaborated by a complicated "caste system" within the white population. Top management lived "in big houses on North Davis Avenue, called 'Nob Hill' by the workers. The office employees and department heads in the company store, the Foremen in parts of the plant, lived on Main street, Gilman Avenue and Camino row. Those employees who had responsible jobs in the sawmill (sawyers, saw filers, and millwrights, etc.) lived on Liberty Avenue and the upper end of Shasta Avenue."[10]

When African Americans moved to Weed in the late 1910s and 1920s, they were housed by the company in a neighborhood officially called "The Quarters" but known by various names: Colored Town, Darktown, Coon Town. Housing mostly consisted of boardinghouses, one-room cottages, and, when demand outran supply, tents, which were rented out by Long-Bell. Most of the new arrivals purchased furnishings from the company store.[11]

Black workers came to Weed for several reasons. Those who had worked for Long-Bell in Louisiana had lost their jobs after the mills they worked for had closed, part of the general decline of the southern timber industry. Others received word—through rumor, through labor agents, or from familiar sources—that there was work for African Americans in Weed. In addition, the spread of the cotton boll weevil in the 1910s severely limited agricultural wage income, an important part of the mixed income strategy upon which many timber workers relied. Moreover, West-South wage differentials in the lumber industry were vast. In 1925, full-time "common laborers" in Louisiana earned on average twenty-five cents per hour, and less than fifteen dollars per week; in California, the same position paid forty-five cents per hour, and over twenty-five dollars per week. Indeed, a skilled edgerman, a position often held by black workers in the South, earned just under thirty-nine cents per hour in Louisiana. Finally, the possibility of secure employment was enormously attractive. As one African American worker who arrived in Weed in 1923 remarked, "Weed was a miracle for black people for work."[12]

Opportunities for work were indeed plentiful, if rigidly structured. Long-Bell's operations were highly integrated, and the labor process was finely organized and specialized. The company hired men to log the forests, build the roads and rails to access the timber, mill the lumber, and manufacture select goods like shingles, boxes, and sashes. Logging camp workers, almost exclusively white, cut the trees, "bucked" them into transportable lengths, and "yarded" the segments to the road or rail. Rail construction workers, often Mexican, graded and laid track. At the mill, the logs were dumped in a holding pond and then sent through the mill. First, boards were sliced off the logs by a head saw operated by the sawyer and maintained by a saw filer. These two positions were considered the industry's most skilled and were the best paid.[13] The boards were sent to the edgerman to be sawn to proper dimension, and this edged lumber was in turn trimmed by an automatic trimmer. The finished lumber was then stacked for drying by "common laborers" and, when dry, planed. From the planer, the timber was either shipped or sent to one of the factories.

In each of these operational arms, the supervisory and high-wage jobs were mostly performed by "native white" workers of western or northern European heritage. The unskilled or "common labor" in the woods was the province of lower-status white workers, nonwhites generally having been deemed unsuitable for logging. In the factories, Italians occupied the skilled positions, and Greek workers did the low-wage work.[14]

Black workers, and younger or lesser-status members of other racialized groups, were employed almost exclusively in the sawmill. The southern arrivals were hired to work alongside Greeks, Italians, and Mexicans as unskilled "common labor," without regard for the experience or skills they brought with them from the South, hoping to earn enough to pay for furniture and rent (and the eighty-nine-dollar transportation cost, had they come from Louisiana at Long-Bell's invitation). These jobs — stacking green lumber or sending dried lumber to the planing mill, for example — were arduous, hot, and often dangerous, and at the lowest wage scale.[15]

As with other groups in Weed, black workers and their families developed a tight and self-reliant community in response both to exclusion from outside and to internal inclusiveness born of similar experience and some shared institutional ties. While there were social divisions among the residents — principally, it appears, between those who had come with Long-Bell and those who had migrated independently — socioeconomic and cultural isolation forced or enabled black workers in Weed to create a set of common lumber town social institutions that were their own. All retail business and community venues were owned by Weed Lumber, and black workers either were barred from attendance or were expected, as at "sit-down" restaurants, to do their business at the counter and leave immediately. Schools were completely segregated. Still, African American residents soon had established their own brothel, barber shop, and "the Club," a pool room and lunch counter that functioned as the main social setting for single men. They also erected a new Baptist church, motivated both by their exclusion from the "white" one that already stood and by their belief that varieties of Baptism were not interchangeable.[16]

The South, the West, and Long-Bell Lumber Company

The migration of African American workers to Siskiyou County is a forgotten thread in the "Great Migration," the exodus of rural black workers from the South that began with, and outlasted, World War I. The movement of thousands to industrial jobs outside the region radically transformed the workers' destinations and their communities of origin. Although the North is virtually always the focus of examinations of technical change, black migration, and industrial structure, the West was also affected by this massive redistribution of labor.[17] Many southern timber workers left oppressive labor conditions and low pay, substantially draining the labor supply of the region's timber industry. The burgeoning western forest industry benefited from this obstacle to southern production, which decreased output, increased labor-management conflict, and in some cases raised wages and productions costs in the South.[18] Not only did these developments increase prices, especially with high demand during the war, but they mitigated some of the competitive disadvantages the western industry faced as a result of remoteness from eastern population centers and high relative wages.

Around this time some southern lumber operators began to expand their operations into the West. At the opening of the twentieth century, Long-Bell was one of the largest lumber companies in the world; its owner, Robert A. Long, one of the most powerful and aggressive southern businessmen of his era, led the western movement. However, the transition was not a simple matter of the transfer of southern production systems to the West. The terrain, a lack of resident labor or extant infrastructure, and the enormous dimensions of the timber all demanded a new way of doing things: industrial forestry in the West required powerful new harvesting equipment, railroad construction, bigger mills, labor force recruitment and stabilization, and, no less important, the maintenance of human communities in isolated locales.[19] All of this meant enormous investment, which in turn meant new means of labor control.

Like some other large lumber companies, Long-Bell had established strong connections to eastern and European financial centers since its incorporation in 1875. Combined with government sales of southern timber land at speculation-friendly prices, access to this capital enabled an extraordinary rate of growth in the 1880s and 1890s, when the company became a significant concern in Louisiana, Mississippi, and Texas. By 1904, continuing a "breathtaking" rate of expansion, Long-Bell owned 228,850 acres of timberland, 61 lumberyards, 4 "giant" sawmills, 9 subsidiaries, 120 miles of railroad, and mines from which 600,000 tons of coal were extracted each year. Capitalization in 1905 stood at $3.5 million.[20]

Long-Bell, with its profitability and ties to powerful investors, far exceeded Weed Lumber's scale under Abner Weed. In 1915, the Weed Lumber Company had 1,500 employees and an annual output of 75 million board feet. After Long-Bell gained majority control in 1916, it focused its energies on large-scale, efficient means of production: powerful new locomotives for its rail spurs, new log carriages in the mill, and log-moving equipment. The most notable changes were the expansion of the log pond and the replacement of Weed Lumber's two sawmills with a modern mill—"the largest mill on the Pacific coast," owned by "probably the biggest lumber company in the world," according to the *Yreka Journal*. These developments increased production to 100 million board feet annually by the early 1920s.[21]

In the early years of industrial forestry, many jobs in the woods and in the mills were considered "unskilled."[22] This was especially true in the South, the most important lumber-producing region in the United States from the late 1890s to World War II, where much of the labor force consisted of African Americans earning low wages. In the West of the 1920s, despite 40 percent greater capital investment per wage earner and a consequent demand for operators of expensive equipment, most workers were also regarded as unskilled, although they were considerably better paid than in the South.[23] As a 1923 Department of Labor report stated, the "higher general level of wages in the logging camps than in the sawmills is due to the disagreeable features of life in the camps and the heavier nature of the work, rather than to any requirement of greater skill. . . . While there are some men who feel something of the artist's interest and pride in their work, for the majority of workers in the mills and camps work is drudgery and endurable only because of the wages paid."[24]

The incentive effects of higher wages appear to have been part of western timber companies' recruitment strategies. Yet despite pressure for continued high returns, encouraged by rapid technological change in the industry and massive investment in Long-Bell's Weed operations during the late 1910s and 1920s, attracting workers with higher skill levels to operate these machines was not a priority. The goal, rather, was to maintain a readily available resident workforce. It is well known that the conditions in western lumber mills and camps were abominable, so abominable, in fact, that a reform movement among operators to stabilize labor focused on improving living conditions. However, these efforts were expended not to attract a necessarily more skilled worker but to attract a "better class" of worker, not "womanless, voteless, jobless" migrants prone to the "destructive type of radicalism" bred by the Industrial Workers of the World: "Labor disturbances in the lumber industry of the Northwest are symptoms of a social disease. They are the natural and expected results of a sawdust-pile, transient, mill-shack-town form of economic development, which has been notoriously characteristic of the development of the lumber industry in the United States."[25]

The Post–World War I Timber Economy

Long-Bell's recruitment and transportation of African American workers to Weed was a response to these conditions. The western timber industry was the province of what the company considered discontented and "maladjusted" workers of "nondescript race," who did not compare "with what had been available in the South." Black workers were highly valued (if ill treated) by southern lumber operators, and their predominance in the workforce of many mills in the South meant that, in contrast to the West, there were experienced nonwhite (in this case, black) workers in virtually all places in the logging and milling labor process. Those directly recruited by Long-Bell were Long's "most trusted employees," workers Long's labor agent considered the "cream of the crop." The principal benefit to Long-Bell, without a doubt, was labor control. As one executive remarked, "[i]n the South labor presented almost no problem. There were no unions to contend with," for African Americans were virtually excluded from membership in organized labor.[26]

A 1917 strike that temporarily shut down the western lumber industry—including the Weed mill—confirmed lumber operators' fears. In response, Long-Bell immediately set about diversifying its workforce, recruiting workers of a wide variety of backgrounds. Aside from "native Americans"—white workers of northern European and British heritage—Italian and Greek communities predated the Long-Bell era. By 1921, however, many more backgrounds were represented in the Weed labor force, which included workers from South America, Mexico, Russia, China, Cuba, India, and Syria, as well as European countries and Canada.[27]

Long-Bell intended to create an unorganizable, stable, and ideally captive labor force in an isolated company town, and for a time, it was very successful, at least in crushing union organization. Not only were workers of many different backgrounds and languages hired at Weed, but this less aggressive tactic was matched by more conventional means of antiunion coercion. The efficacy of these tactics finds testimony in the brief history of the Weed local of the International Timber Workers Union (ITWU), which was established in the late summer of 1919 and successfully organized "practically all employees of the company." By early 1921, however, as a result of various counterefforts, such as an especially effective dismissal of fifty members, including two "principal officers," only one-quarter of the workforce remained affiliated.[28]

From Long-Bell's perspective, interlocking ideological and political economic considerations—i.e., the historically specific demands of hegemony—made a divide-and-conquer strategy very attractive. First, like many of their ruling-class contemporaries, R. A. Long and the Long-Bell executive adhered strongly to a paternalist corporate tradition. They were vehemently antiunion and more than willing to support the use of violence and intimidation to deal with labor unrest. Blacklisting, refusal to bargain, payment in company scrip, even murder: driven by class privilege and the bottom line, Long-Bell resorted to them all.[29]

The second consideration was the fact that the lumber market—always highly seasonal and sensitive to the business cycle—was extraordinarily volatile in the early 1920s. Between March 1919 and March 1920, the average price per board foot increased by more than 130 percent, but by March 1921 it had sunk back to preboom levels. It remained low during the recession of the next twelve months, rose again by 40 percent between March 1922 and April 1923, and then fell steadily for the next sixteen months.[30] This roller-coaster ride was all the more daunting because the 1917 strike at the height of war demand had demonstrated that coordinated action on the part of labor could take a considerable bite out of corporate profit even when all seemed well. In an industry that survived by responding to demand as quickly as possible, labor resistance in good times was a constant source of dread and provoked vicious attacks.

This volatility also manifested itself in other, related ways. The positive demand shock provided by the war and the period immediately following stimulated massive investment in productive capacity throughout the industry; Long-Bell's new mill is exemplary. But with postwar demand and price instability, the resulting overcapacity created "perverse incentives" to overproduction. Wood-products markets were glutted as demand sank in the summer of 1920, and prices fell accordingly. In an almost flawless performance of a collective action problem, rather than curtailing production to reduce supply, many mills continued to function at near-full capacity so as to maintain aggregate returns despite decreasing per unit margins. This of course only exacerbated the problem, and high freight rates added to the difficulties. The recession of 1920–21 put many small producers out of business, and it was only the bigger concerns that weathered it in any form in which recovery was possible. In early 1922, when demand picked up, one local newspaper claimed that "[n]o industry has come through two harder years than western sawmills thousands of miles from markets—an unparalleled depression."[31]

The Strike of 1922

Long-Bell's production fluctuated wildly during this period. In December 1920, the company announced that, for the first time in many years, winter logging operations would be completely shut down and all men laid off. Then, on New Year's Day, 1921, Weed Lumber cut all daily wages by one dollar—approximately one-third of most workers' earnings—explaining that "there is practically no market at the present time for the products of the company and that a readjustment of expenses has become an absolute necessity to meet new conditions." Company store prices were mildly reduced to mitigate the wage reduction.[32]

Following Long-Bell's near dismantling of the ITWU, the working people of Weed generally acquiesced to these decisions. At an April meeting of the town's ITWU membership, "[t]he matter of the wage reduction" was "thoroughly discussed. It was the general consensus that, considering the conditions in the lumber market at present, nothing was to be gained by calling a strike." The next month, the *Sisson Headlight* stated that "reports from Weed are not very encouraging."[33]

By January 1922, however, prospects improved. Freight rates had fallen, Weed Lumber was planning the largest cut in its history, and all sides of the business were expected to "run full force during the entire season."[34] At the end of the month, the *Yreka Journal* reported that R. A. Long was "decidedly optimistic" and that "[a]t present there are no idle men in Weed unless it is by choice, as the saw mill is running on full time, also the factory, the veneer plant, machine shop and planing mill. The cottages are all occupied and judging from the present outlook, Weed will be a busy place during the coming summer."[35]

With the elevated expectations of both labor and management, Long-Bell announced a wage reduction of two and a half cents per hour for "common labor," or more than half of the employees, and an increase in the length of the workday from eight to ten hours, effective 1 March. The announcement was echoed by other large mills in the region: McCloud, Weston, Susanville, and Dorris. The mill at nearby Klamath Falls, Oregon, declared that the workday would be increased to nine hours, with the common laborer's daily wages remaining "at the present scale."[36]

Initially, the reaction of the region's lumber workers was uneven. In Klamath Falls, where the ITWU was more of a force, 400 mill workers struck on 1 March. At the big mill in McCloud, 300 men walked out over the next three days. In Weed, the response came more slowly. Very few of the employees were union members. Local newspapers reported that even though the eight-hour day had been established in Weed since 1918, "no trouble [is] expected in this section by the change." Within a few days, however, Long-Bell's California operations were entirely shut down. By 7 March, 750 new union members from Weed—approximately 80 percent of local mill workers—were on strike, and the number in Klamath Falls had grown to 600.[37]

On 10 March, Weed, Klamath Falls, and nearby Dorris were the only large mills in the "Strike Belt" that had not recommenced production. But the fact that Weed was a company town put the union at a significant disadvantage. J. M. White, manager of the Weed Lumber Company, remarked: "The union organizers have nothing to do with our business, and we will not talk with them now or at any other time." He also stated that the company would not allow strikers to remain in company-owned lodging. Still, the strike continued through March, marked by occasional conflicts with armed guards hired by Long-Bell, many of whom were deputized by local law enforcement.[38]

Despite company power, the union enjoyed considerable support from the community. Benefit dances throughout March and April attracted "large crowds," and the strike spread to other groups of workers in Weed. In late March the carpenters walked out, and in early April the employees of the machine shop struck. But solidarity was not complete. The loggers never struck, and the camps operated at full capacity throughout the strike, the harvested timber waiting in the log pond for the mill to reopen. By the third week, maintenance of the strike had fallen to the married men, the single men having "nearly all left town." Many felt they could not continue to hold out, and by early April the *Yreka Journal* reported that "there are about as many men working as there are on strike." Workers returned to the mills day by day, and new men were hired on an ongoing basis. Manager White reported that there were 283 men in the mill on 20 April, 350 two days later, and more than 400 on 28 April. Those who continued to strike at that point "would not be permitted to return to work by the company." It is unclear exactly when the strike was declared over at Weed, but by early May newspapers were speaking of it in the past tense.[39]

African Americans, the South, and the Meaning of the Strike

The issues in the strike were the eight-hour day and the wage cut. Employers in all communities refused to bargain. In Klamath Falls, the recalcitrance of both parties led the mayor to request the help of the U.S. Department of Labor Board of Conciliation, and the strike was still under way when board representatives arrived on 28 March. Employers claimed the Oregon industry was "entirely dependent on California for its three essentials of existence, financing, market for its output and labor supply." Competitive pressures demanded increased production at lower cost. The union declared that this position was "unjustified" and that workers would remain out in defense of "a principle most vital to the workers of America, the eight hour day." At Weed, Long-Bell cited the hard times of recent years, high taxes and labor costs, competition from the South, and company prerogative. Employees were somewhat less attached to hours, demanding "either the eight-hour working day be restored or the previous hourly wage paid."[40]

These everyday considerations—time and money—constituted the "economic" terrain of the strike. Using the quantitative language of distributive justice, Weed's timber workers made claims against the violation of the established norms of local employer-employee relations. Such claims are the refrain of the history of organized labor, and they are articulated in a language immanent to capitalism. As I noted in chapter 3, on the face of it there is absolutely nothing anticapitalist or revolutionary about protesting wage cuts and the extension of the workday. But there is more going on here, although the urgency of these demands is not rendered false by saying so. The politics of measure as it unfolds here does not mean that quantitative concerns are irrelevant; it only means that in bringing them back into the sphere of the political, i.e., the qualitative, their own critical cultural contents are better understood. For in Weed in the early 1920s, the historical and geographic specificity of white workers' lives can never be divorced from their political practice. Wage struggles can be "about" quantity, but that can never be the end of it; nor can it even be logically isolated. All wage claims are made in the midst of "definite" concrete times and places.

And here, although even this cannot exhaust the "object" of the politics of measure, the wage was freighted with a particularly American cultural dynamic. What terrified western workers was the South, its culture, its political economy, and its people. Unionized white workers claimed that the "trouble at Klamath Falls is believed to be largely due to the entrance of the Long-Bell interests in the Northwest." Other employers took up this argument to defend cost-cutting measures. According to organized labor, Long-Bell—and the operators following its example—were "seeking to lengthen the hours of labor and lower the wages to the level of workers of the east and south, where wages and working conditions beggar description." Weed was a front in a regional-racial battle, "the place selected for the beginning."[41]

The argument was hardly fanciful in light of recent experiences in the region. The tenor of Long-Bell's efforts to break the strike harmonizes nicely with the broader labor relations strategy it pursued in California, and Weed's African American workers represented the racialized infrastructure of that strategy. The recruitment of black workers to Weed constituted part of an attempt—in some ways explicit, in others implicit—to import southern social relations to northern California through the introduction of a low-wage, "unskilled" labor force. The "negroization" of western timber was without a doubt among the company's strategic targets. In that context, African Americans were guaranteed to bear the brunt of western violence, whether "physical" or more subtle. Whatever the success of Long-Bell's strategy, black workers' exploitation and oppression was assured.

Long-Bell's managers, like J. M. White, had worked in the South and were struck by the relative difficulty of maintaining and controlling the workforce in the West. They ruefully noted how comparatively loyal, hardworking, and manageable the mostly African American workers were in the South, and they undertook to impose management systems and strategies that had worked particularly well in the South. Later, when Long-Bell built the town of Longview in southwestern Washington, it refused to hire local workers in an explicit attempt to re-create the successes of Longview's southern sister city, Longville, Louisiana.[42]

Some elements of the company's strategy, like refusal to bargain, were in no way particularly southern but are perhaps better described in the timber industry as antiwestern. Other arrangements, however, while perhaps not explicitly southern, were certainly adopted because of their traditional efficacy in the company's region of origin; Long-Bell may not have been planning to make Weed "southern," but it did intend to make it resemble what had worked for Long-Bell in the past. The importation of African American workers served as the most substantial of these arrangements, for in the transportation of these workers to Weed, Long-Bell brought a group of people who were familiar with a southern social and employment structure that had historically served the company well and who were members of the racialized labor pool that functioned as perhaps the keystone of that structure.[43]

In addition to these efforts, which were founded upon perceived regional differences in production, Long-Bell attempted to maintain a racist paternalism within and outside the workplace that resonated with the cultural norms of its southern executive and contrasted sharply with labor-management relations in the West.[44] The position of the West's historical analogue to the South's African American worker, the racialized low-wage Chinese immigrant, illustrates this contrast. Although the comprehensive residential segregation and labor market subordination imposed upon the Chinese was similar to the African American experience in the South and in Weed, there are important differences. The Chinese immigrant population was generally internally organized by caste and class systems that arrived with the workers. Chinese workers were tied into extensive networks of Chinese employers, labor contractors, and businessmen, who often served as intermediaries between the worker and non-Chinese employers. African American workers in the South and in Weed could not rely on these cultural-commercial systems, and there was no leadership cadre within the black workforce with an influence and economic clout comparable to that of the Chinese. Furthermore, there is evidence that in the hierarchy of racial difference the Chinese were even less fortunate than southern blacks. The American Federation of Labor (AFL), for example, which by the early twentieth century supported the organization of some black workers in separate locals, refused even a segregated membership status to Asians. White working-class leaders like Samuel Gompers, who considered some coordination with black workers economically necessary, believed that any such relation with Chinese was suicidal.[45]

In addition, the status of the relatively immobile southern African American timber worker and his dependence upon his white employer marked him as radically different from western timber workers, who were very mobile and rarely tied to a single company or community. The benefits afforded by a settled, dependent, and nonunion workforce were, from management's perspective, a businessman's birthright, or at least an unimpeachable custom.[46] Western workers' radicalism, social organization, and mobility challenged virtually every important managerial expectation, particularly with regard to wage setting and labor-process decision making.

While the success of this sectional transplantation was mixed, to unionists the fundamentally southern objectives of Long-Bell's strategy were clear. The arrival of "slave-driving Long-Bell operations in northern California" represented the introduction of an industrial cancer to the Northwest. The Conciliation Board in Oregon supported these claims when it found in favor of the Klamath Falls strikers: "[L]et it be clearly understood that evil conditions in an adjoining State cannot justify this board or any human being in promoting or endorsing similar conditions in our own State."[47]

The racism of white and southern European workers abetted corporate efforts to minimize worker solidarity, in effect reinforcing the "southernness" that Long-Bell desired. Notions of "slave-driving" and a southern "evil" are elements of the idiom through which the social relations of production in the United States were understood by working people and workers' organizations. They are saturated with implicit distinctions between the West/North and the South, between labor and capital, and between black and white. As the Weed correspondent to the *Yreka Journal* reported in 1923, "People who are familiar with the Negroes say that in Louisiana they are held in subjection and when they come to California they take advantage of the privileges afforded them and become trouble-some. The southern style may have to be adopted."[48]

Historical understandings of racial and regional difference constructed by the nonsouthern working class in the shadow of slavery and the challenge of emancipation helped this idiom set root and develop in Weed. Insofar as Long-Bell represented a challenge to the sanctity of these differences, it also challenged white workers' conceptions of themselves as free, native, western, and white.

Status, Skill, and Everyday Life in Weed

Among others, historians Alexander Saxton and David Roediger have argued that it is precisely through this process of conscious differentiation that the idea of whiteness became concrete in the minds of white workers.[49] Although the process of conscious differentiation that occurred during this period was certainly not the origin of white racial identity, for the timber workers of Weed it was critical to the social stratification of the community. Not only did contrasts with black workers abet the consolidation of a nonblack consciousness, but they also played into the creation of a racial hierarchy that posited African American workers at the bottom and white, European Americans at the top. Workers of other national origins were slotted in between. Below white workers of British and Scandinavian heritage, Italian workers occupied a middle status, not white, but definitely not black or Mexican. Under them, the hierarchy placed Greeks and a few other eastern Europeans, then Mexicans, then black workers. Relative standing in this structure was an important matter to these middle groups, for segregation by race constrained where one could live, where one's children would go to school, the occupations to which one had access, and more. An Italian mill worker who began working in Weed in the 1930s pointed out to me that Italians "weren't considered white back then"; the achievement of white status in later years represented a significant improvement in the opportunities available to Italians both inside and outside the workplace.[50]

The politics of whiteness in this context, however, was not simply a matter of negative identification. Becoming white or achieving whiteness was driven by more than a simple desire for cultural distance from local blackness. Western lumber workers in the first decades of the twentieth century, the vast majority of whom would today be considered "white," were themselves the object of extreme, quasi-racial social exclusion. They were considered "lazy," "dumb," "of nondescript race," "rough," and sexually "perverted" or "repressed" and had an "impair[ed] . . . instinct of workmanship"; the conditions under which they worked were anathema to "good citizens."[51] A 1916 study by researchers at Stanford University, comparing the "intelligence" of migratory workers with that of prisoners and "street-car men," concluded that workers "showing a mental age of less than 12 years were classed as morons, while those under 11 years were considered feeble-minded. It will be seen that while the median of all three groups was about the same, the range was greatest among the migratories, and that the proportion of low mentality was much higher among that group than among the unskilled workers on the street cars. A group of business men that were tested showed a minimum mental age of about 13 years."[52]

Mobility, birth, political radicalism, education, sexuality, skill: these marked the cultural and biological difference of the lumber worker. The racialization of African American workers was achieved along similar axes, if through differently specified and experienced histories. Skill was a crucial dimension of this process. As Roediger points out, not only did the "performance of 'nigger work' and the consequent association (real or symbolic) with African Americans" make whites vulnerable to "harder driving, increased danger, and stepped up economic exploitation," but the "acceptance of 'colored jobs' also served to heighten the fear of being cast(e) as nonwhite."[53]

Consequently, in combination with the possibility of increased earnings but in no way limited to it, the various motivations to obtain skilled status could be very powerful. The politics of the wage and wage determination served as natural forums in which to articulate these claims. "White" lumber workers of the time, especially through union bargaining, sought to redescribe themselves as skilled, community- and family-oriented citizens. The paucity of lumber jobs defined as "skilled," however, precluded a mass move up the occupational hierarchy, so the problem settled around the definition of skill as the broader sphere of white, well-paid, and secure work.

In Weed, the inferior status and difference of the southern African American worker were essential features of the political economic vision of management and workers. For Long-Bell, these aspects ensured a manageable, competent, but virtually "unorganizable" resident labor pool. For nonblack employees earning the "public and psychological wage" that Du Bois remarked was the principal benefit of whiteness, African Americans constituted a group of workers who were "by nature" incapable of high-wage, high-status work.[54] Bringing racism into the mill through the "objective fact" of skill differentials generated very material earnings premiums that not only increased income but enhanced the status returns of the psychological wage.

The process of keeping African American workers in a subordinate position, however, was not always easy for either workers or management.[55] Producing a consistently "unskilled" workforce defined by irrelevant characteristics like skin color is not a simple task. Ability must be denied, production must be restricted where it would expand, and skill must be understood in such a way that the labor process, accumulation, and the relations of production can change and expand without challenging the notion that these characteristics matter.

In Weed, this was achieved through several mechanisms, each of which had the effect of making the politics of skill coextensive with the politics of race. First, skilled white workers undertook "hate strikes," refusing to work alongside skilled African Americans. For example, in opposition to the employment of skilled black sawyers in the best-paid and highest-status job in the mill, a sit-down strike by white sawyers relegated the most experienced black workers to unskilled, low-wage, unpleasant jobs. Second, unions, which refused membership to African Americans, attempted to redescribe themselves as associations of skilled workmen. Abe Muir, the leader of the Brotherhood of Carpenters and Joiners (an AFL union) in the 1920s and 1930s, spoke frequently of timber workers as "skilled workers who deserved the pay of skilled men."[56] Where successful, this rhetorical strategy made it impossible for black workers to obtain better jobs, and even where it failed, it reiterated a link that legitimated exclusion.

Finally, all of this was embedded in an often naked white supremacy—the everyday logic of racial privilege that structured relationships in the workplace and in the community at large—which ensured that the racialized worker remained low status and disempowered.[57] This worked itself out through a relentless barrage of abuses operating at several scales. It articulated the reaction on the part of white residents and the local state in Siskiyou to any disturbance of the social order—both straightforwardly coercive and more subtly "directive"—with broader, often consonant, regional and national political currents.

At a local level, African American residents were the target of frequent, often violent, harassment by the county sheriff, company management, and the nonblack community. Much of the harassment was justified by police as the appropriate response to African American violations of Prohibition-era alcohol laws and the associated "trouble" caused by black workers in the Quarters. Local newspapers reported with relish Sheriff Andrew Calkins's almost weekly raids on the Quarters' moonshine operations, ridiculing the explanations of his quarry. Black workers drunk on "jackass brandy" were constantly "shooting up" the club and homes throughout the neighborhood.[58]

In addition to liquor violations, citizens and law enforcement argued that they faced an "infestation" of troublemakers, demanding harsh measures to keep blacks in their place. They often acted through a police-supported local vigilantism, and both the vigilantes and the police used force freely in their efforts. At the mill, a white worker fired shots at a black worker; a black worker was beaten by a white clerk at the main company office; after a black laborer fought with a white employee in the planing mill, "several white men procured firearms to be prepared for further trouble." In the aftermath of these conflicts, local justice Judge J. P. Bradley usually ordered the "troublesome" African Americans to leave town.[59]

The local press related these events to readers with a vicious cynicism. A beaten black worker was "sent on his way a wiser and better negro." A confrontation that ended with a black woman being cut with a razor was described as "a great hilarity in Coon Town." Describing an incident in which a "Greaser" (a Mexican) drew a knife on a "coon," the *Yreka Journal* offered "the suggestion that our peace officers make a collection of the various weapons of war which this element of our community favors so numerously." Black workers were frequently reported to be a general disturbance: "[O]f late the Negroes have caused considerable trouble, and each one goes well armed, and the white men are now going armed, expecting trouble at any time."[60]

Not all the means of subordination were so coercive. Other institutional measures reinforced the crude disrespect black workers endured. Enormously popular blackface minstrel shows came through town frequently. Although the psychology of blackface proves very complex, companies like the "Darkey Minstrels" generated and helped legitimate black inferiority in the eyes of their white audience. In more formal institutional arenas, many of the contemporary means for civic participation were denied to blacks. For instance, and aside from the formal political spheres in which they could never participate, there were several white lodges in Weed—Masons, Knights of Pythias, Elks—that were the center of male social life. African Americans were refused membership, and their attempts to incorporate a men's lodge of their own were smothered.[61]

These local racisms harmonized with broader contemporary political developments. The first years of the 1920s were a time of heightened nativism and reactionary conservatism in the West and throughout the United States, and both found fertile ground in Weed. Local whites enthusiastically embraced the intertwined antiblack racism and anti-immigrant feeling that infused slogans like "North America, Last Hope of the White Race." African Americans newly arrived in Weed were refused lodging by landlords who claimed, "[W]e only rent to Americans." To make matters worse, the migration of southern blacks to Weed coincided with the emergence of the Ku Klux Klan as a national political force, and the Klan recruited thousands of members in Oregon and California. While some residents of Weed opposed the KKK's secretive vigilantism, it was sufficiently popular that at least three chapters, or "klaverns," were active in the region: in Tennant, Weed, and nearby Redding. While it is important to note that the politics of the Klan of the 1920s cannot be reduced to the largely antiblack program of the original, it is clear that racism played no small part in its attraction for more than a few local residents.[62]

The strike of 1922 thus did not produce the subordinate racial position of African American workers in Weed and throughout the region; rather, it entrenched that position. Even prior to the walkout, black workers represented the "southern-ness" of Long-Bell and the unfreedom its production practices imposed upon its workforce. The means through which many of them had come to Weed—"imported" by the company—only reinforced the perception of slavishness and servility. Indeed, early in the strike a local newspaper reported that a labor agent was to be imprisoned for defaulting on a contract to "ship a certain number of darkies" to the McCloud Lumber Company.[63]

During the strike, many African American workers initially joined the rest of Weed's mill workers on the pickets.[64] However, those who walked out appear to have been among the first to return to work. Black workers were not welcome to join the ITWU, and they were almost all relatively new arrivals in town. Unlike a significant portion of the other "common laborers," many had families. All lived in company-owned housing, and almost all were in debt to the company, forced to pay for their housing and their furniture, not to mention the costs of getting to Weed in the first place (for which they owed either Long-Bell or a labor agent). Black male workers could not just "pack up their grips" and look to the next town, as many white men did; racism, debt, family, and intimidation made migrating very difficult for most. So they went back to work.

In the wake of the strike, white workers lashed out at black workers. Blacks were beaten and harassed at work and in town. If they resisted, they were often fired, evicted, and driven out of town. "Race riots" were "narrowly averted."[65] In fact, the events for which records still exist seem straightforward enough on the face of it to make some common ahistorical explanations quite tempting. For example, it may seem appropriate to describe the confluence of capitalist interest and worker agency—in the form of intra-working-class violence—with references to "false consciousness," to ask "why didn't they act in their interests?" But to read poststrike attacks on black workers as the product of a "betrayal" of class solidarity, or even of the mere perception of such a betrayal, is to insert a historical discontinuity into the relationship between black and white workers in Weed where there is none.

As Roediger has written of white southern lumber workers, whites in Weed "were not just manipulated into racism." White workers' welfare was very much at stake, and not just on the organizational front. Of course, the need to maintain union solidarity was significant: "[f]or many white workers *scab* and *Negro* were synonymous," and African Americans were clearly purposefully recruited to Weed to diminish labor's power.[66] But job competition explanations rarely reflect the full story. Beyond their dependence upon suspect notions of collectively "rational" calculation and action, they provide only a superficial account of racism.[67] The reproduction of race upon which racism depends requires a historically informed ideological ground on which it can make sense. The arrival of workers of African American "race" in Siskiyou County did not coincide with or bring about regional racism. Racism, and the mechanisms it provided for the racialization of black workers, were already there, providing schemata for the articulation of blackness, as well as for several shades or grades of whiteness.

Skill, Race, and Region

The Legacy of the South

At this point in the chapter, we step into a historical political economy that is both multiscalar and particular to the United States and the legacy of racialized slavery. It demands something of a detour, or at least the introduction of a narrative parallel to the Siskiyou County story, one that is running beneath and through Weed. That narrative only partially constitutes Weed's history, but it is nonetheless as important to the town, and to my explanation of its politics, as its own local particularity. This second narrative thread is the cultural politics of skill in the postemancipation United States, for which an account has rarely been offered. Far beyond the United States, of course, skill has long been deemed the province of particular racial groups, capacities some can acquire but unattainable for others. Indeed, a biologically determined amenability to skill acquisition was a fundamental tenet of the post-Enlightenment age. We can easily turn to so prominent a character as Alfred Marshall for an example. Under the challenging heading "Unskilled labor is a relative term," Keynes's teacher and one of the founders of modern economics wrote: "Very backward races are unable to keep at any kind of work for a long time; and even the simplest forms of what we regard as unskilled work is skilled work relatively to them; for they have not the requisite assiduity, and they can acquire it only by a long course of training."[68]

Times have of course changed somewhat—if not nearly as much as we might hope—and such baldly prejudicial statements are less common and more historically specified since Marshall, but the logic has proved tenacious. In the literature of black-white relations in the United States, it continues to suffuse "culture of poverty" analyses of discrimination, the influential economics of Gary Becker and Thomas Sowell, and the (terrifyingly recent) "Bell Curve" pathology.[69]

Although based in racist fantasy, these circular rationalizations—African Americans are incapable, therefore we will not let them do the work; they do not do the work, therefore they are incapable—have very real outcomes: segmented labor markets, in which a preponderance of black workers perform low-wage, low-status jobs, competing largely with other workers of structurally similar position. Such dynamics are common across the range of social hierarchy. Ruth Milkman describes a similar process through which women's manufacturing work during World War II came to be considered "light."[70] These rationales, little more than self-fulfilling prophecy, have been so ideologically effective that it is now not uncommon for low wages to be used as an *explanation* for African American or female dominance in an industry or sector.[71]

But even the coordinated operation of ideology and racialized violence has not stabilized the racial coupling of "unskilled" and "nonwhite." Frequently, blacks have undertaken the work of better-paid laborers and have been contained among the "unskilled" only by terminological force. In the 1920s,

> [t]he less attractive and lower paid jobs go to the black man. Instances are common in which Negroes receive lower pay than white men for the same work. Sometimes the differential is applied openly, as it was on the railroads prior to federal control and as it still is in many manufacturing plants. Sometimes it is applied by calling Negroes' jobs by different names. . . . There are, of course, Negro molders, machinists, carpenters and blacksmiths, but they are not supposed to work in the same foundries as white craftsmen. If they actually do, in violation of social custom, they are usually classified as helpers.[72]

Noted labor historian Ray Marshall echoes this judgment: "Negroes were generally hired for the lowest-paid jobs, which were generally classified as 'laborer' regardless of the kind of work done."[73] Occupational subordination is maintained by the compression of the African American worker between a systematic proscription against entry to high-wage, high-status ("skilled") jobs on the one hand and a labor-process syntax that is sufficiently flexible and responsive to maintain the association between whiteness and skill on the other.

Insofar as these processes have been shaped by the cultural politics of race in the United States, emancipation is a watershed in the segmentation of black and white workers. Especially in the South, where slaves had dominated many skilled trades—and consequently enabled planters to control the acquisition of skill and the market for higher-wage labor—emancipation led to a massive social expropriation and reclassification of skill along color lines.[74] The influence of this racist restructuring was far reaching. When significant numbers of black workers eventually began to emigrate from the South during World War I as part of the Great Migration, they encountered an industrial system whose principal actors had already developed a hierarchy of production that was ideologically prepared to accept them only if they occupied the appropriate rung: the bottom.

Blatant racism was of course a critical factor in this, intermixed with political and economic concerns. From the perspectives of both white labor and white capital, the black worker was "unfitted by racial temperament for skilled mechanical work." According to employers, African American workers were not only the children of an inefficient, decadent, and parasitic plantation agriculture: they were also former slaves, an unproductive, lazy, and deceitful workforce. The white working class, newly (if unevenly) empowered by union organization, was busily engaged in defining itself as free, native, white, and occupationally and geographically mobile—in other words, not southern, and definitely not black.[75]

Moreover, rapid technical and organizational change, in the form of industrialization, served as racism's shop-floor handmaiden. The obsolescence of knowledge and abilities, and the ongoing and comprehensive reconfiguration of production systems and the politics of organized labor, resulted in a continuous reassessment of what it meant to be skilled and in significant labor market restructuring. This process continues today but certainly accelerated in the early twentieth century. Thus, although the impacts of technology were and are industry- and location-specific—and certainly less significant in agriculture prior to the New Deal—"mechanization is constantly changing the meaning of 'skill,' so that union opposition or craft tradition which has stood in the way of the Negro's entrance into certain recognized 'skilled trades' will count less and less. In the old trades, the union may actually oust him from places he has long filled."[76]

The fallout of early twentieth-century technical change, then, despite some qualified hope that mechanization would reduce barriers to African

American occupational and sectoral mobility, was a complex and contradictory potential that, when confronted with extreme economic volatility and an increasingly entrenched racial order, materialized mostly in the intensified battery of black workers.[77] While African American activist-intellectuals like Sterling Spero and Abram Harris hoped that industrialization's dynamism would increase labor demand to such an extent that new jobs would appear too quickly to be captured by established white institutions, the social division of labor that ultimately emerged effectively maintained skill, status, and wage barriers.

First, African American workers underestimated the influence of systemic white supremacy on the industrialization process. Technical advances were culturally and politically filtered through historical legitimations for keeping the racialized worker at the bottom: "backwardness" explained less capital-intensive and lower-wage production in the South, where the majority of black workers lived; southern employers—the businessmen who paid most of the African American wages in the United States—claimed that the lesser quality of their workforce, and the supposedly lower cost of living, justified their exemption from labor legislation like safety and minimum wage laws; and white workers in both the North and the South fought competition from black workers on racist and economic grounds.[78]

Second, the post–World War I economy was highly unstable, as I mentioned earlier. After a postwar slump, production and employment climbed in the early 1920s and then sank again, a pattern that continued through to the onset of the depression at the end of the decade. On such a roller-coaster ride, job security had a high premium for workers, and even low-status, low-wage jobs became the object of fierce competition, especially in the South. As Lorenzo Greene remarked in 1930, many whites were "glad of the opportunity" to do work "once regarded by them as 'nigger-jobs.'"[79]

Both of these developments were smoothed by the plasticity of the semantics of skill in a context of political economic change. Labor in the South was less skilled because it was not "modernized"—an irony given the ongoing nostalgia for the craft worker—and black workers were neither amenable to nor experienced with the demands of industry. In other words, they were unskilled because they were unskilled. Moreover, new job classifications and occupations that came with industrialization were very often open to definition. Few clearly required years of schooling or experience—indeed, it was often precisely the point of mechanization that they did not—and thus sat on a fence between skilled (or perhaps "semiskilled") and unskilled. Just as blacks were often labeled "helpers" or "called by a different name," so too were the jobs and sectors that they did come to occupy often labeled "unskilled."

From "Undesirable" to "Unskilled"

Most of these jobs, if not clearly skilled or unskilled, were certainly undesirable. Where blacks and whites work close together, the dominance of African American workers in jobs "distasteful to the whites" is a commonplace.[80] Indeed, some argue that this is a fundamental causal dynamic in the history of New World capitalism. The historian Robin Blackburn suggests that, in light of the "many more hugely exacting and unpleasant tasks to be carried out" under the plantation system, European immigrants' concerns for what might today be called "job quality" was so important that it helped justify African slavery and motivate "'white' racial consciousness" in colonial North America.[81]

So, although by itself it surely cannot guarantee the emergence of racial consciousness, the correspondence of higher wages, higher status, and relative comfort in the workplace goes a long way toward preparing fertile ground for ideological explanations of the "common sense" of racially specific "adaptability" to certain types of work. Workers and employers of the postbellum industrializing United States—with a ready-made "lowly worker" in the black southerner, whose very presence in the nation could be attributed to the need for someone to do the dirty, hot, heavy, exhausting work—easily extended the logic of "nigger jobs" from plantation to factory. The fact that political and economic oppression, the boll weevil, and timber exhaustion in the South produced a substantial African American workforce eager for these jobs despite their poor quality only reinforced such notions.[82] Where there was no African American workforce, or in the rare instance in which the racial hierarchy placed someone below the black worker, the stratification was nonetheless effectively reproduced: the worst jobs are still called "nigger jobs."

Then as now, factory safety played a significant part in judgments of job quality. New, frequently quasi-experimental machine-powered production was very often dangerous and unpredictable. When this new type of production was combined with little or no institutional support for accident prevention or worker education, injury and death rates in many industries soared. The American logic of "nigger jobs" meant that, proportionately, African Americans were much more exposed to these dangers. With pointed reference to industrial accident rates among blacks in the United States, one reporter in 1927 pointed out the terrifying fact that it "is only in rural areas of the South that there is now an appreciable excess of births over deaths."[83]

At this stage, I hope it is not too late for us to remind ourselves that African American workers, either in the South or in other parts of the United States, were in no way mere passive objects of these often horrific processes. Many workers knew they had the combination of technique, experience, and capacity to do the high-wage jobs that were the province of whites. There were even instances in which, often through a sort of backhanded compliment, they came to dominate the skilled work in a factory or sector, though almost always with the acceptance of wages lower than those of whites.[84] And it remains possible, as the critic and novelist Ralph Ellison suggested, that many black workers subjected to these abuses were engaged in a fully intentional rejection of white-dominated social and economic systems. In the face of consolidated opposition to the recognition of African Americans' equal rights as workers and citizens, this rejection could take the form, for example, of purposefully undercutting wages, as the black nationalist Marcus Garvey advocated, or rejecting union-sponsored apartheid.[85] The point of this discussion, however, is that in most cases of which we have some minimal historical record, power asymmetries were so pronounced that struggle might mitigate domination but could rarely overcome it. The racism, regionalism, labor, and industrial development of the U.S. cultural and political economy were too intertwined to be successfully confronted very often. The African American worker who performed "nigger work" in southern cotton fields is the regional antecedent of the racialized western worker who died operating the "Nigger-Killer." In each case his specificity is a product of the particularities of history and geography and the articulation, at other levels in the dialectic of capitalist development, of more totalizing dynamics that envelope and contain the incommensurabilities of distant times and spaces.

Conclusion: Making Sense of the "Nigger-Killer"

The economist Maurice Dobb can help us return to Weed from our historicizing detour and can also help us reground the discussion on the political terrain of the wage and the politics of measure—concepts that may seem to have faded into the background at this point in the chapter. Remarking upon the fact that the "disagreeableness" of a job, which should decrease its desirability, has not produced the correspondingly higher wages supply-and-demand economics would lead us to expect, Dobb points out how, instead, the "unpleasant work of the community is among the lowest paid rather than the most highly paid, as is also most of the work involving danger to life and health." Dobb explains this paradox with the notion of "non-competing groups" (an early segmented labor market model), in which artificial scarcity is created by better-off fractions of the working class. He goes on to say that "there is evidently a tendency, in class societies, for occupations which have traditionally been poorly paid to be considered disagreeable, and for those carrying a higher income to be considered more socially respectable or honourable."[86]

With respect to the broader structural features of the labor market, or even within a sector or industry, this analysis is very sound. The statics upon which it relies, however, like the radical institutional economics to which it contributed, restricts an account of the historical dynamics of technology, labor markets, and culture to a level of historical and geographical generality that has little to do with the specificity of concrete life Marx meant to capture with the term "definite." The notion of "traditional occupations" is of limited analytical use in the face of new means of production, different groups of working people with different histories, radical social change, and the contradiction and accommodation between formerly disparate forces of production and distribution that accompany any stream of economic change. As Milkman shows for women workers entering the manufacturing sector during World War II, when there is no "traditional" occupation for women, certain tasks are reconceived or simply deemed naturally appropriate.[87]

For the same reasons, any theory of the wage that assumes a constant set of well-defined objective worker characteristics will always collapse under the weight of historical experience. This is not merely the "inevitable" outcome of the simplifying assumptions that we are so often told we must make to cope with the complications of the real world. The claim that some identifiable qualitative category called skill will explain wage differentials and occupational hierarchy in the capitalist labor process has by no means universal validity, even at some comfortable "general" level of analysis, for it is based on the prior and unacknowledged assumption that the conceptual organization of the labor process is apolitical. The fact that an a priori assumption like this is profoundly antidialectical, while methodologically unhelpful from my perspective, is in many ways the least of its worries. Far more debilitating is its faith in a culture-blind rationality that—however constrained—only further obscures the social forces through which relations inside and outside the workplace are structured and change over time. These forces, as far as I can tell, are supposed to be the object of explanation. To cover them up before we get a good look at them will do us no good at all.

The dynamism of the lumber industry in the 1920s was crystallized in "the Titanic," the deadly skidder in the museum's photograph. Like locomotives earlier, and chainsaws later, the skidder was a revolution in logging technology in its time. Prior to World War I, logs were yarded by horses, sometimes pulling "high wheels," or, later, by "steam donkeys," an inefficient sort of protoskidder. Skidders, and the Lidgerwood Titanic in particular, made many of these older methods seem almost futile. Production volumes at Weed skyrocketed with the introduction of skidders near the end of World War I and peaked during the two years that Weed Lumber operated the Titanic. A massive machine, it was capable of exerting enormous force on the one-and-a-half- to two-inch cable with which it hauled logs. It was also extremely dangerous, and accidents during its operation were more common than in any other part of the production process.[88]

As policy makers often remind us, technological change like this creates new jobs and requires new knowledge and capabilities. That it also demands a redescription of the politics and culture of production is much less frequently discussed. In the case of the Titanic, questions concerning the latter would almost certainly have been as important as those concerning the former. What would be the status of the men who worked the new jobs the skidder required? Were they skilled? Would the wages be good? Working the Titanic was dangerous, even intimidating, but so were many other forest industry jobs. Would these new positions be desirable, dangerous in a "masculine," admirable way? Or were they to be avoided, dangerous in a "risky," low-status way? Their novelty precluded ready answers to these questions. In many industries, for reasons of status and management's interest in the protection of new investments, working with the latest technology is frequently the province of high-wage, skilled workers. Sawyers and saw filers were among the highest-paid workers in the lumber industry both because their jobs demanded experience and judgment and because errors were potentially very costly, damaging expensive machinery and slowing production.

The manner in which these questions were eventually handled by both workers and management reflects both the social—i.e., far more than technical—nature of the response and the centrality of the wage to the cultural politics of western work. The Titanic cost huge sums of money. Operating it required physical agility, sound judgment, and quick decision making. African Americans, as coded by white workers and white capital, had none of these characteristics. Indeed, many white people claimed that black workers were unsuited to work in logging operations altogether and should be confined to the mills and yards; a previous attempt to use black labor "for the woods" was deemed "not a success."[89] Blacks were institutionally and biologically unskilled, and their wages reflected it. But the Titanic was extraordinarily dangerous, too dangerous for white labor. And so it became the "Nigger-Killer," cheap and deadly to operate.

Despite the terrible nickname, black workers were certainly not the only ones killed and maimed working the Titanic. By 1926, Long-Bell had sold the Titanic to lumber operators in Oregon. Not merely dangerous, it had abetted the depletion of their private stands. The company consequently relied increasingly on timber cut from National Forests, and the U.S. Forest Service judged the skidders too environmentally destructive. By 1928, tractors had replaced the Titanic and its smaller relatives in Long-Bell's California operations.[90] The following decades brought continued rapid development in logging and milling technology, increasingly close ties to the Forest Service, and the growing dominance of the West in the national forest industry, all of which served the general dynamism of the sector. The end of the company town era came in 1956, when Long-Bell was acquired by International Paper; timber remained the center of the local economy until the mill closed for good in 1981.

Although many African American workers left or were forced out of Weed in the 1920s, much of the community chose to stay and remains in Siskiyou today. The prosperity and "westernization" of the industry after World War II, and a successful biracial strike in 1941, helped diminish some of the racialized conflict in Weed.[91] Ironically, perhaps, the southern specter reemerged in the late 1970s as union weakness and associated wage differentials, more attractive environmental standards, and cut-over western forestlands all powered the industry's return to the South.

Obscured by the post–World War II boom years, themselves now apparently over, are the processes through which black workers helped constitute this point on the "wageworkers' frontier."[92] They played a role in the persistent social contradictions that articulate skill, status, and race, that give "white" and "black" meaning, inside and outside the workplace. Their role in the construction of the frontier and of the specificity of what it means to be a wage worker at a particular time and place has been largely forgotten, but what is at issue here is not merely historical "facts." If that were the principal problem, we would be considerably better off than we are. The forgetting at issue is not merely an absence, as if the black timber workers of Weed fell off the edge of the table of history and now lie somewhere in the dust on the floor, to be picked up and cleaned off by someone with sufficient energy for the task. Rather, forgetting like this is ideological, and in that sense, it is not a "gap" in our memory but a "roughness" we have sanded down. Neither the historiography nor the popular perception of western wage workers, with only a couple of exceptions, includes African Americans. We miss the black workers of Weed not because the "evidence" is insufficient but because we cannot see them.

This is not merely a contemporary problem. Our own limited historical vision — less an issue of expanse than of magnification, I think — is deeply affected by the concrete relations of domination like those in Siskiyou County and the white supremacy that saturates so much of the western history in which it was embedded. The footloose white timber worker of our imaginations, a Paul Bunyan in California, is not only our own imaginary but one we have inherited. In Weed, the production and reproduction of the (skilled) white worker, a worker who shared commonalities with white workers throughout the United States but who also had his own particularities, represent an alternative politics of measure, different from but related to the American man we met in Los Angeles in chapter 3. Here, the wage as the index of skill maintains its quantitative form but carries such enormous cultural political weight, through the forces of racialization, that in all the historical evidence I can find, the actual range of the wage differentials in Weed is never mentioned. This does not mean the magnitude of racial wage differentials did not matter, but it seems evident that a proxy for a quantitative differential in the wage *rate*, "skill," represented a much more complicated qualitative struggle, within the wage *relation*, over racial hierarchies in the West and throughout the United States. This effort to supersede the quantity-quality opposition, to return the productive quantity to its racialized quality, is further evidence that the politics of measure is by no means entirely emancipatory. It is also testament to the fact that processes of wage determination are embedded in and predicated upon a cultural politics of the wage relation that is inevitably indeterminate, or at the very least, "overdetermined."

It has been claimed that the nature of the relationship between the fishermen and the dealers is one of businessman to businessman, and that the fishermen themselves have insisted on their business status. Every evidence and every action of the fishermen is an indication to the contrary. Fishermen have consistently refused to fish for the market and have demanded to fish for a wage. Even the boat owners have insisted on this status.

International Fishermen and Allied Workers of America, *The Fisheries of California* (1947)

Who Is a Wage Worker?

Worker-Producers & the Wage-Price

If I can say without too much exaggeration that we have exposed some of the dynamic "volume" of what are conventionally seen as the commodities exchanged in the wage relation—money (chapter 4) for human labor-power (chapter 5)—we have nonetheless not yet tackled the stubborn issue of what the wage "denotes." For a principal thread in the cultural politics of the wage is a definitional struggle over what "counts" as a wage. Who is a wage worker? And who will have the power to answer this question? Often these politics may be only indirectly related to working peoples' distributional claims, centered instead on what one might call autonomy or status augmentation, rather than on income maximization. In other words, clashes over what the relationship designated by the wage actually looks like, often originating in a particular group's ambiguous class position, are by no means always about simply "making more money." Put crudely, if given a choice between money and "freedom," there is no historical evidence that workers will consistently pick money.

The key point, though, as I have argued throughout, is that even in cases where "making more money" is not the primary objective—and any historical or ethnographic examination of wage struggles will serve to disarm the cynic's omniscient assertion that it is always the primary objective—the wage remains a political arena of primary importance. Examples abound of workers' efforts to work on the wage as a political site at which to reconfigure their ascribed, or as yet undefined, place in social hierarchies. In the years immediately following the U.S. Civil War, for example, many newly emancipated African Americans, wishing to escape any form of dependence, refused to work for wages, seeking rather to obtain their own plot of land, even if it generated less income. For them, in stark contrast to Frederick Douglass's sentiments quoted at the opening of chapter 1, wage labor meant subordination, not independence. Some of the arrangements they made with white landowners to obtain this autonomy worked very much like wage labor, but it appears that frequently it was the definition, not the practice, that mattered.[1]

In this chapter, I piece together a fragmentary history of the International Fishermen and Allied Workers of America (IFAWA), a trade union on the Pacific coast of North America, to dig deeper into this definitional dimension of wage politics. The IFAWA is not a well-known union. It is rarely discussed in secondary literature, and in fact it came to my attention only because I stumbled across a single mention of it in a footnote to a 1953 article on the Taft-Hartley Act.[2] I grew up in Atlantic Canada, a region in which the ideal of tough, seagoing male independence remains symbolically (if no longer productively) significant, and the IFAWA struck me because it contradicted the closely related convention of the competitive (even selfish) independent smallholder. Of course, having since become familiar with union efforts among fishers across the continent, I now recognize the historical inaccuracy of this caricature. Through my efforts to piece together the history of the IFAWA, I have come to believe that the mere fact of its ill-fated existence, from its establishment in 1939 until it succumbed to various pressures in the late 1950s, obligates us to reexamine the politics of the smallholder's experience. The union's story belies the hegemonic narrative of the fisher's "fiercely autonomous" individualism.[3] Indeed, insofar as the wage is the semantic (i.e., juridical) terrain upon which this conflict plays out, it is the cultural and political key to why this far-from-disinterested narrative gets challenged and how it happens.

In the following pages, then, I first examine the conflict between the union, on one side, and fisheries processors and state and federal governments, on the other, over the juridical or regulatory definition of the wage. In contrast to some of the former slaves in the South mentioned at the opening of this chapter, the IFAWA actively pursued and articulated a wage-worker identity. Its members asserted that the wage was the defining element of capitalist employment relations and, against the small-boat owner's ascribed status as entrepreneur, that the structures and dynamics of the fisheries industry depended upon de facto wage-labor relations of production. Second, I consider this economic redefinition of the wage as a foundational step in the construction of Pacific coast fishers' political economy and ecology. Specifically, I examine the construction of a "worker-producer" identity in light of the bargaining strength and privileged managerial role that identity was intended to legitimate for fishers as participants in a vital and vulnerable natural resources regime.

In both of these frames, the IFAWA's articulation of an explicitly politicized wage relation was central to its effort to assert a *workers'* class position and to redescribe the Pacific coast fisheries' industrial structure according to a "classic" industrial logic — capital versus labor; little guys versus big guys; us against them. The conflict over distribution of income, the legal and organizational status of both the union and its individual members, and the capacity of fishermen to influence the management of fishery resources worked itself out through a conflict over what constitutes the wage as an everyday relation. The stakes in this opposition — working-class identity, "traditional" ways of life, and community and resource sustainability, all in addition, not subordinate, to income — challenge the notion that the wage is simply one among many socially interchangeable means to income earning. They also speak to the importance of the social meaning of the wage as both constitutive of class and productive of class consciousness. The overtly political attempt to insert the wage in fisheries employment relations signaled an emergent working-class consciousness among Pacific coast fishers during the first half of the twentieth century that reflected fishers' "belief" in their working-class status and organizational self-interest.[4]

Clearly, it is up to me to demonstrate convincingly that fishers understood themselves as "wage-earning employees" and processors as "employers." This is especially important because the wide variety of relations that structured the working life of industry participants produced class positions, relations, and strategies that do not readily fit the standard capital-labor dualism; nor do they fit any more comfortably in some emerging "middle class." One way out of this is perhaps available in the social scientific–theoretic treatment of complications in the notion of class evident in the relation of "petty commodity production" to capitalism. Petty commodity production "resembles capitalism in that production is for the market rather than for the direct use of the producer, but differs in that those who control the (nonhuman) means of production also supply much if not all of the labor power, with wage labor playing a secondary role."[5] On the surface, the members of the IFAWA would fit nicely into this group of producers, which is generally assumed to be a historically "transitional" class whose members will eventually sort into proletariat or bourgeoisie.[6] I am not convinced this "categorical" approach is all that useful, however; not only are there are always arguments for and against any particular analytical arrangement, but the effort to repartition social life into ever more narrowly defined and mutually exclusive boxes has two serious disadvantages. First, it betrays a distinctly liberal approach to cultural politics that assumes that if we work hard enough, eventually we will find some "accurate" scientific decomposition that accurately represents "real life." However uncomfortable one might be with the label "poststructuralist," it is difficult to imagine critical social science taking this position seriously anymore. Moreover, even from a more strictly political economic purview, the static empiricism—a cloaked equilibrium model—that underpins such claims is, in the language of the Marxian-Hegelian tradition from which my own work emerges, profoundly antidialectical: it misses the movement, the restlessness of all historical phenomena, and closes our eyes to the fact that all such categories are social artifacts, carefully produced but always "impure."[7] The effects of this indeterminacy play out in the literature: the debate over the position and persistence of petty commodity production is long and wide ranging, but if there is general agreement on anything, it is the analytical anxiety that working people like those who joined the IFAWA are always difficult to categorize.

This chapter has four parts. The first briefly tells the story of the IFAWA, and the second considers the reasons fishers' organization took the form of an industrial union, paying particular attention to political economic and ecological concerns. The third examines in some detail the legal and political struggles of the union to define the wage and its applicability to the small-boat fisher. The fourth and final part links the wage, class, and primary production, key political categories of the discussion, in an attempt to make sense of the IFAWA's short and stormy life. I argue that the wage served a key analytical function in fishers' political economy, and for a dual reevaluation of the literature. First, the characterization of fishers and other smallholders as independent entrepreneurs belies the relations of production and class that hold in the fisheries. Second, organized labor can represent an effective attempt to restructure a particular political economy and ecology.

The Rise and Fall of the IFAWA

The first commercial fishers' union on the Pacific coast, the Columbia River Fishermen's Protective Union (CRFPU), was founded in 1886 in Astoria, Oregon.[8] Although there were several maritime unions on the Pacific coast in the early twentieth century, for many years the CRFPU was one of very few fishers' unions. While there were some "cooperative guilds," "protective associations," and "fishermen's councils," these organizations only partially shared the goals of the CRFPU and the few other unions that emerged in the first three decades of the twentieth century. They did not emphasize collective bargaining for minimum prices, egalitarianism, and relationships with processors characteristic of union activity. Rather, they focused upon the related tasks of "elimination" of foreign vessels from fishing grounds, the burdens of administrative processes imposed upon fishers, and the general representation of fishers' concerns to government and fish processors.[9] Most of these organizations functioned like what would presently be called "industry associations."

In 1937, three fishers' unions amalgamated to create the United Fishermen's Union (UFU) and affiliated with the new Congress of Industrial Organizations (CIO). The following year, three other fishers' organizations affiliated with the CIO.[10] In May 1939, these six unions, and several directly affiliated locals, coalesced to form the International Fishermen and Allied Workers' of America, also CIO-affiliated, representing fishers from California, Oregon, Washington, and Alaska. In the words of a member of the union's Canadian equivalent at the time, the IFAWA was "more of a federation than a single union"; it was constituted to allow affiliated unions and locals to retain significant autonomy and to (ideally) attract all fisheries workers, from boatmen, to "beachmen," to cannery workers.[11] Indeed, in light of the wording of several IFAWA contracts negotiated in the late 1940s, it is evident that the local autonomy it afforded its affiliates was a condition of their participation.[12]

These tactics were effective, especially in the early 1940s: from 8,000 members in 1939, the IFAWA represented more than 19,000 of the approximately 50,000 fisheries workers on the Pacific coast by 1942.[13] Membership reached 22,000 by the end of the war and continued to grow throughout the mid-1940s, especially among fishers, although not as rapidly as the shoreworkers' side of the industry.[14] By 1946, the IFAWA claimed to represent 80 percent of West Coast fishers, and as if to back this up, in the same year the Federal Trade Commission (FTC) noted that the "Pacific North West fishing industry is one of the most highly unionized industries of the country."[15] While my own calculations suggest, more modestly, that in 1949 the IFAWA's membership constituted approximately one-third of the workforce, and perhaps as much as three-quarters of small-boat fishers, organization was fairly successful by most standards of union coverage in the United States.[16]

It will come as no surprise that the IFAWA's emergence in the context of World War II had an enormous impact upon its organizational life. For at least a year prior to the United States' official declaration of war, the IFAWA's leadership believed the war was adversely affecting not only the security and economy of the Pacific fisheries but the union's bargaining position as well.[17] Among the most significant burdens the war placed on fishers was the Office of Price Administration's (OPA) imposition, in July 1943, of price ceilings on all commercially harvested fish. The ceilings were intended to stabilize the fisheries economy, provide cheap wartime food, and enable "maximum production" in the fishing industry.[18] Initially the IFAWA organized to resist these price controls, but by early 1944 union leadership was encouraging the membership to cooperate with OPA in the interests of the war effort, unity, and postwar growth.[19] Along with a suite of "patriotic" war-effort concessions like the "no-strike pledge," this co-operation was consistent with labor's national policy after Pearl Harbor.[20] The motivation to accept price controls was of course the overwhelming support for OPA among consumers. As I explained in chapter 3, World War II political dynamics scripted opposition to OPA as anti-American, and in combination with complications arising from the fact that most fisheries workers (including boat owners) almost certainly benefited from OPA's larger regulatory regime, this was perhaps a sentiment as widely held within the union as without.

At war's end, however, the exceptional sacrifices OPA ceilings demanded of fishers did not go unopposed. Unlike the ceilings on some manufacturing goods—like commercial fishing gear—those on fish prices were not quickly repealed.[21] As late as August 1946—after OPA had been terminated by Congress—the IFAWA was still fighting a "stabilization monstrosity" it claimed cut real wages in half.[22] The eventual removal of price controls the following year gave the IFAWA what the leadership understood to be the fullest freedom to pursue collective bargaining it had enjoyed in its eight-year history.[23]

Yet several obstacles remained, none of them trivial: inconsistent prices along the coast, which "undermined price structures in one region or fleet by fishing in another"; an "influx of fish from foreign countries"; and the "discontinuance of government buying."[24] Moreover, and at least as important, other difficulties loomed: many commercially important fish stocks showed signs of overharvesting, and the FTC and processors were stepping up the pace of already frequent legal attacks, framing the union as "actually" an association of independent businesspersons colluding to raise prices.[25] The latter was particularly burdensome given its coincidence with a related and increasingly vicious anticommunism and antiunionism that abetted and accompanied the passage of the Taft-Hartley amendments to the National Labor Relations (Wagner) Act in 1947.[26]

Despite these difficulties, the IFAWA negotiated some very demanding contracts in 1948 and 1949, particularly in Alaska. Yet enabling "100% organizing," resisting Taft-Hartley compliance, and fighting accusations of collusion in the court changed the demands placed upon the leadership.[27] The FTC's indictments and the doubts they engendered regarding the future depleted membership, undermined strength at the bargaining table, and jeopardized the union's very survival. There was a general feeling among the executive that affiliation with a larger, stronger, more robust union might save the IFAWA and perhaps even reinvigorate it. The International Longshoreman's and Warehouseman's Union (ILWU) seemed the logical choice.[28] The ILWU worked the same waterfronts, was CIO-affiliated, and had proven strength in both the legendary leadership of Harry Bridges and the bloody San Francisco strike of 1934. Limited records make it difficult to gauge rank-and-file support for the merger, but in January 1949, the membership voted "overwhelmingly" in favor of operating as a "coordinated group," a Fisheries and Allied Workers Division within the ILWU.[29]

Ultimately, however, the ILWU's strength did not provide the IFAWA with the resilience and organizational capacity it sought. A series of blows to the fishers' union reduced it to a shadow of its former self by the mid-1950s.

First, after summary trials in early 1950, the ILWU, IFAWA, and nine other unions were expelled from the CIO for "pursuing policies and activities which were 'consistently directed toward the achievement of the program or the purposes of the Communist Party.'"[30] While the specific long-term effects of the expulsion on the IFAWA are difficult to determine because the union disintegrated not long after, writers on the other nine unions have shown how organizational coherence deteriorated with the lack of access to the resources of a national association like the CIO, the exacerbated "red" stigma, and the loss of morale that might accompany such a loss of legitimacy.[31] These certainly weakened the IFAWA's already faltering resistance to federal and industry pressures.

Second, the FTC stepped up its pressure on the IFAWA during and after the CIO trial. Following the 1946 conviction of Local 36 (San Pedro, California) for price-fixing, private suits were filed by "operators" (processors) on the same waterfront.[32] Federal prosecution followed.[33] In 1947, antimonopoly charges were brought against the Sacramento River Fishermen's Union, and its contract with local processors was deemed illegal; in 1949, the FTC again filed suit against the San Pedro local.[34] Between 1953 and 1957, six more complaints were filed by the FTC.[35] These suits were the last straw for the IFAWA.

It did not take very many convictions to convince the dwindling number of unionized fishers that organization and collective bargaining at best only attracted unwanted regulatory attention.[36] There was talk of a "United Front" within the union at least as late as 1952, and in 1958 the division still claimed to represent five thousand workers.[37] But by 1955, what a contemporary described as the "moribund" Fisheries and Allied Workers Division is rarely mentioned in ILWU records.[38] Apart from a couple of brief notes in 1959, it appears the fishers were only a paper organization after about 1957. The IFAWA simply slipped out of sight.[39]

The union's demise is not entirely surprising. Even if it had not been battered by the courts, operators, and the federal government, a cursory description of industrial structure illuminates some of the organizational and structural barriers the IFAWA faced. Fishers on the Pacific coast were boat owners, employees of boat-owning fishers, or lessees of boats and gear owned by a third party, usually a processor or wholesaler.[40] The changing size of the industry over time reflects the market, environmental, and regulatory contexts. From the outbreak of World War II to the mid-1950s, between 33,000 and 50,000 Pacific coast fishers worked on approximately 11,000 to 14,000 boats.[41] These fishers sold their catch to the 500 to 700 processors that dotted the coast, concentrated in significant ports like Los Angeles, San Francisco, Astoria (Oregon), Seattle, and Bristol Bay (Alaska).[42] Individually, processors and boat owners held highly varied degrees of market power: some were single establishment operators, and others controlled several plants, boats, and wholesaling concerns. Some were fishers or former fishers, others large corporations like Star-Kist. Industry concentration varied across the fisheries; tuna packing, for example, was basically controlled by six operators, while some commercial groundfish species were processed by many different establishments.[43] As the FTC reported in 1946, however, wholesalers and processors were highly organized and presented a coordinated market for fishers' products.[44]

Moreover, the composition of the IFAWA's membership broke with tradition in the fisheries. Fishers' organizations on the Pacific coast prior to World War II were locally restrictive and ethnically defined.[45] Whether ethnicity was a condition of membership or not, the "clannish" nature of the fishery is almost always noted in fishers' accounts of the times.[46] The IFAWA, however, was notably culturally diverse, if not at the local level, at least at the highest organization level of the "International." In each port, locals tended to maintain traditional membership characteristics, a function of clannishness at both the union and sectoral scale. Thus, in most cases, the membership was a relatively accurate representation of those who did fish for a living, while as a whole, the union represented a much more diverse mix of industry participants than had been the case with any previous fishers' association: "The fishermen are of mixed national origin, practically every nation of the world being represented. Of those not born in America—only about a third of the total number of fishermen—the largest groups are the Italians, Jugoslavs, Norwegians, Portuguese, and immigrants from the British Isles. The Italian fishermen are scattered in practically every port. The Jugoslav fishermen are largely concentrated in Los Angeles."[47]

As I remarked above, the conventional analytical categories available to clarify the cultural and political economic position of fishers working within this structure are themselves historical products of the boundaries of the debate. We need to step beyond the effort to find a "fit" for the IFAWA's members—capitalist entrepreneurs contracting independently, "disguised wage labor," or some middle location—to bear down on the decisive role for politics and culture that is always there, obscured by cases when the fit is smooth but made so much more evident in such ambiguous instances.[48] Here, fishers' problematic class position produced a cultural-political space in which a vicious struggle took place between, on the one hand, government and business, claiming that fishermen were business-people, and, on the other, the fishers themselves, who claimed they were disguised wage labor. And although this struggle took place in what might appear to be a marginal political economic and geographic sector, the ideological (and thus material) stakes in what Gramsci might have called this front in the war of position were in fact enormous. Against fishers' own claims regarding their economic and cultural well-being, operators and the state defended the hegemony of a conception of the U.S. economy as composed of small, independent entrepreneurs whose perceived autonomy to this day "provides the material basis for the ideology of laissez-faire and democratic politics."[49]

Why the Wage?: Production, Space, and the Political Ecology of Class Consciousness

To better understand the cultural-political dynamics on this ideological front, we need to confront the emergence of working-class consciousness among fishers and the choice of unionization as an organizational form, since it does not necessarily follow unproblematically from that consciousness. A discussion of the idea of a union of smallholders, and of the relations of production and resource management in West Coast fisheries, is therefore in order, as is some consideration of the complexity of that sector's vast spaces of production. These can help explain the emergence, form, and content of the sophisticated political economic arguments, especially the theory of the fisherman's wage, that the IFAWA developed through its own analyses of its historical condition.

Smallholder Unionization and Working-Class Identity

In the history of Pacific coast fisheries, there have been many "marketing associations," some "boat owner associations," and even a few "fishermen's protective associations" but relatively few trade unions.[50] I place a great deal of importance here on the concept of a union, in contrast to other forms of collective association, and it is worth acknowledging the possibility that I overestimate the historical significance of the organizational form.[51] It would be naive to assume, for example, that simply because an organization identifies itself as a union it is in some essential way unlike a protective association. Still, there are critical components of unionism as a political practice that are key to the story of the IFAWA. In contrast to the ways in which nonunion organizational forms operated on the Pacific coast, fisher unionism's particularity resides in its insistence on the institutional priority and political legitimacy of collective bargaining, the integrity of which is maintained by the threat of collective action against the employer.[52]

Any compelling account of the IFAWA's unionism must thus address the fact that small-scale fishers' unions have rarely been very effective or lasted very long.[53] The most common explanations for this lack of success are (a) workers work for somebody else, while fishers work for themselves; and/or (b) small-scale fishers are independent entrepreneurs in competition with one another. It makes no sense to speak of them as "workers" potentially interested in collective action and bargaining. The belief that these explanations are "common sense" is widely shared, even among fishers. Indeed, despite his own commitments, IFAWA president Joe Jurich was himself forced to acknowledge the power of these sentiments: "Many workers in the fishing industry, plus many operators, still labor under the delusion that solid, national organization cannot be built in this industry. Although admitting that lack of national organization is largely responsible for keeping fisheries as the stepchild of the food industry, these people insist that the geographical nature of our industry, its deep-rooted individualism, its intense competitive spirit, its diverse means of production, all of these factors conspire to make organization impossible."[54]

The idea that simple commodity production and working-class identity are incompatible has been challenged often.[55] Yet whether these counterarguments are convincing or not—and many of them are very convincing—few, if any, of them deal with the specificity of the union as institutional form. While they tell us why smallholders might *organize*, they do not explain why they would *unionize*. So, without slipping into functionalism, I want to suggest why the IFAWA's members' institutional response to their collective action problem emerged as a union, and not in some other form. Obviously, the pressures of foreign fishing, stock depletion, and the changing productive and technical nature of the fishery convinced fishers that some collective effort to address the condition of the fisheries—and the livelihoods that depended upon it—was necessary. But why did fishers not form a federation of marketing associations or cooperatives (which were common in agriculture) or follow the historical pattern of independent, community-based collectives?[56] Why would they join a coastwide, multigear, multiethnic, and industrywide organization that seemed almost certain to be unwieldy, oligarchical, and unresponsive to local needs?[57] Moreover, why would they form a union of wage workers, explicitly contrasting members with profit-driven capitalist businessmen? Were these people not independent entrepreneurs, no less motivated by profit?

Admittedly, to say that fishers claimed they were workers elides an important question about the dynamics of political economic conflict on the Pacific coast. Although this chapter is not primarily concerned with social movements as such, the role of the IFAWA as a social movement among working people—as with organized labor's "movement" status more generally—must be acknowledged. Insofar as union organizing is always simultaneously social mobilization, explaining it demands at least a cursory examination of the meaning and function of the symbolic and material structures through which mobilization takes place. According to sociologists like Mustafa Emirbayer and Jeff Goodwin, such "symbolic formations," or "cultural structures," are "narratives, idioms, and discourses" having "emergent properties—an internal logic and organization of their own."[58] While acknowledging that cultural and social systems thoroughly "empirically interpenetrate," they maintain that culture is also *analytically autonomous* with respect to network patterns of social relations."[59] Through this lens, then, we might suggest that the cultural dynamics of a "working-class identity" in the United States, although completely enmeshed in the social relations and everyday practices that constituted fishers' lives, are in important ways analytically distinct, born as they are from a history that is not historically or politically coextensive with the social structures within which fishers were embedded.

Thus far in my account of Pacific fishers' organizational tactics, the meaning and function of working-class identity—as much a part of cultural as social and political economic processes—remain unclear. The historical evidence suggests that most of these tactics are rather straightforwardly explained by material motivations and incentives, but just prior to showing how this is so, I think it helpful to briefly address the symbolic aspects of fishers' adoption and articulation of worker status. This seems an apposite place to do so because cynicism regarding "real" motives lurks around every corner, urging us to ask the inevitable question: Was this "we are workers" stuff only strategic or instrumental representation, or was it a case of class-conscious self-perception, of shared belief; in other words, was it "really" cultural?[60]

Perhaps the most important point to make before trying to "answer" this question is that by itself "self-interest" does not make this question easy to answer—even if one were to take the idea of "interest" as either transparent, consistent, or both. (I will argue in chapter 6 that there is much that is indefensible in the idea of interest, and that most of the rest is based on unsupported assumptions.) On the one hand, of course, we might say there is no reason to expect that any "cultural framing" will be historically produced independently of (self-)interest. On the other, we could respond that although self-interest can certainly be imputed to the story of the IFAWA's self-conscious class positioning, there is no evidence of simple instrumentalism in the wage worker's identity; indeed, to suggest that this is what was at work is basically to assert that we know the answer to all the "why" questions of history before we even ask them: Why? Self-interest! If this is where we begin, then anything other than the rational-choice frameworks of neoclassical economics or "positive" political theory is unnecessary.

Still, given the available records, it is difficult to "prove" that fishers' "truly believed" they were workers. The default, however, should not be to assume that it was all a tactical ruse to garner support, membership, and institutional legitimacy. Limiting the discussion only to the materiality of the context, we can still ask why, if working-class identity was a purely instrumental politics, fishers configured themselves as workers and not as entrepreneurs. Even if we attribute the choice to unionize to the relatively labor-friendly national political economic climate constructed during the New Deal and elaborated during the war, it must be acknowledged that pure instrumentalism would probably have led fishers to abandon the union model—and to question why they ever took to it—especially after Taft-Hartley.

So, although we are unable to ascertain fishers' commitments to their working-class identity, it is possible to wonder at the imputation of an organizational "strategy" that had no obvious income or resource management advantages over, say, fishers' cooperatives, which in fact might have been preferable, from a "rational-choice" perspective, since they allowed price coordination and were legislatively exempted by the 1934 Fisheries

Cooperative Management Act (FCMA) from many of the challenges the IFAWA faced as a union. It was certainly no more difficult, from a procedural perspective, to organize a cooperative or a series of cooperatives than to organize a union. The available record provides clear evidence, then, for the fact and rationality of working-class identity as a strategic representation, but it does not demonstrate that it was necessarily the optimal one, even from a condition of "constrained choice." Moreover, it strongly suggests, particularly on the basis of the politics of a "worker-producer" identity and of the incessant antitrust challenges mounted against the union (discussed in more detail below), that a representation that was no doubt strategic at some level found, at the same time, experiential and cultural resonance among Pacific coast fishers.

In short, union records provide a good reason to believe that the IFAWA's members believed that they worked for a wage and that they were part of a primary-production working class whose interests were distinct from, and often opposed to, those of the capitalist processors for whom they fished. This understanding of their position in the relations of production, and of their relation to the fishery resource and its market, was also firmly predicated upon a textured analysis of the political economy and ecology of the industry, which was in turn founded upon fishers' everyday working lives.

The Pacific Coast as a Space of Production

Class matters to this story. But to tell it in class analytical terms, it is necessary to think not only about the relations of production on the boat, at the wharf, or in the cannery. When looking at a union that covered a vast area, and that would have been ineffective had it not, the spatial and resource management dimensions of the IFAWA's organizational constraints and opportunities are crucial.[61] Unionization among fishers was the result of a conjuncture of contingent and structural tensions, both productive and spatial, which were in turn constrained by the ecological and management regimes that determined the condition of the fish stocks themselves.[62]

To bring class to this discussion without losing sight of these geographical complexities, one need not have much of an orthodox Marxian ontology. At the outset, at least, one need only agree with David Harvey's uncharacteristically open-ended claim that class is an "analytical construct" useful in understanding differential relations to the means of production.[63] For convenience, of course, Marx relied upon what Harvey calls a "two-class model"—capital versus labor—whose relative simplicity, in contrast to concrete history, would allow him "to lay bare the exploitative character of capitalist production."[64] Marx does reify class in the form of an actual group of laborers or capitalists in some of his more programmatic writings, but, as I suggested in chapter 1 (and will come back to in chapter 6), an emphasis on class-as-"thing" misses the conceptual power of the term.[65] We are much better off with the historian E. P. Thompson's oft quoted remark that class is not a "structure" or a "category" but "something which in fact happens in human relationships." In terms that speak provisionally of the cultural relevance of working-class identity to union political mobilization, Thompson says that from this perspective, class is a relation that emerges through the sentiment and articulation of interests derived from "common experiences (inherited or shared)." Usually these interests are understood as opposed to those of others and can produce a class consciousness "in which these experiences are handled in cultural terms: embodied in traditions, value-systems, ideas, and institutional forms"—a historically and ecologically specific, but not culturally or geographically isolated or static, working-class identity.[66]

A Working-Class Commons

Realizing the fact that the precious species of salmon and other valuable food fish are decreasing rapidly and are facing extinction, and that thousands of fishermen and cannery workers on the Pacific Coast of the U.S.A. are depending on the fishing industry for a living, it is our object to use our influence, individually and collectively, urging National and State Governments to enact laws against the unscrupulous tactics in fishing and improper seasonal limits in order to safeguard this great industry.

Columbia River Fishermen's Protective Union,
"Constitution and Bylaws of the Columbia River
Fishermen's Protective Union," Preamble

One way to describe and legitimate the experience of the IFAWA is to understand it as a class-specific response to a crisis of the commons. Bonnie McCay's and James Acheson's influential formulation—"common property should refer to an exclusive as well as inclusive notion of the commonwealth involved" that "encompasses a wide variety of institutional arrangements that delimit access and impose restrictions on use"—highlights the collective resource management aspects of fishers' cooperation.[67] Both on the shore and on the water, the IFAWA delimited and restricted, remaking the essentials of common property resource management in forms appropriate to union action.

On the shore, organizers drew on a variety of sources of organizational potential. They referred to the "solidarity" of fisheries workers, the importance of the industry to the local community, and the value of a shared, "traditional" way of life. As Joe Jurich wrote in 1944, the members of the IFAWA "have learned that the salmon troller has much in common with the sardine seiner; they have learned that the fish filleter has much in common with the tuna packer; they have learned that Puget Sound has much in common with San Pedro. The members of IFAWA have learned that although the workers of the industry live in many different rooms, they have a community of interests which demands a single house for all."[68]

Other times they pointed to the significance of membership to the long-term health of the fishery; management and regulation, by and for fishers, were possible only if all belonged. "Organized fishermen mean production."[69] In addition, they highlighted the injustice of the fisher's plight to attract members: foreign fish on the markets, the exploitative practices of "operators," or the unfair interventions of the "men back in Washington, who know nothing about fishing."[70] Finally, the IFAWA leadership could point to the substantial achievements of unions both within the fishing industry and across North America.[71] As one member, fishing out of Fort Bragg, California, put it, "lack of solidarity" means lower prices.[72]

Notable in all these appeals are two elements frequently associated with collective action to coordinate the commons. First, whether calling upon some shared collective interest, a nostalgic romanticism, or the bald drive to accumulate, the IFAWA excluded in the very act of inclusion. For those who participated in the organization, membership set them apart from what they had been and from those who would not join: members of rival maritime unions, operators, unsympathetic government staff. Any articulation of a "we" simultaneously identifies a "them." As the preamble to the CRFPU constitution put it, one of the principal aims of organization was the "removal of any and all obstructions which are detrimental to our welfare, and which enter into direct conflict with our calling as Fishermen."[73] Second, insofar as these appeals organized the attention of fishers to the issues explicit and implicit in *unionism* as a political-organizational form, they not only legitimized the IFAWA but also constituted the particular version of it that fishers practiced. I think it bears some emphasis that twenty-two thousand members identifying themselves not as "independent businessmen" but as "brothers" represents a significant development in what might be called the "fishers' ideology." Indeed, that these men claimed they shared a "calling" deserves pause. Contrast the sectorally specific histories, memories, and geographies that saturate this phrasing with those in the previous chapters; can we imagine the stillmen of L.A. petroleum refineries speaking of their shared "calling"?

Production, Space, and Class

The kinds of social restrictions that come with an articulated "we" (even one to which one is called), while crucial to systems of resource management and control, are effective only if tied to the geography of the (natural) resource in question and to a mode of collectivity that has some material and symbolic meaning in everyday political life. This resource management endeavor existed within, and contradicted, the larger, quasi-laissez-faire management regime of the Pacific fisheries, generating new conflicts between fishers and operators and government and inscribing older disagreements more deeply. To the state, fishers were entrepreneurs competing independently for access to fish stocks, and this status was coded into the regulatory framework of the industry. For example, like all proprietors, they were exempt from the minimum wage and maximum hour provisions of the Fair Labor Standards Act.[74] Despite this, those familiar with the industry, even within state agencies, understood that the everyday dynamics of fishers' position contradicted this classification. Indeed, with an unwittingly ironic turn of phrase, government representatives countered fishers' identification as employees by defending the interests of those "who give jobs to fishermen."[75]

This is not to say that fishers did not see themselves as independent but that they did so in a manner qualitatively different from the characteristics associated with the competitive entrepreneur status they had been assigned. They understood workerhood, or working-class membership, as structurally determined but politically meaningless unless enacted. As George Johansen of the Alaska Fishermen's Union said to the visiting members of a Senate committee on fisheries legislation: "Under present laws, a union can be prosecuted under the FTC Act, and antitrust laws, if it attempts to bargain for so-called independent fishermen or fishermen who own their own boats and gear. A man who owns his own boat and gear is in an independent position. He wants to belong to a union. Why should he be discriminated against by law if he chooses to have a union bargain for him?"[76]

The story of the IFAWA accounts for the way that, in Thompson's terms, class "happened" in the Pacific coast fisheries and class-consciousness helped motivate the IFAWA. The members of the IFAWA were caught in the contradictions of the meanings of the capitalist mode of production for their way of life, and class—both analytically and experientially—was a product of these dynamics.

These contradictions are most readily visible in fishers' ambiguous attitudes toward technical development. Although the adoption of new technology, from on-board refrigeration to "fish-finders," necessitated the increasing capitalization of the fisheries, and thus the restriction of access, this technology had the potential to make fishers' very strenuous and dangerous work a little easier and safer. Throughout the newsletters, meetings, and correspondence, I found an unromantic welcoming of these expensive productive innovations. "Sardine refrigeration helps labor."[77] "Fathometer finds fish."[78] Yet fishermen both feared and favored technical advances. While welcoming efficiency and safety, fishers remained aware of, and lamented, the impact of improved harvesting technology: as one Seattle fisherman remarked in 1947, "I am moving farther out each year, and the fish are getting fewer each year. In a few years, there will be no fish."[79]

In the face of these conflicting developments, what organizational responses were contextually possible? It would be wrong to paint the fishers as anticapitalist. Members of the IFAWA relied upon the commodity market for their living; they caught fish to sell and were "concerned about the marketing" and the "expansion of the market" of the fish they caught.[80] But, like most participants in common-property systems, they had to ensure a sustainable supply to maintain their living. Furthermore, like many laborers in capitalism, they relied upon an economy to which access was unevenly distributed. The fishers were economically and geographically peripheral to national and international markets. They had neither the time nor the capital to sell their catch directly. To reach the consumer in marketable condition, fish needed to be processed, an expensive and labor-intensive process. Thus, catches were almost always sold to an "operator," who acted as both processor and broker of the product. Given the potential for spoilage, fishers had to sell to the operator closest to the fishing grounds. "Thus the 'perishability' of fish is only a problem for the fisherman."[81]

In many cases, this meant an operator monopsony and the creation of a dependent employment relation, not (as processors claimed) a business-to-business contractual agreement.[82] While certain significant differences remained between fishers and wage laborers (who made up much of the rest of the union in the canneries), in particular the former's frequent role as an employer of nonfamily labor, the integral structure of the fisher-processor relationship was very like that of employee-employer. The fisher, whose income was usually entirely dependent upon one processor, commodified his labor in one marketable form (fish) and was forced to sell to one price-making buyer. In some regions, like parts of Alaska, a portion of the fishers' income was wage-like "run money," meant to diminish the risk of seasonal fluctuations that made companies' and employees' contractual timing imperfect.[83] Often, the processors owned the boat. Almost always, they owned at least some of the gear—nets or lines in particular.[84] Moreover, the processor demanded a great deal of control over when, where, and how fish were harvested and who harvested them, and such discretionary powers were contractually guaranteed. For example, operators could arbitrarily restrict the catch of any boat in any particular twenty-four-hour period of the fishing season.[85] Where the fisher was "independent," the processor was usually the main source of credit, which forced the fisher, if there were other buyers nearby (as there were in some urban centers), to sell his catch solely to that processor as part of debt repayment.[86]

The nature of this relation was very clearly understood by the union; the constitution of the Columbia River Fishermen's Protective Union clearly identified "capital" and the "employer."[87] Fishermen could not forsake capitalist relations of production and remain fishers, but they could try to force operators to maintain the smallholder structure of the industry by monopolizing the labor supply. And monopolizing the labor supply is exactly what a union is designed to do.[88]

> We, the Fishermen of the Columbia River . . . mindful of the fact that a combination exists among capitalists on this river, whose avowed object is to so control the labor market as to deprive us of our share in the general prosperity, and to obtain the product of our labor, without rendering therefor [sic] a fair equivalent. Knowing as we do that if this condition of things is allowed to go unchecked and the few be allowed to control the many, it is only a question of a very short time when we as well as all other laborers must be dependent upon the whim and caprices of a few unscrupulous men. Knowing as we do that any individual effort to maintain our rights and uphold the dignity of Labor is sure to meet with failure, we but feebly imitate the example which capital has set up; to organize and protect ourselves against the unjust efforts of capitalists to reduce us to a state of absolute dependence.[89]

Labor contracts, while acknowledging the seasonality of the industry, formalized the employer-employee relationship in a manner that blatantly contradicts the conventional understanding of the fisher as one who works for no one but him- or herself. Instead, they demonstrate two characteristics very clearly. First, while fishers' legendary independence may hold true, it was manifested not so much by working for themselves but by choosing for whom and how they would work. Second, that choice was significant only if it was made collectively. Fishers pressed the IFAWA and processors for "coastwise schedules" because "fair prices" were impossible without interlocal standardization.[90] Given the mobility of both labor and resource (stocks) in fisheries, that collective had to be relatively large scale; locally specific but uncoordinated responses could easily be undermined.

Clearly, the spatial and productive analyses of fisheries cannot be completely separated.[91] For the Pacific fisheries, as noted above, coastwide organization was the only scientifically viable means of resource management in light of stock and labor mobility. Yet this scale of organization was new to fishers. Note, for instance, that four of the six founding unions of the IFAWA identified themselves as fishing ground–specific: Puget Sound, the Columbia River, Prince William Sound, and Alaska (Bering Sea). This no doubt affected the union's decision to operate in a more decentralized manner. Still, the demands of the resource and a processing monopsony made it clear to the IFAWA founders that locally specific organization was insufficient for fisheries management or economic survival.

Coastwide organization also had to confront another dynamic tension among fishers, one that is often forgotten today: in the mid-twentieth century, many small fishers still operated out of urban centers like Seattle, San Francisco, and Los Angeles. (This is still the case in some parts of western North America.) Furthermore, since a significant portion of Alaska's fisheries labor was not resident in the state, much of the Alaska fishery was urban in the off-season; the Alaska Fishermen's Union, founded in 1902, was headquartered in Seattle for its entire existence. Western coastal cities have often been at the center of radical unionism in the United States, and this was never more true than during the first forty years of the twentieth century.[92] This almost certainly influenced the institutional form the fishers' organization took. It also led to an occasionally marked disparity in the political radicalism of different locals. Strike threats, tie-ups, and conflict were more frequent in the urban locals, and the risks that individual fishers were willing to take seem to have been greater in urban centers, which may be a function of differential exit opportunities in the form of other work or other processors. The union's leadership mostly came from Los Angeles, San Francisco, and Seattle. Also, especially following the ILWU merger, organizational leadership, while sensitive to rural concerns, was substantially involved in national political conflicts that necessitated an urban emphasis, like antitrust suits and the CIO trial. The full implications of the role of the union's urban membership are by no means clear, unfortunately, but they suggest further possible explanations for the rapid rise and fall of the IFAWA.

Whether this speculation is well founded or not, contradictory spatial and productive demands enabled the coastwide fishers' union. Industrial-smallholder, local-coastal, and urban-rural dynamics helped create an organization that struggled to confront conflicting demands: the local particularities inherent in the coastwide concern, the individual fisher's reliance upon a regional resource. This interpenetration of the local and the regional, the general and the particular, is, I believe, the most defensible understanding of the IFAWA.[93] This is one instance of how class happened on the Pacific coast. The differential relation to the means of production between fisheries workers and operators formed the basis of the class relation. Class consciousness manifested itself in an institutional form that could address both concerns for the physical resource and the economic realities of capitalist production by coordinating the harvesters at the relevant scale: a coastwide fishers' union. As with technology, though, the union was neither a plain leap of faith into industrial production nor a "traditionalist" effort to disable it. Rather, it was an attempt to rein it in, to control its development on fishers' terms, and the wage became the political arena in which to do so.

Defining the Fisherman's Wage

[T]he labor of a human being is not a commodity or article of commerce. Nothing contained in the antitrust laws shall be construed to forbid the existence and operation of labor, agricultural, or horticultural organizations, instituted for the purposes of mutual help, and not having capital stock or conducted for profit, or to forbid or restrain individual members of such organizations from lawfully carrying out the legitimate objects thereof; nor shall such organizations, or the members thereof, be held or construed to be illegal combinations or conspiracies in restraint of trade, under the antitrust laws.

Clayton Act, Section 17 (15 U.S.C. 17)

Reining in capitalist industrial development is no simple task, of course. Working within a complex matrix of production and distribution, mechanisms of change and levers of control are difficult to identify and to influence. The most threatening challenge to the IFAWA's legitimacy, the relentless antitrust charges, was at the same time the most intellectually demanding. The government's and processors' assertion that fishermen were independent entrepreneurs earning a return on investment through the sale of commodities gave the union's general strategic strengths—the density of its organization and the immediacy of its members' knowledge of and impact on the resource—relatively little purchase. The FTC did not directly attack the legality of union action, but rather the very political economic basis upon which it stood. Fishermen sold fish, not labor; they received a price, not a wage; they earned a return on capital, not a piece rate.

The IFAWA had hardly consolidated before its legitimacy as a union was first legally challenged. In mid-1939, the Columbia River Packers Association, an association of Oregon fish processors, refused to sign the contract the IFAWA offered. The contract committed the operators to purchase fish from union boats only, and the association alleged that this allowed price-fixing by fishers, which violated the Sherman Anti-Trust Act by restraining trade. The U.S. District Court of Oregon agreed; upon subsequent review, so did the Court of Appeals, Ninth Circuit, and the Supreme Court.[94]

When the case reached the Supreme Court in 1942, the contest had been distilled to the question of whether the original suit constituted a "labor dispute" as defined by the Norris-LaGuardia Act. The union argued that it had a right to bargain accorded by the FCMA, which exempted fishers' associations from antitrust legislation. The Ninth Circuit found that the IFAWA was not a cooperative as defined by the FCMA, that the Sherman Act did therefore apply, and that the IFAWA was in violation.

The importance of this decision for a consideration of the politics of the wage lies in the logic upon which the courts relied, which set the precedent for the rest of the antitrust legal challenges the IFAWA faced in its short life. Quoting Norris-LaGuardia in the Supreme Court decision, Justice Hugo Black wrote:

> That a dispute among businessmen over the terms of a contract for the sale of fish is something different from a "controversy concerning terms or conditions of employment, or concerning the association . . . of persons . . . seeking to arrange terms or conditions of employment" calls for no extended discussion. This definition and the stated public policy of the Act—aid to "the individual unorganized worker . . . commonly helpless . . . to obtain acceptable terms and conditions of employment" and protection of the workers "from interference, restraint, or coercion of employers of labor"—make it clear that the attention of Congress was focused upon disputes affecting the employer-employee relationship, and that the Act was not intended to have application to disputes over the sale of commodities. . . . The controversy here is altogether between fish sellers and fish buyers.[95]

Upon remand, the Ninth Circuit ruled that the IFAWA was "in the same position as sellers of articles generally."[96] According to this interpretation, and in the words of a 1949 indictment, the IFAWA "knowingly and continuously engaged in wrongful and unlawful combination and conspiracy . . . to fix, determine, establish, and maintain arbitrary, artificial and non-competitive prices."[97]

Addressing these charges proved tricky, since the exchange relations that determined fishers' incomes were not easily categorizable. Fishers worked on "shares"; the money paid by a dealer to the boat was divided according to a predetermined pattern. Although there were many different arrangements, shares systems worked through a general convention. Boat owners, whether on the boat or not, usually took a larger portion, some of the money was set aside for maintenance, and employees (non-boat-owning fishers) received somewhat less. If the boat owner was in debt to the processor, then interest and principal were deducted before subsequent distribution of income. When the boat was owned by the dealer, one-third of the catch was usually the "rent" paid, the remainder of which was split among the workers.[98]

The sectoral income distribution determined by this system lends itself to a variety of interpretations. The IFAWA defended itself against antitrust allegations by arguing that a de facto employer-employee relationship held in the Pacific fisheries. It claimed that "the primary economic function of the fishermen is the labor of catching the fish. Fishermen are workers and primary producers."[99] The fact that these wage earners own some of the means of production does not reflect investment but cost; that there was no identifiable relation between the price fishermen received and the price consumers paid underscored this.[100] Before the Ninth Circuit again in 1949, the union proposed that "fishermen acquire no title to the fish but only the right to use or sell them . . . since there is no ownership, the fisherman has only his labor in the fish." According to this interpretation, "the 'worker-producer' is selling his services at wages to be determined by the price of fish delivered."[101] Fishermen argued that any contractual conflict was a "labor dispute relating to fishermen's wages."[102]

As the number and severity of antitrust actions increased over the 1940s, the IFAWA put a great deal of time and energy into a sophisticated political economic analysis designed to underwrite its arguments concerning members' wage-worker status. The central analytical category in this work was the "wage-price," i.e., the wage rate implicitly associated with any given price at which fishermen sold their catch to dealers.

The "wage-price" is an impressive and theoretically interesting conceptual move, echoing Marxian value theory while rejecting one of its critical derivative claims. The "wage-price" is not easily compatible with Marxian "labor-power." It consciously avoids the idea of commodified labor as "capacity to work," calling upon the explicitly noncommodity nature of labor defined by the Clayton Act. Fishers do not sell mere labor time, to be used according to the dealers' whims. Their labor is an "economic function" of a very specific and voluntary nature.[103] Many of them believed a fisherman's life and work were in one's blood; Columbia Fishermen pledged an oath to "remove all obstructions" that "conflict with our calling as Fishermen."[104]

At the same time, the "wage-price" builds fishers' labor into the value of the commodity by collapsing the distinction between commodity and labor in a way that does not reduce labor to commodity but reduces the commodity to labor. In a way that is particularly appropriate to primary production and echoes Marx's notion of the commodity as "congealed labor time," it builds the act of fishing into the material existence of the fishery resource. There would be no marketable fish without the particular efforts of the fisher. The fisher's earnings, therefore, are remuneration for the fish in which their labor is embodied—a wage-price for labor-fish.

The idea of a wage-price allowed the IFAWA to pull the small-boat fishers away from the entrepreneurial pole in the businessperson-worker binary. Still, its arguments rely implicitly on that opposition. If the wage-price is not a price, then it is surely a wage, characteristic of the employer-employee relation within which collective bargaining is a protected right.

> Payment by shares, it is argued, place[s] fishermen in the position of independent businessmen. But it is only superficial. For many years the mining of coal was paid for on a tonnage piecework basis, and miners were required to furnish their own tools, equipment and explosives. There have been numerous cases where the wages of coal miners, as well as other workers, have been tied to the price of the product. There is no substantive difference between the piece rates of fishermen in Alaska who are paid a specified amount of money by the canneries who own the boats for each fish caught, and the piece-rates of fresh market fishermen in California who are paid a specified share of the total catch which the dealers have agreed to but at a specified price. There is no law which can compel fishermen to go out fishing when prices are not posted in advance and adhered to later. If it is legal to compel dealers to post prices, the fishermen see no reason why it is not legal to require that such advance agreements be put into writing and extended over longer periods in order to stabilize production. Thus the fishermen have by their own actions refused to remain in the industry as entrepreneurs and have insisted on payment in piece rates which are similar to those in other industries. Payment in piece rates in no way changes the status of the fishermen as wage earners and primary producers.[105]

Wage, Class, and Natural Resources

It is one thing to say class happens, but it is another to say that workers or capitalists know it is happening; class can be a useful analytical construct even if one searches in vain for class consciousness. Such a search among Pacific fishermen, however, is not futile. Indeed, an emergent class consciousness among fishermen—"wage earners and primary producers"—is one of the central historical themes in the story of the IFAWA. The union's efforts discussed above reflected this emergence, while they also helped it take place.

The very existence of the IFAWA demonstrates that its membership was aware of the fact that different groups will exploit resources differently, according to their "interests." Processors, factory fishers, and governments all approached fisheries management in a particular way. It is also clear that small-boat fishers who joined the IFAWA did so at least partially to participate in the development of harvest regimes and techniques that would be distinct from those practiced by atomistic "independent entrepreneurs" or by the rapacious "absentee capital" and "large corporations" that, they claimed, had "gutted [their] fisheries and ruined [their] economy."[106] Here is the "primary producer."

Moreover, this class ideology was not only a response to potential resource scarcity and sustainability; it was equally a declaration of political economic and cultural difference. For example, before the U.S. District Court of Southern California in 1947, the IFAWA disputed an antitrust indictment by arguing that the jury was biased because it was not adequately representative of class diversity in the community. According to the court's summary, the union claimed that "an 'economic class' (arbitrarily designated by the defendants as proprietors, managers and officials) constitutes more than 50 per cent of the grand jury and the trial jury panel . . . whereas this so-called 'economic class' actually constitutes but approximately 15 per cent of the population."[107] In addition, the union argued that "laborers, people working by the day or hour, members of labor unions and Negroes were systematically and intentionally discriminated against" during jury selection.[108] In this challenge, fishermen are both wage workers and members of the working class.

The significance of the wage, both as marker of workerhood and as a political category around which the union and its claims could be organized, emerges alongside this consciousness. While the social meaning of the wage is clearly productive of class, it is not a case of "if A then B," wage then class (or class consciousness). Rather, the wage, or wage-price, served as the mechanism through which the simultaneous nature-work-production instant that is fishing was linked to the broader political economy. Class and the wage each helped make, and make sense of, the relation between primary production and work in capitalist societies.

"Class War Has No Place in America": A Political Ecology of the Wage

The story of the IFAWA is particularly well suited to my efforts to lift the lid on the wage, since it is unusual that the qualitative stakes in the wage are formulated so explicitly by both "sides." The legal battles over fishers' place in the chain of production relations were framed plainly as a conflict over what constitutes a wage and thus who is a wage worker. The political economic meaning of these battles for the different parties—i.e., the distributional claims—is generally not difficult to recognize, and in cases where it might be, the union itself provides helpful interpretive material. It might even be tempting to contrast the positions of the processors and government on one side and the IFAWA on the other as roughly an opposition between neoclassical (de jure) and institutional (de facto) wage theories. To do so, although perhaps fruitful for some purposes, would miss the point of this discussion.

Rather, the tale of the IFAWA as told here is best understood as a cultural politics of the wage, a politics of measure. The struggle over the meaning of the wage on the Pacific coast is not simply a clash of theories of wage determination, of the wage-as-quantity. It is a struggle over the qualitative content of the wage relation, a story of fishermen's efforts to politicize quantity, to knot the slippery thread of value, and overcome the quantity-quality opposition. In this context, the wage is a central site in a very broad conflict between different groups' culture and politics and their respective theories about how they work and how they should work.

Even more compelling, however, are the facts of the case at hand. From my perspective, they are worth restating, for even in the process of reassembling the story of the IFAWA, I occasionally lost touch with the appropriate time register. I found myself wrapped up in the intricacies of daily life in the union and on the water. As I mentioned earlier, the archives told tales that resonated with those that circulate as my own family's history. I would flick forward five years, then back another eight, without much thought. Rereading the fragmentary records of the antitrust and Taft-Hartley pressures, though, I am reminded of their astounding relentlessness. This all happened in less than twenty years. The FTC indictments began as soon as the union was organized and did not let up until the union was only a paper shell. Moreover, these impositions took place, at least initially, in a context in which labor had nominally relinquished a great deal of its strength for the war.[109] Willingly, it did so through the no-strike pledge; unwillingly, through measures like the "Connally Amendment," which enabled the government to "take over and resume production in any plant where production has been interrupted," just as the secretary of the navy did in the case of the struck oil refineries in 1945.[110] Admittedly, the fishers were not the only ones under scrutiny, but this does not obviate the immediate question: Why so much time, energy, and persistence directed against the fishers?[111]

The IFAWA was a radical union, which almost certainly did have communists in the leadership. Many unions did at the time. Taft-Hartley compliance was an issue with working people throughout the United States in the postwar period.[112] The government and processors said the IFAWA was a "fishermen's trust." It is a painful irony that the Sherman Act, designed to curb the power of megacorporations like U.S. Steel, was turned against a group of working people; nevertheless, the antitrust suits underscored the potential for fishers to collectively intervene in fisheries resource management. Recognizing their class-specific shared reliance on the fishery, the fishers formulated organizational objectives that would have, if successfully met, created a de facto working-class commons on the Pacific coast.

The only way the government could justify antitrust measures was if the fishers were not supposed to organize. As Justice Fee of the Ninth Circuit, ruling on the IFAWA's "conspiracy," wrote in a decision that would have astounded even Gramsci in its committed ideological testimony, "Class war has no place in America. The very contention itself contains a paradox." Indeed, the very act of fishers' unionization "proved the possibility of abuse of the freedom accorded by democratic institutions."[113] The fishers' configuration of their class identity was simply denied by the dominant conception of the relations of production. The claim that "the relationship involved is that of buyers and sellers of fish" required not only a denial of the employment relation fishers felt was evident in the fishing industry but an ascription of entrepreneurial independence, of a "freedom," that the fishers themselves intentionally rejected.[114] The hegemonic socioeconomic discourse—atomized, competitive businessmen-harvesters—into which the IFAWA's membership did not fit is remarkably like that double-edged liberty that Marx described as "free labor." As Bonnie McCay notes about some New Jersey fisheries, the government understood open access to natural resources as "the structure of laissez-faire competition" in both product and labor markets. To the extent that it was successful in maintaining such a regime, the government refuted the counterclaim implicit in unionization and in common-property regimes: the demand for social equity.[115]

The reasons for dismissing these claims are tied up in the cultural politics of capitalism and highlight the enormity of the ideological stakes in the FTC's efforts to destroy the IFAWA. As Alain de Janvry has powerfully argued, the existence of petty commodity producers or a petty bourgeoisie plays an essential legitimating role in laissez-faire (liberal) economic systems: "In the pluralist interpretation of democratic politics, the state acts in the interest of society as a whole by reconciling the demands of various interest groups. These groups compete on an egalitarian footing for access to and control over public institutions. And it is this political equality that gives meaning to majority rule. Implicit in this 'citizen sovereignty' interpretation of the state is a Jeffersonian-style petty bourgeois society where economic and social power are fairly evenly distributed."[116] Consequently, the ideological basis of western capitalism is to a great extent "grounded on the actual or presumed existence of a significant petty bourgeoisie."[117]

De Janvry discusses co-option and separation as two (among several) strategic means through which this hegemony can be maintained. Co-option would require confining struggle to forms that can be addressed by the state's mediating institutions. When this does not work, as with the unionization of "independent" fishers, the separation of a class of working people to "create" a petty bourgeoisie becomes an attractive option. This explanation describes the facts of the IFAWA's history well. It has its own peculiarities, but de Janvry is arguably on the mark.

Wider possibilities for the study of work, class, and nature emerge from the discussion in this chapter. The Pacific coast fishery is an ecologically determined political economy—a particular regional political ecology—and the social response to it was at least partially shaped by the constraints and opportunities of the environment in which it operated. If I have convincingly argued that the social response was the realization of class membership and the emergence of class-based organization in the form of a fishers' union, then the IFAWA is evidence of class as a political-ecological relationship, and the wage as the political space through which it was realized.

Because nothing is known but what has
passed through labor, labor, rightly and
wrongly, becomes something absolute,
and disaster becomes salvation.

    Theodor Adorno, *Hegel: Three Studies*
    (1963)

The Wage & Workers' Interests

With some historical ground beneath us, I would like to return to the critique of wage theory to extend and problematize it. For while the first-cut effort I laid out in chapter 2 helped prepare the terrain for the immanent political economies of chapters 3, 4, and 5, there remain at least two important conceptual questions I have delayed engaging. First, how do we bring these histories, theories, and their respective internal dynamics together? How does the cultural politics of the wage in the West work itself out as a politics of measure? Second, if indeed it is the politics of measure unfolding here and elsewhere, what is the object of that politics, if not our old nemesis utility (or some version thereof)? Are workers merely pursuing their "interests," or can we still talk about "interest" at all?

Toward a Wage Theory "without Guarantees"

It is perhaps only good fortune that Piero Sraffa was close with Antonio Gramsci, but we should thank our lucky stars for it.[1] Sraffa, the economist, understood how many lines have to be drawn, how much has to be hidden from view, to make "the economy" make sense as a bounded object of analysis. Gramsci's analytical goal was to erase those lines, to uncover what is hidden, exposing the extent to which the "economic" is endlessly punctured by the "noneconomic." He is in many ways the theorist of the exogenous—or better, the theorist for whom everything is endogenous. I think it impossible that Sraffa's essential role in the cultivation and preservation of Gramsci's intellectual and political work is not due at least in part to his recognition of the limits of his own often purely formal analysis and of the irreducibly political-cultural embeddedness of all economic activity.[2]

Gramsci is best known as the theorist of "hegemony," the social processes and conditions by which a group—a "historical bloc"—exercises economic, political, and ideological power in society, power that works itself out not through mere "domination" (i.e., coercion) but through a political economic "leadership" to which other groups actively consent: "The fact of hegemony presupposes that account is taken of the interests and tendencies of the groups over which hegemony is to be exercised, and that a certain balance or compromise equilibrium should be formed—in other words that the leading group should make sacrifices of an eco-nomico-corporative kind. But there is no doubt that although hegemony is ethico-political, it must also be economic, must necessarily be based on the decisive function exercised by the leading group in the decisive nucleus of economic activity."[3] Gramscian thought has become increas-ingly influential since the 1960s, and "hegemony" (if often in a grossly simplified form) is now a crucial component of the contemporary social scientist's vocabulary. Aside from its own explanatory force, the concept's attraction partially resides in the extent to which it abets the move away from the economism that weakens some Marxian theorizing. Not surpris-ingly, then, most of the attention to Gramsci has emphasized his cultural and ideological writing, out of which his understanding of "the economy" presumably flows.[4]

Yet hegemony's specific relevance for this discussion—a theory of the wage as a fundamental ideological, i.e., consensual, relation—is troubled by Gramsci's few direct remarks on the wage relation. In his one extended comment on the wage, in the notes on "Americanism and Fordism," he ar-gues that high wages in the United States are an "ingenious" combination of "persuasion and consent"; they are "the instrument used to select and maintain in stability a skilled labour force suited to the system of production and work."[5] But even if we must read Gramsci sympathetically, keeping in mind the terribly oppressive conditions in which he wrote the *Prison Note-books*—violence, hunger, isolation, depression, and illness—the uncritical rational individualism in which this analysis is based must be excised if we are to reconstruct "economic" concepts like the wage in a theoretically and politically incisive manner commensurable with the best of Gramsci's contributions. The claim that high wages are an "objective necessity" of capitalist exploitation relies upon a functionalism that implies an unchar-acteristic simplification of social relations.[6] It leads Gramsci to pass over the dynamic working-class agency, the active struggle for compromise, that plays such an important part in the construction of hegemony under capitalism, in the United States no less than elsewhere.

While never forgetting the importance of the consent to which Gramsci points, Adam Przeworski's extension of Gramsci's materialist theory of what might be called the "wage of consent" goes some way toward such a theoretical reconstruction of the "decisive nucleus of economic activity," while at the same time recognizing that nucleus's dialectical inseparability from the "totality of economic, political and ideological relations."[7] Przeworski makes sure to remind us that "ideological hegemony can be maintained only if it rests on a material basis": Gramsci's famous remark that in the United States "hegemony is born in the factory" is, for him, a materialist claim before it is an ideological one.[8] The reproduction of wage earners' consent requires a "minimally necessary" level of wages. Here we have something like "persuasion." But then Przeworski adds that the wage does not in fact work as political closure, a purchase of workers' complicit silence (or active support), as Gramsci's brief comments suggest. Instead, the wage of consent suggests an opening by pointing out the fundamentally political determination of an "economic" threshold beyond which crises arise. In his words, "the consent-reproducing level of wages depends on the economic militancy of wage-earners."[9]

It bears emphasis here that I have no interest in reproducing Przeworski's flawed, antidialectical, and ultimately untenable methodological individualism. It stands upon a very un-Gramscian quasi-rational model of workers' politics, which for him reduces to "economic militancy," a corollary of which is a conception of the wage as mere quantitative measure of relative power in bargaining outcomes. These premises are subject to the same debilitating weaknesses, discussed in chapter 2, that limit the neoclassical analyses from which his methodology is borrowed. Fortunately, with regard to the elements of his analysis relevant here, his "plea" for such methodological orientations is in the end a conservative afterthought.[10] Despite his narrow and arbitrary assertion (it is not a theory) of workers' "natural" interests—an antianalytical move that is extraordinarily common in orthodox and critical social science and from which I suggest an escape route below—some of his insights into the wage can be readily mobilized in the effort to reconstruct it as a cultural-political site. In fact, in many ways Przeworski triangulates at least two of Sraffa's and Gramsci's key theoretical contributions to a cultural politics of the wage, despite his own apparent interest in delegitimizing the very concept of cultural politics.[11]

First, he develops Sraffa's critique of the Marxian-Ricardian conventional wage in a specifically Gramscian manner. Since "there is today sufficient evidence that wage levels are not determined endogenously by the system of production alone," the problem for continued capitalist accumulation is not the reproduction of labor but the "requirements of legitimation."[12] These "legitimation wages" (to coin a phrase) are perhaps the crucial fiber of the "economico-corporative" "compromise equilibria" that constitute hegemony. Legitimation is dynamic, produced partly by the crude purchase of workers' consent but also by workers' own efforts to carve out a space without which the very notion of legitimation cannot even be entertained. In other words, the wage is neither solely a tool of capitalist mystification nor a transparent distributional mechanism. As the preceding chapters demonstrate, the politics of the wage can in no way be reduced to the mere maintenance of stable relations of production.

In light of the arguments against equilibrium in chapter 2, Gramsci's reference to "compromise equilibrium" merits brief consideration. The first thing to note is that these are "unstable" by definition, and the realm in which they might hold is explicitly distinguished from the strictly "economic."[13] Indeed, an essential premise of this political formula for hegemony is that wage rates and shares are indeterminate, in the full Sraffian sense, if for no other reason than to provide the necessary flexibility in political economic means to allow what Gramsci calls the "economic" component of hegemony to operate. The crucial point, however, is that in this account the legitimation wage is again not the outcome simply of capitalist calculus—in contrast to the neoclassical "efficiency wage," which is a tool to attract and keep good workers—but also of working-class struggle. Nonequilibrium (as opposed to disequilibrium) wage rates, and wage differentiation across time, space, and social group—an oft noted empirical characteristic of the U.S. West, as I discuss below—are in this sense sine qua non for the reproduction of capitalist relations of production and accumulation. "Compromise equilibria" constituted in the political realm of capitalism depend upon an indeterminate wage rate or share (or both).

The second way in which Przeworski can triangulate Sraffa and Gramsci for the purposes of a cultural politics of the wage is the extent to which he might reconcile Sraffa's antideterminist theory of income distribution under capitalism with Gramsci's concern for the consent-and-coercion dynamic that so thoroughly influences it. As Przeworski notes (in stark contrast to the reductionism of his consent-reproducing wage level), "[P]atterns of income distribution are important for they construct the immediate experience of social relations and thus serve to validate competing ideologies. But they do not explain, they must be explained. That some people obtain incomes larger than some yet smaller than others does not account for their role as a historical subject in the process of transformation or preservation of social relations. The question is precisely why did class struggles result in the situation in which particular categories or places in the capitalist system obtain particular shares of surplus as revenue."[14]

This stakes out ground that Sraffa elegantly steps around, pointing out that he had virtually nothing to say about it. "Sorry," he seems to be saying, in the almost regretful tone he uses at the point in the *Production of Commodities by Means of Commodities* at which he says wages are determined outside the system of production, "but I have done all I can. Please ask Gramsci." And indeed, the problem of the material basis of Gramsci's class-hegemonic *political* theory is crystallized in Przeworski's remarks. What is that "totality of economic, political and ideological relations" that not only produces a patently uneven distributional "situation" but makes that situation "common sense" both to those who end up with the "short end of the stick" and to those with the long? What is the particular combination of consent and coercion—both of which, it must be remembered, assume working-class agency—that produces and legitimates unequal outcomes and opportunities, i.e., limits political vision?

These questions and our responses to them are critical, for they provide a theoretical basis for a working-class politics of the wage that is not reducible to the technical problem of wage determination yet refuses to lean on either an unsubstantiated "false consciousness" or on its neoclassical negative image, constrained utility maximization.[15] Gramsci argues that "[s]elf-deception may be an adequate explanation for a few individuals taken separately, but it is not adequate when the contrast occurs in the life of great masses. In these cases, the contrast between thought and action cannot but be the expression of profounder contrasts of a social historical order."[16] And Przeworski asks: "Is it not an absurdity that wage-earners would obtain less than the product without expecting that profits will eventually be transformed into an improvement of their material conditions? Is it not an absurdity that they would consent to capitalist relations, that they would not use their political rights for 'social emancipation' if there did not exist a real possibility for realizing their material interests in some foreseeable future?"[17] The implication—that the working class has "its own conception of the world"—is explicit in Gramsci and Przeworski and underwrites Sraffa's theory of indeterminate distribution. And it is, in all senses of the word, a conception that is continually "waged" by and for the working class.

Concrete History: Working-Class Political Economy in California

Even along the lines of an orthodox analysis of wage determination or wage rates in the U.S. West, the Sraffa-Gramsci concoction proves a powerful analytical frame, and it generates some intriguing questions with merely a cursory glance. In the interplay between formalism and open-endedness, the combination of Sraffa's narrow abstraction and Gramsci's historical specificity has insightful things to say about how the wage actually works, both quantitatively and qualitatively.

Consider, for example, the most commonly noted characteristic of wages in the West before World War II: they were higher than in the rest of the United States. The suggested explanations for this phenomenon that emerge from the other "schools" of wage theory are relatively predictable. Neoclassical theory attributes high wages to labor scarcity or to the relative skill sets of western workers in comparison with workers elsewhere. These were indeed important influences, as the histories here make clear. Institutionalist economists and sociologists put some meat on these neoclassical bones with a consideration for labor market isolation and unionization, and these are also formative factors in each case, although it is certainly the case that isolation need not necessarily drive wages up, as the case of Weed's workers makes clear. Marxians might uncover the workings of some western conventional wage, determined by the higher costs of living in the region and the particular political and social contexts of the West. To use the story of the oil workers as a case in point, one could potentially see these relations manifested in the struggle over the "ability to pay" and in the often extraordinary radicalism of western workers.[18]

These economic analyses of western history do not necessarily contradict one another.[19] To them we can add the wage's double content, that it meets conventional-subsistence needs but may contain surplus. Workers' efforts can improve wages by altering the social forces influencing the conventional wage, in effect lengthening the golden chain. However—and this is a key point—workers can go further than this, configuring not simply the accepted norm of subsistence but the meaning (in Sraffa's sense) of the legitimation wage and the political content of legitimacy. In so doing, they can affect both the wage rate and the wage share—the division of the surplus—challenging the fundamental dynamics of the distribution of income under capitalism. This is part of the politics of measure, a struggle over the social meaning of capitalism's obsession with quantity.

However, even if we remain within the realm of that obsession, the great advantage of the reconstructed concept of the wage that I have tried to trace here is that, unlike the ideas of wage politics that undergird other approaches, in this analysis the movements of this politics of measure are made visible and some of the specific ways in which it plays out in everyday life are identifiable. In the West, this approach finds fertile historical ground. First, it suggests we discard any conception of a western conventional wage or of competitive equilibrium wages determined in the regional labor market. Indeed, if there are dominant characteristics of western labor markets prior to the mid-twentieth century, it is their isolated and *non*equilibrium "states" (a word whose fixity seems to contradict the point I am trying to make). Workers earned more in the West, but wage rates were far from consistent across the region (even for the "same work"), they fluctuated dramatically, and entire sectors were susceptible to complete structural-distributional transformation in relatively short periods of time—witness the recruitment of Chinese labor for the railroads, for example.[20] Wages were high in the West, but in terms of the wage share and of intraindustry occupational wage rates, they were nonetheless extraordinarily volatile.

In a similar vein, a recognition—one is tempted to say admission—of the possibility that profit rates are determined outside the system of production is unavoidable in light of the regional politics of the wage. Workers' wage claims were not necessarily based upon the right to a productivity-based wage; nor were they always just a struggle over the price of the labor commodity, however "persuasive." They were, however, almost always a site of often violent cultural assertion, articulated in terms of the absolute distribution of income, coursing with a frequently unwieldy combination of vociferous race-inflected class politics and populist anticapitalism. Workers fought for a share of the surplus in addition to subsistence allowance at least partly because there was neither precedent nor functional logic to the region's profits, especially in the resource sectors that effectively industrialized the West. The efforts of the Oil Workers International Union (OWIU) to use its augmented political economic power under the World War II command economy to restructure the division of the postwar surplus in L.A. is perhaps the clearest example of these developments presented here, but the fisheries and forestry sectors also provide ample historical substance.

Second, and perhaps most important for this project, high wages in the West were a cultural characteristic, even cultural precondition, of those who enjoyed them. Indeed, high wages in the West were both a result of and a critical ingredient in the recipe for cultural hegemony produced by the interactions of western capitalists and workers for whom independence and small-property ownership were primary objectives.[21] In turn, the culture of high wages in the West partly determined not only the politics of wage determination but the politics of culture itself: what it means to be exploited or exploiter, male or female, white or nonwhite, American or foreign. This is another way of saying that the politics of the wage is more than capitalists' instrumentalism. As Przeworski remarks, criticizing

Braverman-like models of capitalist victory: "Neither 'ideological domination' nor repression is sufficient to account for the manner in which workers organize and act under capitalism. The working class has been neither dupe nor passive victim. . . . Even if itself molded by capitalist relations, the working class has been an active force in transforming capitalism. We will never understand the resilience of capitalism unless we seek the explanation in the interests and actions of workers themselves."[22]

But if we leave the obsession with quantity behind, an understanding of the wage tied to Sraffa and Gramsci—a theory of the wage "without guarantees," to paraphrase Stuart Hall—can contribute to measured and empathetic consideration of the contradictions of workers' everyday lives. Bound up in a mode of production that is both curse and gift, one that simultaneously generates freedom and unfreedom, working people rarely face easy choices and, paradoxically, must consent. With opportunity and constraint so immanent in the wage, it is unsurprising that workers take seemingly contradictory stances toward wage earning—pride and shame, skepticism and hope, militant opposition and enthusiastic participation—and toward capitalism generally. Some of the literature on this contradiction is appreciative of the multiple forces that influence the daily lives of people who work for wages. It ranges from the work of Przeworski, to functionalist accounts of working-class "tastes for necessity," to theories of the "possibility of upward mobility," to social psychological discussions of the power of the "emotional grip" of capitalist social structures.[23] The principal lesson of this work, regardless of approach, is that working people in capitalist societies do not consistently act in the ways that theory predicts because they are responding to an array of personal and social conditions that are radically inconsistent, indeterminate, and often incommensurable.

We must also be sure to see through the homogeneity of high theory, into the differentiation of the working class. The wage is a political and cultural arena for the production of individual and group identities that are always historically and geographically particular. For the OWIU, citizenship and gender, crucial categories of union members' identities, gave the wage a cultural and political weight that put a great strain on wage negotiation. In Weed, a skill-based discursive politics of the wage effectively repackaged conflicts over fundamental racializing hierarchies. For Pacific small-boat fishermen, the very definition of the wage relation became critical to the culture of small-boat fishermen on the Pacific coast. Simultaneously, this class-based cultural debate served as the focal point for struggles over exploitation and the return to labor.

To politicize the wage in this way is in some ways to echo Anthony

Giddens's point that "conflict consciousness is in a certain sense inherent in the outlook of the worker in capitalist society; 'revolutionary consciousness' is not."[24] For in grounding the wage in both capitalist *and* working-class politics, it is possible to consider the ways in which workers have or have not transformed capitalism and the ways in which the wage has played a role in the transformation of relations not only between workers and capitalists but among working people themselves. It is also possible to understand working-class political cultures as not merely constructed in opposition or according to the dictates of the wage relation but as including and incessantly reshaping the intersection of the qualitative and quantitative dimensions of that relation—a politics of measure immanent to working-class life.

This is an outline of what I would describe as a cultural and political economy of the wage. It emerges from existing wage theory, shares an explicitly social emphasis with Marxian and radical institutionalism, but reaches beyond the constraints of these approaches, not following but urged forward by the work of someone like Sraffa. It explicitly introduces culture to these politics, highlighting the ways in which the wage is not simply a politicized outcome but a historically specific political forum; as I said earlier, it is political and cultural through and through.

Yet behind these arguments a larger question looms: if indeed I am to be believed, and the wage *is* a crucial site of the cultural politics of capitalism—what does the wage signify on the historical stage? What does the wage, as a cultural-political arena, represent? The victory of the mystifiers? The improbable achievement of the powerless? And if, as I have argued, it is not a question of straightforward false consciousness, then what kind of "agency" or "practice" constitutes the wage and struggles over it? The figure of the duped worker animates much of the critical work on exploitation, but the historical caricature is no longer useful, if it ever was. This is not to say that wage workers have all the information they need or that their decisions always reflect a considered political worldview. There is probably nobody this accurately describes, worker or not. It is to say, however, that there is an absolutely essential relation between the wage and any formulation of the question of why workers do not act in their "interests." The desperate recent attempts in the progressive media to answer this question in the wake of the U.S. federal elections of November 2000 and 2004 underscore the persistent political problems from which it arises.[25]

The Problem of "Interests"

Rather than struggling to answer the question of why workers do not act in their interests, we need to realize that the question is unworthy of the problem at hand. The difficulty, I think, lies in the very notion of "interest," and perhaps more particularly in "class interest"—a phrase some say has no referent.[26] We need to take up this oft elided problematic of critical scholarship on the cultural politics of capitalism, for, although far more frequently noted in its absence than elaborated in any positive sense, a theory of interests underwrites all work on class, the wage, and labor politics. Indeed, it is implicit in every emancipatory critique of labor's subordination under capitalism and in every liberal or utilitarian defense of status quo inequities.

Yet here I am on very unstable ground—as are we all. Because to think this through, we have to embrace uncertainty, in a dialectical sense: i.e., not uncertainty in the sense of the insecurity that suffuses so many people's confrontation with the bounded volatility that is capitalism (although this is of course always at play) but uncertainty in the existential, tentative sense. Although we do not stop to reflect on it very often, "interests" are not "about" the present; they are about the future. They are essentially anticipatory; to have an interest is precisely to be concerned with something to come. In other words, then, to think through the problem of interests—a concept that, when we stop for even a moment to worry, announces itself as one of the most taken-for-granted notions in the vocabulary of critical social science—we have to suggest or even anticipate what people want out of a time that has not yet arrived. We have to work with "mights" and "perhapses," not only because that is all we can do "for now" but because that is an inviolable analytical condition when thinking about the future.

Moreover, for me, this argumentative ground trembles all the more because it demands at the very least a minimal engagement with theories of the subject that challenge fundamental political concepts like class, ideology, and freedom. My position here thus feels particularly precarious because these concepts have special relevance for a theorization of the wage and an explanation of workers' politics and because they have come to play an essential role in my own self-conception as a Marxist scholar.

To deal with these complexities, with the histories recounted here in mind, the question-formulation that I think might best meet present purposes is not "What are interests?" but, rather, "What kind of agency drives the articulation of workers' interests?"—consisting as that articulation clearly does in seemingly incommensurable, complex, and historically particular mobilizations of race, gender, class, and citizenship. This allows me to get at interests while avoiding what Ernesto Laclau and Chantal Mouffe rightly dismiss:

> The problem with these approaches that start from a restricted definition of the working class, is that they are still based on the concept of "objective interests"—a concept which lacks any theoretical basis whatsoever, and involves little more than an arbitrary attribution of interests, by the analyst, to a certain category of social agents. In the classical view, class unity was constructed around interests, but it was not a datum of social structure; it was a process of unification, resulting from the impoverishment and proletarianization which went hand in hand with the development of the productive forces. . . . The objective interests were historical interests, insofar as they depended upon a rational and necessary movement of history accessible to scientific knowledge. What cannot be done is to abandon the eschatological conception of history, and to retain a notion of "objective interest" which only has sense within the former.[27]

What I propose is a theory of worker interests under capitalism based in the cultural politics of the wage, for the wage produces and constitutes the relation between the individual worker and the mode of production. Insofar as the wage as it is conventionally conceived in capitalism implicitly assumes and projects workers' class-specific "interest"—"economic advantage," in Albert Hirschman's words, or increasing relative or absolute real wages (or both)—it paradoxically constructs the wage as a crucial site of the politics of the working class, i.e., of the possibility of difference, whether or not these politics are "class politics."[28]

Remembering Class

I imagine hackles raised at this characterization, "class reductionism" on readers' lips, the (legitimate) demand that race, gender, and other axes of social difference be recognized for their relative autonomy under capitalist social relations. Indeed, the analytically independent workings of these axes are fundamental to the histories that give this project substance, as I have emphasized throughout. But from accurately noting the futility of reading race and gender as epiphenomena of class, it is a big—and myopic—leap to any of the following: (a) dropping class altogether, (b) diluting it to leach out power, or (c) eschewing it as "a concept whose links are [too] loose."[29] Although the challenge so-called post-Marxism brings to class primacy is in many respects enormously important, attacks on class have overshot their targets, with sometimes devastating political and theoretical consequences.

Many of the problems with the arguments against class analysis, and associated claims regarding the supposed supersession or destabilization of class by social movements old or new, are a function of the fact that they actually miss the point of the concept of class and thus cannot understand its purchase or its possibilities. Class gets forgotten (or willed away) by a fixation with "movement organizations" based in "identity politics," geography, gender, ecological concerns, and so forth. But class is clearly a relation that need not be "organized" in this or any other sense; that is Marx's point, I think: class-in-itself (as opposed to class-for-itself) is still class. The optimistic fixation with contemporary social movements misguidedly ignores (or is unaware of) the nonorganizational, "conjunctural" solidarity of shared material conditions and structural position, not to mention the very concrete obstacles it creates within these "new" social movements. The critique of class thus comes very close to limiting politics to political organization—as if the latter were not a subset of the former—which would surely be a theoretical and political disaster, as I have, echoing many others, demonstrated throughout. Indeed, the very notion of multiple subject positions, key to much of the post-Marxist literature along these lines, would not indicate that class has gone away or been rendered irrelevant, as its authors often suggest, but that it is *always there*, historically specific in form *and* content.[30]

The wage founds such class relations under capitalism. Of course, it is axiomatic that class cannot subsume all of workers' politics, culture, and "subject positions"—as white man, as African American, as woman, as Mexican immigrant. But this need not lead to abandoning the site of class politics or to claiming that class is politically irrelevant (à la Laclau and Mouffe). In fact, as I hope I have made clear, to do so is to dismiss the wage (and much else) with a wishful flourish.[31] Instead, as the existing (shared) political fulcrum for wage workers, and for many who at any moment do not work but wish to, the wage is of crucial symbolic and material importance beyond its patent material dimensions. In absolutely irreducible ways, the wage claims workers' interest under capitalism and in doing so establishes the site of working-class politics. The fact that "interests" are not "objective," as Laclau and Mouffe say (and throughout all of this it is important to remember that we are still in the dark as to what "interests" are), in no way means they are therefore entirely "subjective," i.e., a product of individual worker consciousness, unconscious desire, or "subject positions." Capitalism is still there, if not fully determining then at least helping shape everything, and it has not gone away. The wage thus looms large as the structurally determinate site or medium of interest—and I mean "of interest" in both senses: it is one of the most important arenas, if not *the* most important arena, in which what we might call interests are expressed, and it is the arena of particular interest here.

And of course it is true that, as the histories recounted in the previous chapters demonstrate, workers rarely settle for "objectively" ascribed interests, regardless of who suggests their "obviousness." Thus, while wage earners embrace the wage relation in every case I discuss, and while they work through it to assert, among other things, a particular politics of value, they never acquiesce to the politically neutral and qualitatively empty conception of the wage held or posited by employers and the state, a conception that is "common sense" to contemporary economics and economic policy. On the contrary, they embrace the wage because at the level of the social (which is always also political economic) it functions as perhaps the principal locus of the production of both exchange value and use value. Indeed, the everyday, absolute necessity and practicality of the wage under capitalism are irrefutable proof that its significance could never be limited to some bounded economic sphere—even if such a sphere can in fact exist, and the whole point is that it cannot. The wage is the way that millions of workers "get by" in the capitalist order (or wish they were getting by, if they are not working), and "getting by" is more than the mere circulatory shuffling of dollars from purse to till or landlord. The wage produces part of who workers *are*, in the deepest existential sense, and suggests how much they are *worth*; to imagine that it might somehow be a purely quantitative distributive "means" is to suggest a radically disembedded individual, a worker whose politics of value emerges outside or apart from what he or she does in the world. Consequently, other, "nonclass" interests are attracted to and instantiated in the wage relation precisely because it is the origin of any (structural) equivalence the working class might possess, whether it be attributed by capital, hoped for by workers, or realized.

All of which is to say that Stuart Hall is right (I am tempted to say "as usual"): "race is the modality in which class is lived" hits the nail on the head—just not hard enough. Race is indeed *a* "modality in which class is lived," but it is not the only one. Gender and citizenship are also among these modalities, and we may be able to add to the list. In any case, class does not "wither"; in fact, it always matters insofar as it constitutes the political terrain upon which the heterogeneous working class has no choice but to meet and struggle against other workers and with capital. This is how race can be the modality through which class is lived—in workerhood itself. Class is the ground of working-class politics, even if those politics are neither class conscious nor class-based (but are instead oriented toward gender or race, however "objective" their solidarities).

Thus, class *is* all these other politics, culture, and subject positions. It can be purely "itself" only in orthodox "Second International" Marxian terms where all workers' interests are identical: in other words, nowhere. So to point out that these other interests—even if we could ever define them—are always there and conflicting is still not to show that class is no longer an essential political arena. Instead, class is always and only these very conflicting subjectivities. It is the commonality of these struggles. Adam Przeworski's comment that class is the result of struggles over class formation is apposite here. Class is inevitably historical and experiential, akin to E. P. Thompson's remark that "class happens."[32] It does not happen in a singular bounded "event" after which it is here for good, but rather it is always happening. There is no resolution or closure. And, as I argued in chapter 1, in the capitalist mode of production, the wage is fundamentally about class (among other things): you cannot talk about the one without talking about the other.

Fredric Jameson says that unlike categories such as race, gender, and ethnicity, "class as such can never be a mode of interpellation."[33] This is far too quick a judgment on a couple of fronts. First, the wage posits an interest, which class (even if that is not what it calls itself, or is called) hails, thus interpellating the working-class subject. Althusser's famous account of interpellation demands not only a theory of conscience, as Judith Butler suggests, but also, and perhaps more urgently, a theory of interest.[34] Second, and no less important, because class is made up of all these other subject positions, they often interpellate through class; they use class as their ideological "apparatus," not least because many of these other subject positions have no more "materiality" than class, and often less. The regular American working Joe is a (racialized, gendered, and nationalist) interpellating ideological figure that does not decenter or destabilize class as historical subject. On the contrary, it actually works through and by class; it brings class into being. There is no class outside these other subject positions; they are the cultural-political modes through which "class is lived."

Articulating this complexity and specificity is never straightforward, and although it is a persistent theme in the politics of North American wage work, the effort has often failed, or at least fallen far short. But the reasons for this failure are not, I would argue, those commonly identified—false consciousness, lack of working-class solidarity, relative high wages (on a global or regional scale), mobility—although all of these have mattered more or less in any one time and place. The problem of the wage as political site, and of the supposedly "nonrevolutionary" or quiescent working class in contemporary capitalism, is not so much one of workers' inability to understand (or the willful obfuscation of) their "true" interests. Instead, the problem is the almost overwhelming obstacles to the determination of a noncapitalist political subject by interests that are never fully articulated—indeed, whose interests may be indeterminate, not yet articulable, by definition. I believe this is of profound significance, for it uncovers some of what one might call the cultural-political fabric of contemporary working-class politics and brings us back to where we started. This irreducible indeterminacy, this not-quite-yet-ness, is both the content of the inescapable problem of ideology and the form of the working-class politics of measure under capitalism. It can never meet the demands of the "vague and brutal commandment of clarity" against which Adorno raged throughout his career, a fact we should celebrate with equal rage, for that is precisely where its transcendent promise lies.

Wages and Interests in the Time of Capital

The effects of all these forms of progress on the relative wages of
the worker result quite automatically from commodity production and
the commodity-character of labour-power. . . . Thus the struggle against
the fall in relative wages also implies a struggle against the commodity-
character of labour-power, i.e., against capitalist production as a whole.
Thus the struggle against the fall in relative wages is no longer a struggle
on the basis of the commodity economy, but a revolutionary, subversive
attack on the existence of this economy.
Rosa Luxemburg, quoted in Roman Rosdolsky,
The Making of Marx's "Capital" (1977)

What falls out of this constitutive indeterminacy is an enormously complex dialectical movement. On the one hand, we have a concept and politics of "interests" that for all intents and purposes are falling "forward" in time, propped up only by a future whose content they must paradoxically produce. The fact that whatever content these "interests" have is pieced together from the past comes as no surprise. On the other hand, we have a future of which perhaps the only thing that we know for certain is that it is absolutely necessary for any meaning in the political present. In other words, we are faced with what is perhaps *the* antinomy of political life: to shape a future—which should by its very definition be the most radically different idea of all, for it has yet to even *be*—out of a past that cannot help but contaminate the future, curtailing the immanent possibility of something that is "not yet" as soon as we can give it an "is."

The concept of "interests" as commonly used—as ahistorical object of desire (i.e., freedom), biologically encoded instinct (i.e., survival), culturally determined goal or achievement (i.e., wealth/status)—not only cannot overcome this antimony; on the contrary, it petrifies it, hardens it into standardized code that at once dehistoricizes capitalism, enshrines "objectivity," and fundamentally misapprehends politics. For what is missing is not only the humilities that should inform critical practice in the face of both the unknowable future and the diversity of human life, essential as these are on their own. (How can I possibly claim to know someone's "interests" now, let alone what they will be?) What is also missing is an acknowledgment of what we could call, dragging Hegel back into the discussion, a dialectical sensibility, a recognition that the categories are not given but are historicized in the very act of operating or even thinking them. In the face of an uncritical blindness to history itself, we must constantly remind ourselves that "the nature of history is precisely that every definition degenerates into an illusion: *history is the history of the unceasing overthrow of the objective forms that shape the life of man. . . .* From this standpoint alone does history really become a history of mankind. For it contains nothing that does not lead back ultimately to men and to the relations between men."[35]

This is not to make the rather straightforward, even bland point that individual or collective "interests" are historically specific, although this is of course true, if we are willing to grant the term some formal meaning. Rather, it is to say that the very concept of "interest" is historically specific. It emerged in the context of an Enlightenment rationalism that is historically bound up in capitalism, one among the vast array of conceptual buttresses to what Marx, in the *Grundrisse,* calls "Robinsonades," origin stories of autonomous men founded on Rousseauian myths of primordial individualism.[36] In other words, the fundamental Hegelian and Marxian lesson—that our categories of thought are themselves historically conditioned, caught up in the historical movements they purport to describe in all their illusory objective "immediacy"—is to think again about the particular form of rational and individualized intertemporal commitment posited by the idea of "interests." Not only do we not know what a particular group's or person's "real" interests are; we cannot appeal to any naturalized link between past, present, and future without tautologically willing that link into being.

The wage emerges in this context as one of the ways in which this past-present-future link is constructed in capitalism. The wage relation appears to be a functional means through which capital and workers assert, contest, and address workers' interests. As such, it becomes a locus of working-class politics, even, as I said above, if those politics are not "class-based"; think, for example, of women's "equal pay for equal work" movements. Yet the wage is not nearly so transparent or two-dimensional as this would indicate. In fact, insofar as the wage is understood as workers' interest under capitalism, the crucial ways in which the politics of the wage in fact produces workers' orientation to the future are obscured.

This is not a false consciousness argument. First, false consciousness requires some ultimate "immediate" reality, the "true consciousness" of which would mark all others' falsity. In any fundamentally political analysis, this is hardly a defensible claim. Second, from the fact that the concept of interests is the trajectory through which the politics of the wage is so often conceived and worked out, in no way does it follow that investigating the historicity and dynamics of "interest" is rendered irrelevant. Indeed, as both Marx and Hegel argue incessantly, it is just such historically specific categories that must be illuminated and explained.[37] To destabilize interests is not to argue that it is the "wrong" way for workers to engage in the politics of wage; it is, rather, to try to think about why it can be the "right" way—even, often, the only way.

It is this indeterminacy, and the concrete ways in which wage workers respond to it, to which the politics of measure is addressed. I mean this in two senses. The politics of measure as analytical concept provides a useful means to understand these dynamics, *and* the politics of measure as political practice takes shape in precisely these indeterminate contexts. It encapsulates a dialectical sensibility in both these senses, too: it is open to the constant, contradictory, and infinitely complex movements of history, and it describes a dialectical politics.[38] The latter is the ongoing effort to "overcome reification" (in Georg Lukács's words), to explode the static and naturalized categories of political life produced by capitalism and confirmed by orthodox economics: "As long as man concentrates his interest contemplatively upon the past *or* future, both ossify into an alien existence. And between the subject and the object lies the unbridgeable 'pernicious chasm' of the present. Man must be able to comprehend the present as a becoming. He can do this by seeing in it the tendencies out of whose dialectical opposition he can *make* the future."[39]

Therefore, the politics of measure describes the cultural political constellation out of which "interest" is produced; it represents the very possibility of something called "interest." It is not so much the arena in which given "objectives" are pursued but that in which wage earners work to give some content to the ultimately indeterminate (which is not to say subjective) concept of interest. This by no means takes the wind out of working-class politics. On the contrary, acknowledging the lack of an a priori and static interest—i.e., high and rising real wages, founded upon rational utility optimization—helps illuminate and explain the dynamism of the politics of the wage that is so evident in the three previous chapters. Even in three spatially and temporally proximate histories, the diversity of the qualitative "content" of the wage, and its cultural and political economic implications, are enormous. In all cases, what is "at stake" in the wage, workers' "interests," is not logically predetermined but is a product of the interplay of a host of forces that are irreducibly historically and geographically specific.

Indeed, on the terms of the critique of political economy initiated by Marx—as opposed to critical or radical political economy—there is a sense in which, at any particular conjuncture in the history of capitalism, the politics of measure is an immanent theory of value. In other words, workers' "interested" engagement articulates an immanent political economic theory, as I suggested earlier. In addition, the effort to overcome the rigid hegemony of the quality-quantity separation in the wage, to "make the future" by dialectically returning quantity to quality, speaks to alternative conceptions of value itself. These conceptions of value break with the obvious categories within which labor politics conventionally operate, and they make the wage and value at once indeterminate and heterogeneous. And insofar as these conceptions are spoken and heard, the immanent contradictions of the wage are recruited not simply to the campaign for more money but simultaneously to the cause of the supersession of the wage itself.

Further, it is worth reiterating that the struggle to tie what I have called knots in the thread of value—and to do so from within the wage relation, as the oil workers, timber workers, and fishermen all did—is not about the struggle over some structurally determined dialectical moment in which quantity and quality "converge." It is about the production of those dialectical moments—making the future—by tying a knot that serves as a historically specific political space in which it is possible to have an interest. I hope it is clear that this is completely compatible with the persistent demand for better wages, shift premiums, benefits, and so forth that animate the three historical chapters. As Rosa Luxemburg says in the quote that begins this section, efforts to secure higher wage rates are completely commensurable with the politics of measure and are, more often than not, its medium: "Thus the struggle against the fall in relative wages also implies a struggle against the commodity-character of labour-power, i.e., against capitalist production as a whole." The point is that, under capitalist relations of production, wage rates are not all that is at stake. Rather, they are often the only available vocabulary with which it is possible to speak or construct a comprehensible sentence about an alternative future whose radical possibility is categorically denied by capitalism a priori.

In history, in social life, nothing is fixed,
rigid or definitive. And nothing ever will be.
    Antonio Gramsci, *Il Grido del Populo*
    (1918)

Conclusion
The Wage, Our Daily Bread

Part of the motivation behind this book comes from a frustration I share
with many others with the relative paucity of theories of contemporary
capitalism that do the necessary critical work *and* identify political possibility in the process. I do not mean to lay the blame for this at someone
else's feet, but theory that is critical in this sense—which is what, to name
only a few of the most famous theorists, Marx, Luxemburg, Gramsci, and
Adorno were trying to do—would both avoid the bland and unreflexive
normativity that makes most liberal political theory so vapid and reject
the ethical emptiness that characterizes the desire-driven "positivity" of
much that is currently "hot" in social theory. Of course, even within the
radical or Marxian tradition, which is where I believe the best such work
has been done, the frustration persists. As Paul Willis remarks, "[i]t seems
to me that a theory of struggle between the classes and the projected proletarian overthrow of capitalism is a strange thing indeed—especially
today—without a theory of advanced capitalist working class consciousness and culture *sui generis*. . . . The form of this must, I would argue, be
of the contradictory and unintended results of the relatively independent
working class attempts to 'see into,' and adapt to, the real conditions of its
existence which actually reproduce, albeit somewhat changed, these conditions in, as it were, a reverse dialectic."[1]

As much as I wish it were so, this book does not answer Willis's call for
"a theory of advanced capitalist working class consciousness and culture
sui generis," but I like to think that it does some useful work toward it.
The concept of the politics of measure, and of the cultural politics of the
wage more broadly, presents an opportunity to reconstruct wage struggle,
and what is at stake in wage struggle, in ways that suggest some paths out
of the bind we refasten every time we ask "Why don't they act in their
interests?"

These paths seem to me desperate theoretical necessities. For much, if not most, of working-class political agency is comprised of efforts to alter the relations of production, exchange, distribution, and consumption *within* the political and ideological framework of capitalism. Still, and despite an orthodox fixation with distribution shared by many radical political economists—what Postone calls the "critique of capital from the standpoint of labor"—even in this context "interest" is not a quantity; nor is it quantitative.[2] In fact, the absurdity of the focus on quantity is made glaringly obvious when we try to put into words the idea that working-class interests are, or are realized at, some distributive threshold, i.e., something like: "workers' interests are (realized by) this or that level of revenue or money or property or power or whatnot." The fact that this phrasing sounds almost exactly like the way capital commonly describes ownership—"they have a 10 percent interest in the business"—only drives the point home harder. As soon as we try to say what "interest" actually *is*, we are reminded again of its constant tendency to surpass itself, to move dialectically, as it were. It defies definition, which is precisely what it needs to do. For it is, in fully dialectical fashion, true specificity, true quality (which is in no way to say pure individuality). We can no more pin it down than we can stop time itself. More accurately, interest is close to what Adorno calls "nonidentical": "the Utopia of the qualitative—the things which through their difference and uniqueness cannot be absorbed into the prevalent exchange relationships."[3]

It is worth emphasizing that such a conception of interest is not "anti-materialist," even in the unfortunately common and categorically false sense that equates the "material" with the disciplinary domain of economics. On the contrary, it involves the identification of a theory of "interests" with a theory of subjectivity in which both form (i.e., the concepts of interest and subjectivity themselves) and content are historically specific to the mode of production. That mode of production, capitalism, is not only one in which workers are the "internal" agents of material production but one that takes the very shape it does because of the political agency of those workers. This is merely a rather inelegant restatement of one of Gramsci's basic lessons—capital reproduces neither the form nor the content of capitalism on its own—which is cause for concern and for hope, whether or not one's aims are revolutionary. The politics of measure is, among other things, the never finished effort to come to grips with this situation, one in which the "interests" measure makes possible are produced but never fixed. To call on Adorno again, interests are one of those categories we can reflect on only "by reckoning into their determination the impossibility of nailing them down as well as the necessity of continuing to think them."[4]

Wage theory, as a conceptual arena within which some of this can be confronted, consequently has the potential to do a great deal of explanatory work. That capacity varies within and across time and space, and each of the histories recounted here might serve as a useful test of historical validity and theoretical limitation. The point of such a review, of course, would not be to find a theory to match each story, i.e., Keynesianism is the theory for chapter 3, institutionalism for chapter 4. Instead, the focus should be to consider what wage theory is good for, what dynamics it can help explain, and what previously foreclosed possibilities it can enable us to see.

One of the premises of this discussion is that economic structures like markets are not the elementary social phenomena but are embedded and produced in social life. There is of course nothing novel in this. Culture and politics are the subsoil we are trying to reach, not economic decision making; the idea that the former are a product of the latter seems to me, for lack of a better word, bananas. Getting down that deep means using different tools where the ground demands it. Certainly we may enlist many approaches on the way down, as I have. If we encounter smooth, responsive labor markets at the surface, we may chip away with neoclassicism for a brief while; if we see imperfections everywhere, we will probably lean on Keynesian or institutional theories while we gather our thoughts. We can certainly begin in this manner. But superficial beginnings are all they will ever be. We can get farther down, beyond determination, with Marx and Sraffa, and this is where I want to be, where I believe we need to be. They are certainly limited in their own ways, as I have discussed, but part of the process of this book has been to go beyond these limitations when they become obstacles.

This is not to say that it is all contingency, that there is no "generally" useful theory. There are dynamics that matter in most cases—"no production will be thinkable without them," as Marx says—and one would be hard pressed, for example, to claim that supply and demand have no influence on labor markets and wage determination.[5] Rather, the point is that although supply and demand matter, they only matter insofar as they are already a part of the cultural politics of labor markets, the wage, and employment relations generally. Without social context, the market is inconceivable, as Karl Polanyi has shown us seven ways to Sunday. Supply and demand for labor are not natural but *social* forces, as much a product of cultural politics as the wage itself. They would not equilibrate if undisturbed because they would not exist. Pure economic theory is as fictional as it is pure.

With politics built into the wage, the analysis moves beneath the quantitative surface of the wage. The extent to which Marxian theory informs my analysis is evidence of its capacity to work in this deeper soil. Any approach to the wage in which it is understood as both political relation and distributive quantity shares considerable ground with Marxian wage theory, and clearly such an immanent approach is characteristic of all the groups of workers in the previous chapters: one need not bring sophisticated social theory to bear to agree that members of the IFAWA fought for a wage as a political goal, not simply an economic share; Los Angeles oil workers contested wage rates at least partly because of what it meant for their masculinity and their American-ness; and African American workers in Weed were stripped of their skills by a racist and racialized conception of waged work. In each case, the wage became a key arena in the organization of political life.

Nevertheless, although these stories depend on the fundamental "traditional" Marxian axiom that the wage matters politically and this argument forms a ground against which the stories are told, we have to go much further if culture is a concern. In the recognition that the wage is politically multidimensional, and that these dimensions are substantially a product of cultural politics, we reach the limits of Marxian wage theory, if not Marxian social theory, as I mentioned in chapter 2. To confront the fact that the wage is an exploitative social instrument of capitalists and a powerful and indeterminate, i.e., nonequilibrium, political tool of working people, Sraffian wage theory provides a solid initial footing. As the "left-Keynesian" economists Amit Bhaduri and Joan Robinson remark on Sraffa's conception of the wage: "The rate, or better the ratio, of exploitation is not determined by the technical specification of the system. It is an independent element in the situation which may be explained by the fortunes of the class war. This freedom of the distribution parameter enabled Sraffa to break out of the 'iron-law of real wages.' . . . In principle, a given technical situation is compatible with any proportion of relative shares."[6]

However, if Sraffa's argument severs any attachment to a conventional wage, as Bhaduri and Robinson say, it nonetheless remains beholden to a social theory with no clear place for cultural differentiation. To escape this bind, as Sraffa knew, we have to come back down to earth. Then we can see how the politics of the wage can be consistent with gender, class, or racial dynamics, even if a larger share of the economic pie is not a principal aim of struggle. We can see the ways in which labor market relations are saturated with the social meaning that always configures market structure and function in a continuous dialectic. We can see how "a given quantity of money . . . means utterly different things to different people," while we specify this insight by looking at particular pecuniary relationships at particular places and times.[7] At the most general level, we can see that the wage is not pure quantity, or pure outcome, but a political site, bound up in and influencing the dynamics of capitalist societies both within and beyond the point of production.

This book shows how this works historically by looking at one region and sector more closely, and through it the cultural politics of western work is illuminated in new ways. It demonstrates that the western wage is not only a particular product of the way that capitalism plays out in the West; it is also a crucial influence on the development of western resource capitalism, a cultural and political economic force shaping regional forms of production, consumption, and social stratification. The particularity of work and workers in the U.S. West is not merely a product of geography and history; western geography and history are themselves a reflection of these workers, their work, and the way they politicized the wage relations that constituted it.

In this light, the cultural politics of the wage emerges as one of the central sites of workers' historical agency in the U.S. West. Each of the conflicts detailed here take place *within* the confines of capitalist labor politics. Clearly, capitalism, in the U.S. West and elsewhere, would look very different if it had not been shaped by workers' immanent efforts to change it. But the existence or the justice of the wage relation was rarely in question, and it is perhaps even less in question today. The AFL-CIO's recent "America Needs A Raise" campaign (begun in 1996) is as committed to the fundamental "fairness" of the wage qua relation as any employer: "Anyone who puts in a fair day's work should receive a fair day's pay."[8] Contrast this with the words from the IWW constitution I quoted in the preface: "Instead of the conservative motto, 'A fair day's wage for a fair day's work,' we must inscribe on our banner the revolutionary watchword, 'Abolition of the wage system.'" Indeed, the wage can be more than a point of consent: it can even be held up as preferable to other social relations of production, as in the case of the IFAWA (chapter 5).

I have undertaken to understand some of these immanent efforts, and not because they are foolhardy or "reformist." Beginning with the wage, and the powerful role it plays in workers' everyday lives, I have shown how attempts to reshape it, to redefine it, to change its real value, to debate its very meaning, are also instances of working people trying to challenge the givenness of their place in the capitalist hierarchy of race, class, gender, and citizenship—even if they are not always challenging the givenness of that hierarchy. The workers in question take capitalism for granted (at least in the short term), and some even cheer it on, but they focus on the wage as a lever of positive potential change within capitalist relations of production. I rely heavily upon the tools of radical political and cultural economy, but I do not read a historic programmatic role for the working class in any of the stories. Nevertheless, I have tried to suggest that, however particular the stories, what is at stake here, and what is going on culturally and politically, is not limited to the region in question or even to the United States. This is a firstly a book about the dialectics of the wage. I have examined some histories of the U.S. West to make my case, but I believe the book identifies more generally applicable historical and theoretical concepts, like the politics of measure, which allow some insight into to the cultural politics of capitalism elsewhere.

Moreover, if I may say so, the book also suggests other potentially fruitful paths of investigation, like the cultural politics of the wage in other historical contexts, and the meanings of additional phenomena commonly considered "purely economic." Aside from the evident geographic and historical range of possible study, the former path might, for instance, point to an examination of the politics of the wage in a situation of wagelessness, unemployment or slavery. It is likely that such research would detail a cultural politics of the wage that can help flesh out the substance of the transition from slavery to wage labor for workers of many different backgrounds in the United States, the case of Frederick Douglass being perhaps a good place to start. The latter path might lead to a consideration of the cultural politics of investment, saving or economic growth. Each are critical categories of everyday activity and change, the quantitative dimensions of which have an enormous impact upon individual and group well-being. It is certain, I believe, that the manner in which they become important in economic life—one might even say the manner in which they become "economic"—is significantly determined by some of the same dynamics that are the substance of this discussion of the wage.

One further, more case-specific direction in which this book might lead is toward a reflection upon the relationship between the cultural politics of the wage in western natural resource industries and the meaning of environmental justice. These stories illustrate the conflict over the distribution of the West's natural abundance among different claimants. Capitalists, the state, and many different groups of workers were involved in the struggle over who would profit, socially and economically, from the West's astounding riches. As it stands, however, the phrase "environmental justice" refers almost exclusively to a concern for the inequitable social-geographic distribution of environmental "bads" like air or water contaminants across groups defined by race, class, or citizenship.[9] As a result, the political sphere focuses on issues like facility siting, cleanup obligations, and hazardous waste management.

While these are essential concerns from a social justice perspective, the emphasis on the "bads" of environmental justice limits the opening for a historically informed analysis of the problem, overlooking the fundamental causal role of the inequitable distribution of environmental "goods" and natural "wealth" in the origins of environmental injustice.[10] In other words, what we have now is a concept of "negative" environmental justice; but without a theory of "positive" environmental justice we are hobbled in any effort to comprehend the development and persistence of the full range of differential relationships between groups and their physical environments, and of the long-term effects that effort might have on struggles to destabilize social hierarchies. A broader definition that would recognize these accounts as contests over environmental justice would energize the debate and give it a long-term relevance that can do nothing but augment the validity of the claims of the dispossessed.

Some Final Thoughts

When Marx called the wage the "golden chain" in the first volume of *Capital*, he meant to remind us of the chain more than the gold. To his mind, the gold usually attracts too much attention, helping us forget that it is a *chain* that glitters: "A rise in the price of labour, as a consequence of the accumulation of capital, only means in fact that the length and weight of the golden chain the wage-labourer has already forged for himself allow it to be loosened somewhat."[11] His analysis is thus very attentive to the concrete everyday contradictions that produce the situation in which the golden chain is forged. What he did not take the time to account for, however, is the ways in which those same everyday contradictions also accord the chain not merely an economic meaning but a cultural-political weight, and a significant one at that. The wage, that "vital category" of social life under capitalism, can never be contained within the "economic," neither in its pecuniary nor its symbolic dimensions. It is far too important to be linked to only one "sphere" of life, if indeed that sphere were ever separable from all the others (a premise fundamental to liberalism). It is part of the fabric of capitalist society, one whose value—what we might call its "goldenness"—arises not only from its importance in exchange. The wage's goldenness is also of a kind with a golden key, a golden crown, and a golden ring. These are some of the means, the power, and the humanity in our lives. I do not mean that the fact that these symbols are gold is less "materially" determined than the symbol of gold itself—only that goldenness has slipped its bounds somewhat: it is an economic *and* cultural medium of value (and of production, exchange, distribution, and consumption) at the same time.

This is no less true of the golden chain, however much unfreedom is most definitely forged into any chain. It too is made up of the stuff of means, power, and humanity. It too has cultural, economic, and thus of course political possibility that is as restricted as any chain, but as utopian as anything golden. Rattling the golden chain, then, the struggle over the wage, is not just noisemaking. It shakes the very foundations of that to which it is affixed, as Rosa Luxemburg saw. Sure, workers could spend their days pounding at those chains, sawing away at the links; some do, and bravely. But the failure of the many to do so—like the workers whose histories are contained in this book—is not quiescence, or at least not necessarily. The idea that without the ring of hammers and the hum of hacksaws hopes for radical political change are dormant is not only disabling; it is wrong. And while it may seem that I am flogging a dead horse here, I would venture to suggest that this kind of "we need hammers and hacksaws" thinking is still very much a part of the Left's political critique, and that it is precisely what animates the question "Why don't they act in their interests?"

Of course, as is clear from the stories I have told, what I have called the politics of measure is by no means a necessarily emancipatory or inclusive practice. Race, gender, class, and citizenship are some of the range of exclusions that work through it and force us, if we have not already done so, to face the fact that what a good ol' vanguardist Marxism would hope is "false consciousness" is often not really all that false. Indeed, as I have tried to show, there is usually a "logic" behind it that is not spurious or uncritical but is rather a more dialectical logic, an immanent critique of historical movement that is not captured by the static "rationality" to which the word "logic" now seems solely to refer, even among Marxists. Nevertheless, the politics of measure through which this dialectic is worked out is also evidence of myriad challenges to the rigid quantity-quality opposition upon which capitalism depends. And insofar as it thus contains the possibility of overcoming that opposition, it describes a political practice I think we cannot yet do without.

All of which brings me back to the wage, our daily bread. For I am certain (or as certain as the dialectic will allow) that "the relations in which people exist are the 'real relations' which the categories and concepts they use help them to grasp and articulate in thought."[12] The wage is one such relation, one with which many of us live and which we are for all intents and purposes forced to embrace. "The proletariat," as Adorno says, "does have more to lose than its chains."[13]

But as a dialectical sensibility will bring out again and again, this combination of coercion and consent absolutely does not imply closure.

Certainly, the wage brings with it a historical burden, one we might now ponder longer over before taking it on, knowing what we do (although given the options at the time, I doubt it). The problem, however, is the inseparability of all of this in everyday life, the curse and the gift that is the unequal wealth around us in capitalist societies. For it is true to the point of being pedantic to state that when someone says that a job has "good wages," most of us know exactly what is meant, and, however fervent our radical sympathies, if it is not true of our jobs as well, we wish it were. And at the same time, I think it is equally obvious to say that a "good wage," no matter how good, is never, and never will be, "enough." The notion has no meaning in the realm of the qualitative. The very idea that the wage could be "enough" would suggest, against the grain of politics itself, that the problem is somehow one of quantity, that we have the answer right, just not the amounts. This is not so, and it is precisely the reason why Marx or the Wobblies (among others) called for the abolition of the wage. The problem is not merely distributional, i.e., wages are inevitably too low. It is, rather, in all senses of the term, categorical. However much or little of this sentiment we share, we must grasp the truth of the wage in it.

Notes

Abbreviations

BLS
　U.S. Department of Labor, Bureau of Labor Statistics

Calif. CIO–IFAWA
　Congress of Industrial Organizations, California Council, Research
　Department, and International Fishermen and Allied Workers of America

Doe Library, Berkeley
　Collections available in Main Stacks, Doe Library, University of California,
　Berkeley

IFAW
　International Fisherman and Allied Worker (San Francisco, Calif.)

IFAWA Papers, Bancroft
　Papers of the International Fishermen and Allied Workers Union, Bancroft
　Library, University of California, Berkeley

IFAWA Papers, ILWU
　Collected Papers of the International Fishermen and Allied Workers Union,
　International Longshore and Warehouse Union Library, San Francisco,
　Calif.

IOW
　International Oil Worker (Denver, Colo.)

KC
　Kheel Center for Labor-Management Documentation and Archives,
　Cornell University, Ithaca, N.Y., Collection 5092, box 1

KFEH
　Klamath Falls Evening Herald (Klamath Falls, Oreg.)

LAT
　Los Angeles Times

LH
　Labor Herald (published by California CIO, San Francisco, Calif.)

Local #1-128 Archives
　Records of Local #1-128, Oil Workers International Union, Norlin Library
　Archives, University of Colorado, Boulder (series, box, and folder numbers
　indicated by S.#/B.#/F#)

MSH&SH

    Mount Shasta Herald & Sisson Headlight (Sisson, Calif.)

NPN

    National Petroleum News (published by American Petroleum Institute)

OLP

    Oregon Labor Press (Portland, Oreg.)

OWIU

    Oil Workers International Union

SB

    Sacramento Bee (Sacramento, Calif.)

SDN

    Siskiyou Daily News (Yreka, Calif.)

SH

    Sisson Headlight (Sisson, Calif.)

SN

    Siskiyou News (Yreka, Calif.)

SUR

    Seattle Union Record

YJ

    Yreka Journal (Yreka, Calif.)

Preface

1. *YJ*, 19 February 1919, 3. This was far from an isolated incident, as local newspapers and other sources make clear: *YJ*, 12 February 1919, 3; *SH*, 6 October 1921, 3; *KFEH*, 1 May 1922, 1; 19 May 1922, 1; *MSH&SH*, 27 July 1922, 5; *YJ*, 9 August 1922, 2; Weintraub, "IWW in California," 108–10; and Tulin, "Digest of California Criminal Syndicalism Cases," IFAWA Papers, Bancroft.

2. The Industrial Workers of the World was an organization of mostly "unskilled," often migrant workers founded in Chicago in 1905. Although it was for a time an important force, particularly in the West, it did not survive World War I in anything like its prewar form. In many ways it was more a syndicalist movement than a union, and the "Wobblies'" expressed goal was to "abolish the wage system" by forming the "structure of the new society within the shell of the old." To this end, they often fought uncompromisingly (if not always cohesively) against the state, capital, and other unions. The historiography of the IWW is immense. The classic account is Dubofsky's *We Shall Be All*. Among the many other accounts, see Buhle and Shulman, *Wobblies!*; Foner, *Industrial Workers of the World*; Hall, *Labor Struggles in the Deep South*; and the Wobbly leader Bill Haywood's *Big Bill Haywood's Book*. I should note that the IWW still exists, although it must be said in a much less formidable form. It does have a slick Web site, though, which has a great deal of excellent material (including the constitution and other historical documents) and is definitely worth a visit: <www.iww.org>.

3. I write "North America" with a purpose: the Wobblies and their One Big

Union had a significant presence in western Canada in the early twentieth century. See Leier, *Where the Fraser River Flows*.

4. Marx, *Value, Price, and Profit*, 62.

5. On the history of struggles over the length of the working day, see Roediger and Foner, *Our Own Time*. As both Roman Rosdolsky and André Gorz have pointed out, these efforts to shorten the workday run into difficulties in an age of rapid technological change and the increasingly elastic substitutability of capital for labor. Today, it seems, workers fight more often to prevent the working day from contracting even further. See Gorz, *Farewell to the Working Class*, and Rosdolsky, *Making of Marx's "Capital,"* 287.

6. Marx, *Capital*, 1:769.

7. Auerbach, Desai, and Shamsavari, "Transition from Actually Existing Capitalism."

8. In Foner, *Story of American Freedom*, 66.

9. Roediger, *Towards the Abolition of Whiteness*, chap. 5.

10. Thompson, *Making of the English Working Class*.

Chapter One

1. Moore, Pandian, and Kosek, "Cultural Politics of Race and Nature," 2.

2. Young, *Justice and the Politics of Difference*, 86.

3. Ibid.

4. There are, of course, a few who claim that racial wage disparities are not political but simply represent "irrational" "tastes for discrimination." See the paradigmatic work of Gary Becker, *Economics of Discrimination*: "[I]f someone has a 'taste for discrimination,' he must act *as if* he were willing to forfeit income in order to avoid certain transactions; it is necessary to be aware of the emphasis on the words 'as if.' An employer may refuse to hire Negroes solely because he erroneously underestimates their economic efficiency. Ignorance may be quickly eliminated by the spread of knowledge, while a prejudice (i.e., preference) is relatively independent of knowledge" (16).

5. Blauner, *Racial Oppression in America*; Omi and Winant, *Racial Formation in the United States*; Roediger, *Wages of Whiteness*; Almaguer, *Racial Faultlines*.

6. Deutsch, *No Separate Refuge*; Peck, *Reinventing Free Labor*, 167–68.

7. Wright, *Old South, New South*.

8. Biernacki, *Fabrication of Labor*, 12.

9. Dore, *Taking Japan Seriously*.

10. Du Bois, *Black Reconstruction in America*; James, *Black Jacobins*; Cox, *Caste, Class and Race*; Fanon, *Wretched of the Earth*.

11. Rex, *Race Relations in Sociological Theory*; Blauner, *Racial Oppression in America*; Hall, "Race, Articulation, and Societies Structured in Dominance"; Reich, *Racial Inequality*; Stoler, "Racial Histories "; di Leonardo, *Exotics at Home*; Reed, "Unraveling the Relation of Race and Class"; Singh, *Black Is a Country*.

12. It is worth emphasizing that I pass this judgment only at the most general level. Anyone familiar with, for example, Du Bois's or James's writing could

point out how sensitive both were to what might be called a race-class dialectic. Nonetheless, I think it is not inaccurate to read *Black Reconstruction* as a detailed exhortation to see the commonality of black and white exploitation. The case for reading *The Black Jacobins'* argument for the political centrality of the periphery along these lines is much less clear-cut, but James's later writing suggests a relatively "orthodox" argument for class primacy.

13. Hall et al., *Policing the Crisis*, 394.

14. Gilroy, *Against Race*; Holt, *Problem of Race*.

15. Holt, *Problem of Race*, 22.

16. Saxton, *Indispensable Enemy*; Saxton, *Rise and Fall of the White Republic*; Barrera, *Race and Class*; Weber, *Dark Sweat, White Gold*; Wells, *Strawberry Fields*; Almaguer, *Racial Faultlines*.

17. Barrera, *Race and Class*, 214.

18. Wells, *Strawberry Fields*; Thomas, *Citizenship, Gender, and Work*; Peck, *Reinventing Free Labor*; Ruiz, *Cannery Women, Cannery Lives*; Deutsch, *No Separate Refuge*. For a brilliant theoretical discussion of the relation of citizenship and labor, see Cooper, Holt, and Scott, *Beyond Slavery*, 1–32.

19. Harvey, *Limits to Capital*, 35.

20. Almaguer, *Racial Faultlines*, 207.

21. Walker, "California's Golden Road."

22. McWilliams, *California*, 25.

23. On natural resource production in the rest of the Pacific West, and California as its driving force, see, for example, Robbins, *Hard Times in Paradise*; Robbins, *Colony and Empire*; and White, *Organic Machine*.

24. Walker, "California's Golden Road." Paul David and Gavin Wright have made similar arguments for the United States as a whole. See David and Wright, "Increasing Returns."

25. Schwantes, "Concept of the Wageworkers' Frontier."

26. Adorno, *Hegel*, 109.

27. Spivak, *Critique of Postcolonial Reason*, 247–48.

28. Throughout the book, I resort to a distinction between the analytical and the political that has its costs. I recognize that analysis—a term I use to avoid the class pretensions and academy centricity implied by "intellectualizing" or "scholarship"—is always a political act, no matter if the analysis makes claims to "objectivity." I choose to go with it nonetheless because I believe that the analysis–political practice link is two-staged: analysis comes first, and political practice comes second. Thus, particular theories, categories, or historical conclusions can have related but not identical implications for the two different moments.

29. For a recent selection, see Allmendinger, *Imagining the African American West*; Comer, *Landscapes of the New West*; Klein, *Frontiers of the Historical Imagination*; Peck, *Reinventing Free Labor*; Rothman, *Devil's Bargains*; Saxton, *Rise and Fall of the White Republic*, esp. pt. 3; and Spurgeon, *Exploding the Western*.

30. That said, I acknowledge that there are ironic and important complications that arise from reasserting the dominance of white masculinity, even for

the purposes of destabilizing it. It is akin to the problem Spivak identifies when she writes that "there is something Eurocentric about assuming that imperialism began with Europe" (*Critique of Postcolonial Reason*, 37).

31. Adorno, *Hegel*, 99: "The traditional categories do not remain intact within the dialectic; the dialectic permeates each of them and alters its inherent complexion."

32. At least in its most fundamental Hegelian form: see Taylor, *Hegel*, 129: "It is important to stress here that Hegel is not proposing a dialectical 'method' or 'approach.' If we want to characterize his method we might just as well speak of it as 'descriptive.' . . . For his aim is simply to follow the movement of his object of study. . . . If the argument follows a dialectical movement, then this must be in the things themselves, not just in the way we reason about them."

33. Lukács, *History and Class Consciousness*, 204.

34. Hall, "Marx's Notes on Method," 137.

35. There is a long-running debate regarding the extent to which Marx draws on Hegel in his work. I am thoroughly convinced by the "yes, enormously so" argument, but the link is definitely not Marx = Hegel-does-political-economy. As many have pointed out, and as Postone puts succinctly in *Time, Labor, and Social Domination*, 81: "Marx did not 'apply' Hegel to classical political economy but contextualized Hegel's concepts in terms of the social forms of capitalist society. That is, Marx's mature critique of Hegel is immanent to the unfolding of the categories of *Capital*—which, by paralleling the way Hegel unfolds these concepts, implicitly suggests the determinate sociohistorical context of which they are expressions. In terms of Marx's analysis, Hegel's concepts of dialectic, contradiction, and the identical subject-object express fundamental aspects of capitalist society but do not adequately grasp them." This is the sense in which, in Fredric Jameson's phrase, "in reality Marx *includes* Hegel"; I completely agree. See Jameson, *Marxism and Form*, xv, emphasis in original.

Even among those who believe Marx remained more or less Hegelian there is no agreement regarding the ways in which or the degree to which Hegelianism matters. The most notable Marxist to declare Hegel essential to Marx is Lenin, but other well-known writers have followed suit, e.g. Rosdolsky, *Making of Marx's "Capital,"* chap. 5; Banaji, "From the Commodity to Capital"; Taylor, *Hegel*, 547–62; Ollman, *Dance of the Dialectic*. There are, however, anti-Hegelian Marxist opponents, the most famous of whom are Louis Althusser in *For Marx*, 89–116; Galvano della Volpe in *Logic as a Positive Science*; and Lucio Colletti in *Marxism and Hegel*. For a more strictly methodological argument against Hegel's importance to Marx, see Mattick, "Marx's Dialectic."

36. In a detailed examination of the problem of "determinism" in Marx, William Corlett develops a very helpful distinction between "logical" and "causal" determination and argues convincingly that Marx's theory of history adheres to the former and rejects the latter. Corlett's subtle reading is buttressed by Adorno, Jameson, and Marx himself. See Corlett, *Class Action*, 119–28; Adorno, *Negative Dialectics*; Jameson, *Marxism and Form*, 360–62; and Marx, *Grundrisse*, 105–6.

See also Elson, "Value Theory of Labour"; Hall, "Marx's Notes on Method"; and Postone, *Time, Labor, and Social Domination*.

37. For example, see Marx, *Capital*, 1:93.

38. Postone, *Time, Labor, and Social Domination*, 29.

39. Lukács, *History and Class Consciousness*, 208.

40. Marx, *Grundrisse*, 85–86, 100. The problem of "totality" is not small, and the wariness or outright hostility to the concept shared by many contemporary thinkers is often justified. It is, after all, only a few letters from totality to totalitarian. Without taking us into an enormously complicated debate, I would just like to point out that totality, the historical whole that is not merely the sum of its parts, is *not* universality, homogeneity, or eternity. Rather, the emphasis on totality "stems from a methodological insistence that adequate understanding of complex phenomena can follow only from an appreciation of their relational integrity." Insofar as the relations of production, for example, can be understood dialectically, then they must be understood as interconnected in an infinitely complex whole, rendered ultimately unthinkable by the impossibility of ever standing "outside." See Jay, *Marxism and Totality*, 23–24.

Much is lost, I believe, without access to the holism of the dialectic, a complex relationality that can theorize in the most practical way by uncovering levers and paths we could not see. There are "poststructural" politics that are brilliantly developed analytically and have much to offer—I am thinking particularly of Judith Butler's work—but I would argue that when "returned" to the concrete world they hope to effect, they often resonate closely with the "open" Marxian analysis I advocate here (a point that someone like Butler would probably freely admit). Indeed, in the end most of these critiques, either without acknowledgment or unaware, lean heavily on a Marxian critique of liberal capitalism that is incomprehensible without the notion of totalization. See also Jameson, *Political Unconscious*, 281–92.

41. Jameson, *Political Unconscious*, 9.

42. Jameson, *Marxism and Form*, 307. As Hegel says, "the mind perceiving the contradiction does not commonly know how to relieve it or to keep it free from its onesidedness, and to recognize in what seems conflicting and inherently antagonistic the presence of mutually necessary moments" (*Phenomenology of Mind*, 68).

Chapter Two

1. Simmel, *Philosophy of Money*, 259, emphasis in original.

2. Parker, "Motives in Economic Life," 213–14.

3. Rothschild, *Theory of Wages*, 173.

4. Marglin, *Growth*, 105. This insight has a Keynesian heritage.

5. See, for example, Piore, "Fragments of a 'Sociological' Theory of Wages." This plays out as a kind of "weak" Polanyian account of wage formation, one that foregrounds the "embeddedness" argument but ignores the implications of Polanyi's more complicated theory of labor as a "fictitious commodity." For more on the concept of fictitious commodities, see Polanyi, *Great Transformation*,

and Prudham's fascinating "application" of this approach to forest labor and markets in the western United States, *Knock on Wood*. I try to draw out some possible limits to this approach in an engagement with Prudham's book; see Mann, "Reflections on Scott Prudham's *Knock on Wood*."

6. Fredric Jameson makes this connection in his introduction to Jacques Attali's *Noise*, vii. For a devastating critique of musicology's commitment to disembedded, ahistorical analysis—probably a surprise to most of us outside the discipline—see McClary, *Feminine Endings*.

7. These ideas are developed more fully in chapter 6. It is perhaps worth noting here that these comments are not unrelated to Antonio Negri's remarks on the chapter on wages that Marx planned but never wrote. That chapter "would have been the chapter on not-capital, thus on not-work," for the laws of the wage "flow from the condensation into a subject of the revolt against work contained in capitalist development" (Negri, *Marx beyond Marx*, 72, 131).

8. Against the common mechanistic and ahistorical reading of the labor theory of value, based on the (incomplete) notes that make up *Capital*, vol. 3, this historicized conception of value is not only more analytically useful but it is, for whatever it is worth, a more accurate reading of Marx. For fascinating analyses, see Postone, *Time, Labor, and Social Domination*, esp. 24–27, and Karatani, *Transcritique*, esp. 185–200. As Postone demonstrates very compellingly, Marx's mature work is not a critique of capitalism from the perspective of labor but a critique of the category of labor *in* capitalism.

9. Hegel, *Hegel's Logic*, 134, 145, 149. I refer throughout to the later, or "shorter," *Logic* that constitutes one part of Hegel's *Encyclopædia of the Philosophical Sciences* (1830). The earlier, "greater" *Science of Logic* (1812–14) is a different beast, altogether more complex and obscure. The differences between the two are sometimes significant but are not important to my admittedly coarse appropriation of some of Hegel's concepts.

10. Ibid., 157.

11. Ibid., 158–59.

12. Ibid., 160, 158.

13. I see this political struggle to supersede the quantity-quality opposition as closely related to the *salto mortale* (mortal leap) that Karatani (after Marx) reminds us value must take in capitalism (*Transcritique*, 190). I would add, however, two important addenda that Karatani neglects in his efforts to tie Marx to Kant (as opposed to Hegel). First, despite Karatani's brilliant exposition of the Kant-Marx relation, the mortal leap does not constitute a critique of Hegel (*Transcritique*, 189). In fact, it is central to Hegel's conception of materiality, as he himself remarks in the section on measure in the *Science of Logic*, 370. There, he goes out of his way to dismantle the idea that "nature does not make leaps." Second, the *salto mortale* cannot take place on its own in some abstract realm of value, i.e., it is a *social* process. Indeed, I think it possible that some of Karatani's distrust of Hegel might be remedied by a reexamination of the section on measure—a section I believe was crucial to Marx.

14. Marx himself noted the great importance of the *Logic* in an oft cited 1858 letter to Engels: see Marx and Engels, *Selected Correspondence*, 102. In *The Making of Marx's "Capital"* Rosdolsky calls the *Grundrisse* "a massive reference to Hegel, in particular the *Logic*" (xiii). The connections have been more fully developed by others as well. For example, Jameson, *Marxism and Form*, 359–74; Taylor, *Hegel*, 550–52. See also Nicolaus's excellent foreword to Marx, *Grundrisse*, esp. 24–44. I have taken these issues up in more detail in the sections on the problem of method in chapter 1.

15. Postone, *Time, Labor, and Social Domination*; Laclau, *On Populist Reason*, 141.

16. Any such overneat compartmentalization is fraught with problems, since it is impossible to do justice to the complexity and subtleties. A few caveats are thus in order. First, with the exception of some brief words on Marx's and Sraffa's shared roots in the early nineteenth-century work of David Ricardo, I do not review pre-Ricardian classical wage theories independently. Instead, I consider only those "classicals" aware that the supply-demand scissors may significantly affect the wage, whether they reject that possibility or not (economists before the "marginalist revolution" did not work with demand theory but assumed wages were a function of the cost of production). Second, the theories themselves are presented as more or less distinct, generating insights particular to method and conceptual apparatus. Occasionally this leads to what might seem, from the perspective of someone familiar with the literature, to be oversimplification. I cannot always deny the charge but offer a modest defense. Without glossing over contradictory elements, I highlight only those issues that are relevant to the project as a whole, to explain their significance to the cultural and political economy that is the argument's focus and the structure upon which it hangs. Where a more discipline-specific engagement might dig much deeper, at times I move along.

17. Marx is no help to the dismissers here: indeed, the seriousness with which he engaged the work of his predecessors and opponents—think of how closely he read Malthus, for example—exemplifies the critical necessity I am trying to describe.

18. Cohen, *Self-Ownership, Freedom, and Equality*.

19. Weiss, *Efficiency Wages*.

20. This theoretical division of labor is not strict, of course. Many Keynesians and especially "neo-Keynesian" economists are interested in the wage rate, and many orthodox macroeconomists try to explain the wage share.

21. Antonio Negri, with characteristic energy, remarks that Keynes (and Polanyi) "insist maniacally on the necessity for equilibrium (neoclassical in the case of Keynes, institutional in the case of Polanyi) as the soul of the collective, of the planned, of the State" (*Time for Revolution*, 41).

22. Marx, *Capital*, 1:759 n. 50. On the relationship between the wage and skill, see chapter 4. In recent, and enormously influential, theories of "skill-biased technological change," the growth in wage differentials is examined in light of

technological innovation, which is assumed to be exogenous. The factors in wage determination are specified, using econometric analysis, to identify their relative weight. Advanced technologies like computers prove to be associated with higher-wage occupations, and thus computer-literate workers in these occupations enjoy a "wage premium" due to "capital-skill complementarity."

23. Hicks, *Theory of Wages*, 1. It is worth noting that Hicks later repudiated this orthodox idea of the wage; see *Theory of Wages*, 2nd ed., addendum.

24. Although Hicks was writing before World War II, his is a systematic analysis of competitive labor markets on a theoretical foundation that is no less powerful today. It was laid down in nineteenth-century western Europe by W. S. Jevons and Léon Walras, who, along with Carl Menger, are considered the fathers of the "marginalist revolution" in economics. Marginalists reoriented economic analysis toward consumer demand (as opposed to production) and strictly identified the realm of economics with the market. Their work marks the point at which economics divorced itself from political economy, claiming a disciplinary status equal to that of the other "sciences." Jevons, *Theory of Political Economy*; Walras, *Elements of Pure Economics*; Menger, *Principles of Economics*. For an excellent description of the "Jevonian Revolution," see Dobb, *Theories of Value*, esp. 167–73.

25. Akerlof, "Labor Contracts as Partial Gift Exchange"; Akerlof, "Gift-Exchange and Efficiency-Wage Theory"; Stiglitz and Grossman, "On the Impossibility of Informationally Efficient Markets"; Solow, *Labor Market*.

26. Solow, *Labor Market*, 33–34. Although it sometimes surprises noneconomists, orthodox economists long resisted the idea that the labor market is essentially different from other markets, and some, like the adherents of the strict market-clearing approach of the Chicago school, still do. For radical economists, especially those that work in the Marxian tradition, labor-power's difference from other commodities is fundamental, for at least three reasons: "by its *evanescent* nature, by the impossibility of *accumulating* it, and by the fact that the *supply* cannot be increased or decreased with the same facility as with other products" (Marx, "Wages," 419, emphasis in original).

27. Solow, *Labor Market*, 50.

28. There is a degree of social content in neoclassical modeling beyond which the label neoclassical no longer fits, and Solow presses his face against the window but refuses to go outside. After his initial theoretical leap, he retreats to a modified "prisoners' dilemma" game in which rational individuals maximizing intertemporal welfare choose whether to underbid in the labor market.

29. Although just one of many possible examples, Marilyn Strathern's influential account of gift exchange in Melanesia, *The Gender of the Gift*, shows how deeply political such economic-circulatory processes are.

30. Bewley, *Why Wages Don't Fall*, 430.

31. Much of the discussion on Keynesian wage theory in this section is also applicable to the lesser-known but contemporaneous work of the Polish economist Michał Kalečki and his followers.

32. Keynes, *General Theory*, 236–37; Marglin, *Growth*, 89.

33. Keynes, *General Theory*, 161–62; Robinson, *Essays in the Theory of Economic Growth*, 87.

34. Marglin, *Growth*, 320–21. Keynes's wage theory bears a close resemblance to "wages fund" theories associated with some classical economists like J. S. Mill and disparaged by later economists like Marx and Alfred Marshall. Keynes himself acknowledged this link, claiming that wages fund ideas "embodied an important truth" that economists since Marx have been too quick to dismiss. See Keynes, *Applied Theory of Money*, 127–29.

35. Assuming continuous substitution (or simply variable factor proportions). In practice, this means that production technique will shift so that marginal productivity will equal the (already) given real wage: this is the "Cambridge theory of distribution," named after the British university that was home to its most famous adherents — Nicholas Kaldor, Luigi Pasinetti, Joan Robinson, and Keynes himself. See Marglin, *Growth*, 320–21, 330, and Solow and Stiglitz, "Output, Employment, and Wages."

36. "The effect of combination on the part of a group of workers is to protect their *relative* real wage. The *general* level of real wages depends on the other forces of the economic system." Keynes, *General Theory*, 14, emphasis in original.

37. Marglin, *Growth*, 475. This is the theoretical position behind both Keynes's and Kalečki's arguments regarding the "downward rigidity" of money wages. Keynes, *General Theory*, 303–4; Kalečki, "Money and Real Wages," 34–39; although they shared a pessimism regarding working-class powerlessness in a fully functioning capitalist economy, Kalečki's last published work sounded a more cautiously hopeful egalitarian note. See Kalečki, "Class Struggle and the Distribution of National Income."

38. Indeed, part of the argument of this book is that it is not at all over but persists within capitalist social relations, like the wage, that are thought to be empty of struggle, history, or culture.

39. It is worth noting that these ideas were not at all new, suggested in several instances by Marx (among others), a debt that Keynes spent his career dodging. Marx, *Grundrisse*, 287, 419; Marx, *Theories of Surplus-Value*, bk. 2, 505. See also, for example, Marx, *Capital*, 3:614–15: "The ultimate reason for all real crises always remains the poverty and restricted consumption of the masses, in the face of the drive of capitalist production to develop the productive forces as if only the absolute consumption capacity of society set a limit to them."

40. Przeworski, *Capitalism and Social Democracy*, 37.

41. See, for example, Douglas, *Real Wages in the United States*, and Ware and Means, *Modern Economy in Action*.

42. Althusser and Balibar, *Reading Capital*, esp. 126–44. For radically different assessments of Althusser on Gramsci, see, for example, Anderson, "Antinomies of Antonio Gramsci," esp. 34–39, and Preve, "Louis Althusser," esp. 126–32.

43. Aglietta, *Theory of Capitalist Regulation*, 116–17.

44. Brenner and Glick, "Regulation Approach"; Tickell and Peck, "Social

Regulation after Fordism." For an excellent overview of the regulationists' approach, see Davis, "'Fordism' in Crisis."

45. Aglietta, *Theory of Capitalist Regulation*, 186–208. Aglietta is in fact unclear in his explanation of the reference wage. At one point he claims the nominal wage is inflexible under Fordism (196), but he then points out the indexing system by which wages were pegged to the cost of living (197). Furthermore, he does not even begin to address the fact that the nominal wage clearly did not remain stable in the Fordist era (from approximately World War II until 1973). This is perhaps a product of eschewing some of Marx's wage analysis in favor of that of Keynes. For an excellent explanation of rising real and nominal wages under capitalism, see Roman Rosdolsky's reading of Marx's demonstration that "it is possible, given increasing productivity of labour, for the price of labour-power to fall constantly, and for this fall to be accompanied by a constant growth in the mass of the worker's means of subsistence" (*Capital*, 1:659). Rosdolsky shows how this is "the theoretical formula which lies at the heart of the increases in real wages which have largely taken place in the latter half of the nineteenth and the twentieth century" (Rosdolsky, *Making of Marx's "Capital,"* 289 n. 19).

46. Brown, "Institutional Model of Wives' Work Decisions."

47. All institutionalists, that is, with the important exception of the "new institutional economists," whose current project is the reconciliation of institutional interests in incentives and organization with rational choice theory. In the United States, institutionalism proper can be traced back to the pre–World War II work of economists like John Commons and Ronald Coase, who were broadly interested in what Coase called the "supersession of the price mechanism" in actually functioning economic institutions. Here I focus on post–*General Theory* institutional wage theory, which is not only better developed but also far more influential. I think that it is not too much of an oversimplification to say that the "new" institutionalism is heavy on the Coase, light on the Commons, and not only is new institutionalist work on the wage rare but, when one does find it, it is a simple "incrementalist" version of neoclassical microeconomics. Commons and Associates, *History of Labor in the United States*; Coase, "Nature of the Firm," 388–89.

48. Jacoby, *Modern Manors*, 5. See also Jacoby, "Development of Internal Labor Markets."

49. As Kerr puts it, contrary to neoclassical arguments, the "wage market," i.e., "the totality of jobs" "for which the same wage is paid," is not coextensive with the "labor market," the area within which "workers move comparatively freely from one job to another." Kerr, *Labor Markets*, 38–39.

50. Ibid., 34.

51. This was by no means a new idea; see Commons and Associates, *History of Labor in the United States*, 34.

52. The institutionalists' work was attacked ferociously by the neoclassical establishment of the United States in the postwar era. Working hard to undermine

collective bargaining and justify the suite of policies associated with the Taft-Hartley Act, some of the most prominent names in the profession berated both unions and the scholars who supported the industrial relations system. For a collection of representative papers, see Bradley, *Public Stake in Union Power.*

53. The node from which more recent work has branched is Peter Doeringer and Michael Piore's enormously influential *Internal Labor Markets and Manpower Analysis*. Echoing earlier but underdeveloped conceptual work by Kerr and Lloyd Fisher, *Internal Labor Markets* develops a theory of the "dual labor market," one fragmented into primary and secondary markets. The former is characterized by relative high wages, job security, and opportunities for upward occupational mobility. The latter is the domain of low-wage, contingent, and "dead-end" work. Radical economists were quick to pick up on the ways in which this theory helped explain social hierarchy within and between labor markets and the reproduction of broader social division. See also Fisher, "Harvest Labor Market in California," esp. 469–71, and Kerr, *Labor Markets*, 30 n. 16.

54. Dobb, *Wages*, 142–46; Gordon, Edwards, and Reich, *Segmented Work, Divided Workers*; Brown, "Institutional Model of Wives' Work Decisions."

55. There are, however, important exceptions, like Fisher's "Harvest Labor Market in California" and Taylor's masterpiece, the three-volume *Mexican Labor in the United States.*

56. Given its explicit historicity, it is no surprise economic historians are drawn to the institutional framework and have produced some very sophisticated analyses of U.S. labor history. Gavin Wright's work is an excellent example. He argues that the political economy of the U.S. South is largely a function of the isolation of southern labor markets between the Civil War and World War II. More recently, Wright extends the institutionalist claim to the nation in general: "conflict in American labor history has not been a direct tug-of-war between capital and labor over division of the surplus" but "has instead been over the scope and operation of labor markets." This position is very compelling, the violent battles over the union hiring hall providing one of the best-known examples. See Wright, *Old South, New South*; Wright, "Labor History and Labor Economics," 328; and Kimeldorf, "World War II."

57. Gordon, Edwards, and Reich, *Segmented Work, Divided Workers*, 8. This is as succinct a description of the institutionalist legacy as one could hope to find.

58. For an example of the application of this productionism, see Reich, *Racial Inequality.*

59. Samuelson, "Wages and Interest," 906–7.

60. Marx, *Value, Price, and Profit*, 58.

61. Lapides, *Marx's Wage Theory*, 6.

62. Marx, *Wage-Labour and Capital*, 32–33.

63. Harvey, *Limits to Capital*, 49. For an example of a slightly "sympathetic" misreading, see Robinson, *Essay on Marxian Economics*, 32–44. This seems like the right place to acknowledge my debt to Harvey's comprehensive account of Marxian wage theory in chapter 2 of *Limits to Capital*. Indeed, we should be

enormously grateful for *Limits to Capital* even if Harvey had only written the first two brilliant chapters (and we should be doubly grateful that he did not stop there).

64. Samuelson, "Wages and Interest," 910–11. The caricature of wage theory Samuelson willfully misattributes to Marx is properly associated with Marx's sometime friend and political rival Ferdinand Lassalle (1825–64), whose "iron law of wages" described the subsistence wage in the restricted, just-getting-by sense. Marx in fact devoted a lot of energy to attacking such ideas, labeling them "nonsense" in his denunciation of Lassallean socialism (*Critique of the Gotha Programme*, 534). For a detailed account of the content and context of the "iron law of wages," which Lassalle laid out in his "Open Reply Letter to the National Labor Association of Germany" of 1863, see Bernstein, *Ferdinand Lassalle*, 134–47. Bernstein is himself an important figure in the history of radical political theory, perhaps most famous for being the object of Rosa Luxemburg's withering attack on "revisionism," i.e., nonrevolutionary social democracy.

65. The point is made so often that any particular citation is arbitrary. This one comes from Marx, *Capital*, 3:999; for a series of others, see Harvey, *Limits to Capital*, 45–50.

66. Ricardo, *On the Principles of Political Economy and Taxation*, 96–97: "[T]he natural price of labour . . . essentially depends upon the habits and customs of the people."

67. Marglin, *Growth*, 316.

68. Marx, *Wage-Labour and Capital*, 27. See also Marx, "Wages," 415: "Average or normal price of labour; the minimum is valid only for the class of workers, not for the individual."

69. Marx, *Capital*, 3:998. The volume 3 "version" of the "social wage" is strikingly similar to the Keynesian "residual wage fund," and the contrast between the two ways of designating aggregate working-class income is an accurate indicator of the contrast in the politics of the individual thinkers. In each case, those who are understood to truly move history are implicitly identified.

70. Marx, *Grundrisse*, 85: "Some determinations belong to all epochs, others to only a few. [Some] determinations will be shared by the most modern epoch and the most ancient. No production will be thinkable without them; however, even though the most developed languages have laws and characteristics in common with the least developed, nevertheless, just those things which determine their development, i.e., the elements which are not general or common, must be separated out from the determinations valid for production as such, so that their unity — which arises already from the identity of the subject, humanity, and of the object, nature — their essential difference is not forgotten. The whole profundity of those modern economists who demonstrate the eternity and harmoniousness of the existing social relations lies in this forgetting"; Marx, *Wage-Labour and Capital*, 32–33. On Marx's break with Ricardo's ahistorical wage theory, see Garegnani, "Sraffa's Revival of Marxist Economic Theory," 74.

71. Marx, *Value, Price, and Profit*, 58.

72. Marx, *Capital*, 1:769.

73. The term "labor-power" has become the standard translation of the German *Arbeitskraft* and the French *force de travail*, but Marx also occasionally used the terms *Arbeitsvermögen* or *puissance de travail*. Slightly different translations are possible with all four of these terms, so some fluidity in reading is appropriate. Marx, *Capital*, 1:270; Marx, *Wage-Labour and Capital*, 17; Marx, *Le Capital*, 130. (The French edition of *Capital*, vol. 1, is the only translation Marx "approved"; indeed, disappointed with the work of translator J. Roy, he rewrote large parts of it.)

74. Marx, *Capital*, 1:677.

75. Harvey, *Limits to Capital*, 45; Marx, *Capital*, 1:680.

76. Marx, *Wage-Labour and Capital*, 18; Marx, *Capital*, 3:969.

77. Gramsci, *Prison Notebooks*, 310–12.

78. Aglietta, *Theory of Capitalist Regulation*, 200. Michael Burawoy, for instance, argues that "the defining essence of the capitalist labor process is the simultaneous obscuring and securing of surplus value" (*Manufacturing Consent*, 30).

79. Burawoy, *Manufacturing Consent*.

80. Edwards, *Contested Terrain*; Reich, *Racial Inequality*; Barrera, *Race and Class*.

81. Bowles, "Production Process"; Bowles, "Endogenous Preference Formation"; Bowles and Gintis, " Revenge of Homo Economicus"; Bowles and Gintis, "Walrasian Economics in Retrospect."

82. Some of it, like Bowles's elaboration of "endogenous preference formation," acquiesces to the neoclassical emphasis on demand far more than many Marxians would like. Others, like John Roemer or Erik Wright, have criticized the emphasis on the wage as anachronistic because it disables analyses of other forms of exploitation or more complex class hierarchies. See Bowles, "Endogenous Preference Formation"; Roemer, *General Theory*; and Wright, *Classes*.

83. For a recent example, see Boyte, "Pragmatic Ends of Popular Politics," 349.

84. Aronowitz, *False Promises*; see also Burawoy, *Manufacturing Consent*.

85. In addition to Aronowitz, see, for example, Radosh, *American Labor*; Braverman, *Labor and Monopoly Capital*; Gordon, Edwards, and Reich, *Segmented Work, Divided Workers*; Reich, *Racial Inequality*.

86. Rowthorn, *Capitalism, Conflict and Inflation*, 182–230; Willis, *Learning to Labor*; Cohen, *Karl Marx's Theory of History*, chap. 5.

87. Hall, "Problem of Ideology," 38–39.

88. Roemer, *General Theory*, 115; Bowles, "Production Process," 25. Marx did recognize the theoretical possibility of intersectoral equilibrium but thought it was empirically very unlikely. See Dobb, *Theories of Value*, 162–63.

89. See the famous "1857 Introduction" to Marx, *Grundrisse* (sometimes called Notebook M).

90. It is worth noting here that the "dynamics" captured by these models—as

the mere shift between static equilibria—are not dynamic in any meaningful historical sense. This is the analytical equivalent of showing every tenth frame in a film, pausing the projector to fix each image for an instant. One gets no sense of the time and space between, of the constant motion in which each frame is embedded. This is arguably not just a simpler version of the film or history but something else all together. Indeed, if one were to press the metaphor a little bit more, one might wonder at who would be depicted in the frames.

91. Marglin, *Growth*, 320.

92. Although this is not the place to argue it, I would suggest that the former is as incompatible as the latter with a close reading of Marx. For a fuller treatment, see Mann, "Interests and the Political Terrain of Time."

93. Roemer, *General Theory*, 29.

94. Ibid., 108–9. The significance of the reserve army in labor market function is the elephant in the room in orthodox labor economics—everyone knows it is there, but it is rarely mentioned. A signal exception—in which, incredibly, Marx's development of the idea more than a century before goes unmentioned—is Shapiro and Stiglitz, "Equilibrium Unemployment as a Worker Discipline Device."

95. For example, Meek, "Mr Sraffa's Rehabilitation of Classical Economics." Sraffa apparently believed his chief contribution consisted in these two analytical achievements. See Sraffa, *Production of Commodities*, 93–94.

96. Sraffa, *Production of Commodities*, 12.

97. Ibid., 33.

98. Samuelson, "Sraffa's Other Leg," 570–74.

99. Sraffa, *Production of Commodities*, chap. 5.

100. Dobb, *Theories of Value*, 260–61.

101. See Rowthorn, *Capitalism, Conflict and Inflation*, 210.

102. Sraffa, *Production of Commodities*, 9–10.

103. Ibid. This is a somewhat different reading of Sraffa than that offered by Harvey in *Limits to Capital*, 40. However, the two interpretations are complementary, not logically inconsistent.

104. Dobb, *Theories of Value*, 261.

105. Sraffa, *Production of Commodities*, 33.

106. Ibid.

Chapter Three

1. The "working man" in the United States in more recent times has received very interesting treatment in David Halle's *America's Working Man*, esp. chap. 10, and in Michèle Lamont's *The Dignity of Working Men*. Halle is less interested in the political weight of "Americanism," which is critical to this chapter, and Lamont briefly discusses nationalism but does not emphasize the content of Americanism. Dana Nelson's discussion of the flawed fraternity of U.S. "national manhood" in the early nineteenth century shows some of the ways in which white manhood became conflated with American citizenship, if not Americanism. See Nelson, *National Manhood*, and Kessler-Harris, *In Pursuit of Equity*,

on the fundamentally gendered structure of economic citizenship in the United States. For a more theoretical discussion of working-class studies and the implicit masculinity of the "quintessential worker," see Rose, "Class Formation and the Quintessential Worker."

2. Kessler-Harris, *In Pursuit of Equity*; Kessler-Harris, *Woman's Wage*. George Mosse considers the ways in which World War I similarly destabilized European masculinity in *The Image of Man*, 107–32.

3. Milton, *Politics of U.S. Labor*; Davis, *Prisoners of the American Dream*; Aronowitz, *False Promises*, 226.

4. Przeworski, *Capitalism and Social Democracy*, 77 n. 30.

5. Among geographers: Herod, "From a Geography of Labor to a Labor Geography," and Mitchell, *Lie of the Land*; historians: Saxton, *Indispensable Enemy*; Lichtenstein, *Labor's War at Home*; and Roediger, *Wages of Whiteness*; sociologists: Milkman, *Gender at Work*; Lamont, *Dignity of Working Men*; and Kefalas, *Working-Class Heroes*; others: Davis, *Prisoners of the American Dream*.

6. Herod, "From a Geography of Labor to a Labor Geography," 16–17.

7. Lichtenstein, "Class Politics," 267. Although the phrase was coined by Toqueville, the most influential statement of anti-class-conscious "American exceptionalism" is Lipset's "Radicalism in North America."

8. Gerstle, *Working-Class Americanism*; Gerstle, "Working Class Goes to War." The argument I am making is perhaps too easily associated with "consensus" history's nationalist mythmaking. Some historians suggest these years involved organized labor's irrevocable acceptance of "the great trade-off entailing the exchange of political power for money" (e.g., Milton, *Politics of U.S. Labor*, 155). Yet U.S. workers' patriotic (if complex and contradictory) support for the war is increasingly evident in World War II labor history. Although a superficial picture of working-class prowar sentiment was brilliantly torn apart in the early 1980s by historians like Martin Glaberman, George Lipsitz, and Nelson Lichtenstein, recent social history has reasserted workers' active engagement in state-sponsored activities on the home front and their significant ideological commitment to the "Americanism" that emerged during the New Deal and buoyed both the war effort and Cold War politics. For the former, see Glaberman, *Wartime Strikes*; Lipsitz, *Rainbow at Midnight*; and Lichtenstein, *Labor's War at Home*. For the latter, i.e., accounts of working-class support for the war, see Gerstle, *Working-Class Americanism*; Leff, "Politics of Sacrifice"; Lichtenstein, "Making of the Postwar Working Class"; and Lichtenstein, "Class Politics."

This new work, however, complicates working-class participation in the war effort. As Gerstle shows in *Working-Class Americanism*, the politics of Americanism in the 1930s and 1940s did not rely on nationalism alone but combined several powerful and often contradictory ideological threads. The working-class Americanism behind the war effort, while partly produced by the state's massive ideological apparatus, was at the same time a product of workers' political agency. The resulting ideas of American-ness were a complicated mix of four "dimensions": nationalist, democratic, progressive, and traditionalist. In the labor politics of the mid-1940s, these dimensions were inseparable. The nationalism that at least partially motivated the purchase of war bonds was tied directly to a commitment to egalitarian democracy; the progressivism that anticipated an ever improving standard of living also defended the "rightness" of idealized traditional social structures like the patriarchal family and white supremacist racial hierarchy.

9. Lichtenstein, "Class Politics," 267–69.

10. Goldin and Margo, " Great Compression"; Lichtenstein, "Class Politics," 268.

11. See also Glickman, *Living Wage*, 84.

12. Stimson, *Rise of the Labor Movement in Los Angeles*, 420–27; Perry and Perry, *History of the Los Angeles Labor Movement*; Soja, Morales, and Wolff, "Urban Restructuring"; Davis, "Sunshine and the Open Shop." However, work not yet published by Jeffrey Stansbury (personal communication, 3 April 2003) contradicts the dominant characterization of pre–World War II L.A. as the quintessential open-shop town.

13. In 1945, almost 15 percent of the International's fifty thousand members belonged to Local 128. See Rothbaum, *Government of the Oil, Chemical and Atomic Workers Union*, 22, and OWIU, *Proceedings of the Ninth National Convention*.

14. Local #1-128 Archives, S.1/B.21/F.4; S.1/B.21/F.5.

15. Bratt, "Profiles," 181.

16. Viehe, "Black Gold Suburbs."

17. *LAT*, 7 September 1948, II-4.

18. Viehe, "Black Gold Suburbs," 8–9; Hise, "'Nature's Workshop,'" 86.

19. BLS, *Wage Structure: Petroleum Refining, 1948*, 7–8.

20. Kidner and Neff, *Statistical Appendix*, 586.

21. California State Reconstruction and Reemployment Commission, *Third Report*, 4; Scott, *Metropolitan Los Angeles*, 40.

22. Kidner and Neff, *Economic Survey*, 102.

23. *LH*, 20 April 1945, 1.

24. Many expected a postwar recession. The OWIU and its rival the International Union of Operating Engineers held this view, as did many prominent economists, fifty-four of whom signed a letter to the editor in the *New York Times* (26 April 1946, 26). See International Union of Operating Engineers "Resolution No. 4."

25. *LH*, 13 July 1945, 1.

26. As Roman Rosdolsky has pointed out, the fact that since the defeat of fascism the reduction rather than the expansion of the working day is on capital's agenda is one of the more significant (if less remarked) postwar changes unions faced in bargaining. See Rosdolsky, *Making of Marx's "Capital,"* 287.

27. Murray, *CIO Case for Substantial Pay Increases*; Seidman, *American Labor*, 217.

28. *IOW*, 15 November 1945, 8.

29. *IOW*, May 1945, 2.

30. KC.

31. *IOW*, 24 June 1946.

32. Bratt, "Profiles," 181; *LH*, 25 May 1945, 1.

33. Scott and Mattingly, "Aircraft and Parts Industry," 52.

34. National Bureau of Economic Research, Macrohistory Series 08084c [Unemployment]; Gordon, *Employment Expansion and Population Growth*, 128; California Department of Industrial Relations, Division of Labor Statistics and Research, *Labor in California, 1945–1946*, 52; California Department of Industrial Relations, Division of Labor Statistics and Law Enforcement, *California Labor Market Bulletin*, 3.

35. California State Reconstruction and Reemployment Commission, *Report and Recommendations, 1945*, 4.

36. Oil workers fared better than many of the region's workers. See BLS, "Workers' Experiences during the First Phase of Reconversion," 17, Doe Library, Berkeley.

37. Local #1-128 Archives, S.4/B.1/F.20. My calculations yield considerably different results: a 28.7 percent increase in the cost of living and a 25.8 percent wage increase (based on data from California Department of Industrial Relations, Division of Labor Statistics and Law Enforcement, *California Labor Market Bulletin*, 3). I believe this is due to the union's use of a strategic mixture of price indexes from the local, state, and national scales that maximized the difference between cost-of-living and wage increases.

38. Hoch, "Oil Strike of 1945," 120–23; Dunlop, "Review of Wage-Price Policy," 156. At least on the surface, the unions had President Truman on their side. In Executive Order 9599 (18 August 1945) he threw his weight behind "the maintenance of purchasing power," to which he later (30 October 1945) added Executive Order 9651, in which he declared that companies had the "ability to pay" workers better without raising prices.

39. Local #1-128 Archives, S.2/B.59/F.45.

40. Ibid., S.4/B.1/F.20; S.1/B.21/F.5.

41. Ibid., S.4/B.1/F.20. The Office of Price Administration (OPA) granted industry only small price increases on refined products during the war, which mostly affected wholesale industrial fuels prices (ibid.; BLS, "Primary Market Prices and Indexes," table 2, and BLS, "Indexes of Primary Market Prices," both in Doe Library, Berkeley).

Despite "a rapid and continuing expansion in the total demand for refined products in the Pacific Coast area," the retail price of gasoline in L.A. remained eighteen cents per gallon from 1942 until OPA's demise in mid-1946 (Bain, *War and Postwar Developments*; Cassady and Jones, *Nature of Competition in Gasoline Distribution*, 171).

42. Local #1-128 Archives, S.4/B.1/F.20; BLS, "Work Stoppages," 20; Hoch, "Oil Strike of 1945," 124; Department of Labor, Oil Panel, "Report and Recommendations," 1, Doe Library, Berkeley; Local #1-128 Archives, S.2/B.59/F.45.

43. Seidman, *American Labor*, 222.

44. Department of Labor, Oil Panel, "Report and Recommendations," I, Doe Library, Berkeley.

45. *NPN*, 5 December 1945, 8–10; KC; OWIU, *Facts about the Wage Dispute*.

46. OWIU, *Facts about the Wage Dispute*.

47. Testimony of President Knight, in Department of Labor, Oil Panel, "Report and Recommendations," 8, Doe Library, Berkeley.

48. *IOW*, April 1945, 8.

49. *LAT*, 7 September 1948, II-4; Kidner and Neff, *Los Angeles—The Economic Outlook*, 8.

50. Local #1-128 Archives, S.2/B.59/F.45; S.4/B.1/F.20; *LAT*, 2 October 1945, II-4.

51. *NPN*, 3 October 1945, 8; Local #1-128 Archives, S.2/B.59/F.45; *NPN*, 26 September 1945, 4; *LAT*, 3 October 1945, 1; 2 October 1945, II-2.

52. Aglietta, *Theory of Capitalist Regulation*, 117, 67, 197.

53. As did Marx: Antonio Negri points out that workers' opposition "tries continually to broaden *the sphere of non-work.*" See Negri, *Marx beyond Marx*, 71, emphasis in original. "The worker's participation in the higher, even cultural satisfactions, the agitation for his own interests, newspaper subscriptions, attending lectures, educating his children, developing his taste, etc., his only share of civilization which distinguishes him from the slave, is economically only possible by widening the sphere of his pleasures" (Marx, *Grundrisse*, 287).

54. *The Nation*, 29 December 1945, 724. The emphasis on demand predated Keynes and played a critical role in the populist "consumption" economics of depression-era activists like Caroline Ware and Gardiner Means (*Modern Economy in Action*). See also Douglas, *Real Wages in the United States*, and Jacobs, "'Democracy's Third Estate.'"

55. *IOW*, 24 June 1946, 12.

56. Local #1-128 Archives, S.4/B1/F.20; *IOW*, February 1946, 9; OWIU, *Facts about the Wage Dispute*, emphasis in original; Local #1-128 Archives, S.4/B.1/F.20; S.4/B.1/F.21.

57. Local #1-128 Archives, S.2/B.59/F.43; *IOW*, 15 November 1945, 8.

58. Oil workers, like many other white male union members throughout the United States, were no less troubled by the entry of millions of African American workers in the wartime labor force. The dynamics of these racial politics, both inside the union and within the larger industrial labor markets of Los Angeles, were very different from those concerning gender and require a full consideration in their own right. I suggest a possible way to conceive these politics elsewhere; see Mann, "'Discrimination Costs You Dough.'"

59. Lambert and Franks, *Voices from the Oil Fields*; Lynch, *Roughnecks, Drillers and Tool Pushers*; Sellars, *Oil, Wheat & Wobblies*.

60. Matthews, "'Roughneck' Oil Worker."

61. Local #1-128 Archives, S.2/B.59/F.43; *NPN*, 2 May 1945, 39; Local #1-128 Archives, S.2/B.59/F.43.

62. Local #1-128 Archives, S.2/B.59/F.43; S.4/B.3/F.56; S.4/B.10/F.67.

63. By late 1945, this prophecy was (self-)fulfilled across the industry, L.A. included (*IOW*, 15 November 1945). See, also Milkman, *Gender at Work*, chaps. 7–8; May, "Rosie the Riveter Gets Married"; Kessler-Harris, *In Pursuit of Equity*; Collinson and Hearn "'Men' at 'Work.'"

64. *IOW*, 25 March 1946, 2. These objectives fit nicely with the same state-sponsored ideological enlistment process that helped generate working-class support for the war. Government propaganda in the labor media included depictions of strapping factory workers beneath the slogan "I'm a Fightin' Man Too! Watch My Smoke!," an image that not only buttressed the masculinity of labor politics but endorsed and reproduced oil workers' claims to "pumping the dark blood needed for the arteries of war" (*IOW*, April 1945, 16).

65. *IOW*, 12 August 1946, 2; OWIU, *Proceedings, Seventeenth National Convention*, 5; *IOW*, August 1945, 13.

66. Mosse, *Image of Man*, 4, 8; see also Stoler, "Racial Histories."

67. Ehrenreich, "Decline of Patriarchy," 288.

68. KC, 12, 24, 26.

69. Ibid., 22, 69.

70. *IOW*, October 1945, 16; OWIU, *Facts about the Wage Dispute*.

71. *The Nation*, 2 February 1946, 119.

72. OWIU, *Proceedings, Seventeenth National Convention*, 10–11.

73. *IOW*, September 1945, 4.

74. *IOW*, 24 June 1946, 12.

75. Local #1-128 Archives, S.2/B.43/F.14; S.2/B.59/F.45; S.4/B.1/F.19; Leff, "Politics of Sacrifice"; Lichtenstein, "Class Politics." "Little Steel" permitted wages in industries under WLB jurisdiction to be adjusted upward up to 15 percent to take account of inflation between 1941 and 1942. Wage increases beyond this threshold were disallowed without board approval on the grounds that they were inflationary. Although refinery wages did rise through this ceiling, the WLB's reluctance to grant "justified" wage increases was roundly criticized, especially since there was no limit to corporate profits. However, corporations were subject to a wartime federal tax on "excess profits," payments that they were able to claim as "carry-back" tax credits after the war. See National War Labor Board, "Wage Report to the President," 4–7, Doe Library, Berkeley; Local #1-128 Archives, S.4/B.1/F.20.

76. OWIU, *Proceedings, Seventeenth National Convention*, 10; Jacobs, "'How about Some Meat?'"; Lichtenstein, "Class Politics," 269–70.

77. Jacobs, "'How about Some Meat?'"

78. Despite oil industry protests, the "no-strike agreement, which formed the *de facto* basis for the War Labor Board, was widely understood to apply only to the period of actual hostilities" (Dunlop, "Review of Wage-Price Policy," 154).

79. Were oil workers simply attempting to maximize real wages? Wage bargaining is not overdetermined by income maximization; nor is income maximization necessarily even the ultimate objective. Although maximizing the mem-

bership wage bill was an immediate goal, the OWIU understood it as one part of broader objectives. The politics of wartime and immediate postwar taxes on workers' wage income are an excellent example of the wage-based, explicitly interclass distributive struggle the OWIU and other unions undertook. Income taxes during the war, and into the first years of peace, were higher than ever before. After-tax real wages in manufacturing were lower in 1945 than in 1940, despite previously unmatched pretax wage rates. That a substantial proportion of workers' wages was going to the government would seem to be a cause for grievance. Yet, in all the OWIU literature, or in Local 128's bargaining and communications, criticism of tax rates is virtually nonexistent. The "politics of sacrifice" may explain this during the war, but after, with the union focused on wages and earnings, oil workers still did not target taxes. Instead, their focus was a new politics of productive industrial citizenship. So they explicitly attacked the injustice of the distribution of income between capital and labor, not, as Ross argued, the relative wage structure. Ross, *Trade Union Wage Policy*; Piore, "Unemployment and Inflation"; Mulligan, "Pecuniary Incentives to Work," 1042–44.

80. Local #1-128 Archives, S.2/B.59/F.45.

81. Goldin and Margo, "Great Compression," 23–24. Goldin and Margo argue that wage compression also persisted because of a rising minimum wage, an increased supply of educated workers, and growing demand for unskilled labor during and following the war.

82. Local #1-128 Archives, S.2/B.43/F.18; BLS, "Wages and Hours of Labor in Petroleum Refineries," 1311; BLS, *Wage Structure: Petroleum Refining, 1948*, 11; BLS, *Wage Structure: Petroleum Production and Refining*, 28; BLS, *Occupational Wage Survey*, 22.

83. KC, 5. The 18 percent increase agreed upon at the end of 1945, for example, worked out to a 22.5-cents-per-hour increase in the average petroleum refinery wage in Los Angeles in December of that year. Although it is conjecture, it is likely that the union would have agreed to a 22-cent increase just as, if not more, readily. Since all available evidence demands that we dismiss any argument about "money illusion," this would indicate a strategic rationale for a non-percentage-based increase.

84. Dobb, *Wages*, 138–59. This argument goes back at least as far as Adam Smith's *Wealth of Nations*: "The wages of labour vary with the ease or hardship, the cleanliness or dirtiness, the honourableness or dishonourableness of the employment" (115). However, Local 128 would not have accepted the logical corollary, that the more agreeable refinery jobs should be less well paid. The point was to diminish wage differentials and maximize the average.

85. Local #1-128 Archives, S.2/B.43/F.20; S.2/B.59/F.45.

86. Ibid., S.1/B.21/F.5.

87. Ibid., S.2/B.43/F.20.

88. Ibid., S.2/B.43/F.20: 4.

89. *LH*, 4 May 1945, 4; *IOW*, 24 June 1946, 12.

90. Although escalator clauses were first used in the United States following World War I, and again during the inflationary period prior to U.S. engagement in 1942, they became ubiquitous only after World War II.

91. BLS, "Cost of Living Adjustment Clauses," 2, Doe Library, Berkeley; Local #1-128 Archives, S.2/B.43/F.20: 4; S.4/B.3/F.65.

92. Green, "Labor in the Western Oil Industry," 17; Aglietta, *Theory of Capitalist Regulation*, 205–7.

93. *The Militant*, 18 May 1946, 4; *IOW*, 24 June 1946, 12.

94. Murray, *CIO Reemployment Plan*, 8; Robinson, *Accumulation of Capital*, 48–49; See also Rosdolsky, *Making of Marx's "Capital,"* 289, and Marx, *Theories of Surplus-Value*, bk. 3, 312.

95. Schultze, *Recent Inflation in the United States*, 65; Piore, "Fragments of a 'Sociological' Theory of Wages," 383.

96. *IOW*, 22 December 1947, 4.

97. OWIU, *Proceedings, Seventeenth National Convention*, 44.

98. *IOW*, January 1946, 16.

99. Local #1-128 Archives, S.1/B.21/F.3; S.4/B.1/F.22.

100. *LAT*, 3 October 1945, II-1.

101. *NPN*, 26 September 1945, 7; *LAT*, 2 October 1945, II-4.

102. Local #1-128 Archives, S.1/B.21/F.6; *IOW*, 5 May 1947, 9; Local #1-128 Archives, S.1/B.21/F.9; *LH*, 23 November 1945, 1; 23 March 1945, 3; Local #1-128 Archives, S.1/B.21/F.6.

103. *LH*, 20 April 1945, 1; 9 March 1945, 1; California State Reconstruction and Reemployment Commission, *Report and Recommendations*, 151; O'Connor, *History of Oil Workers International Union*, 256. Although the Murray legislation was eventually enacted in the form of the toothless Employment Act of 1946, the state bill was never passed. See also Brown, "Unemployment Theory and Policy," 175–76, and *LH*, 25 May 1945, 1.

104. Congress of Industrial Organizations, California Council, *Taft-Hartley Plot Unfolds*, 31; Lichtenstein, "Class Politics," 270–71.

105. *IOW*, 23 June 1947, 11.

106. *IOW*, 9 June 1947, 7, 1.

107. Poulantzas, *Fascisme et dictature*, 166, my translation.

108. Davis, *Prisoners of the American Dream*, x. Davis serves as something of a foil throughout this conclusion not in spite of but because of the fact that his is in my view the most compelling history of the U.S. working class. Engaging with it begins the conversation at a degree of sophistication that is largely possible because of his work.

109. KC, 49; see also Cohen, "Labour Process to Nowhere."

110. Davis, *Prisoners of the American Dream*, 52.

111. Przeworski, *Capitalism and Social Democracy*, 55.

112. For example, Milton, *Politics of U.S. Labor*.

113. Levenstein, *Communism, Anti-Communism*, 208.

114. Hall, "Race, Articulation, and Societies Structured in Dominance," 335.

Chapter Four

1. My attention was called to the photograph, which is in the collection of the Weed Historic Lumber Town Museum, by Lawrence Shoup, in his *Speed, Power, Production, and Profit*, 74. While this chapter's concerns are not those of Dr. Shoup's research, I am in considerable debt to him for providing one of only two historical accounts of African American labor in the northern California lumber industry. I am equally indebted to the author of the other, James Langford, for "The Black Minority of Weed — Its History, Institutions, and Politics."

2. Griliches, "Capital-Skill Complementarity"; Alchian and Demsetz, "Production, Information Costs, and Economic Organization"; Weiss, *Efficiency Wages*, 55–57. I offer a more theoretically detailed critique of orthodox economics' ahistorical conception of skill in Mann, "Social Production of Skill."

3. On "split" or "segmented" labor markets, see Bonacich, "Advanced Capitalism and Black/White Relations," and Gordon, Edwards, and Reich, *Segmented Work, Divided Workers*.

4. Thomas, *Citizenship, Gender, and Work*, 196–200.

5. Offe, *Disorganized Capitalism*, 59.

6. Du Bois, "Shasta and Siskiyou," 9–10; *SN*, 12 April 1917, 8; Langford, "Black Minority," 9.

7. *YJ*, 12 July 1922, 5; Langford, "Black Minority," 9; *YJ*, 12 July 1922, 5. One historian of the timber industry contends that a third group of African Americans arrived in Weed after an unsuccessful attempt to settle them in Longview, Long-Bell's new company town in southwestern Washington, but she provides no sources to support the claim. See Todes, *Labor and Lumber*, 61.

8. Weed, "Weed," 29; Weed Bicentennial Committee, *Weed*, 14; *MSH&SH*, 26 July 1923, 3; Langford, "Black Minority," 15; Gilman, "City of Weed," 1.

9. Weed, "Weed," 33; *YJ*, 15 November 1922, 3.

10. Linville, "Unions," 41.

11. Weed, "Weed," 44; Langford, "Black Minority," 11; *SDN*, 16 October 1924, 1; *YJ*, 12 July 1922, 5.

12. Langford, "Black Minority," 1; Wright, *Old South, New South*, 159–62, 204–5; Green, "Brotherhood of Timber Workers," 168; Danny Piggee, quoted in Langford, "Black Minority," 1.

The differences in weekly earnings were somewhat diminished by longer hours in the South. BLS, *Wages and Hours of Labor in the Lumber Industry in the United States*, 20–21, table A.

13. Shoup, *Speed, Power, Production, and Profit*, 81–82; Howd, *Industrial Relations*, 34–35.

14. Linville, "Unions," 85.

15. *SB*, 14 March 1922, 8; Langford, "Black Minority," 9, 19; *YJ*, 15 March 1922, 2; McClelland, *R. A. Long's Planned City*, 65.

16. Langford, "Black Minority," 15–18. According to local newspapers, there were two "factions" in the Weed black community, the "Long-Bell Negroes" and "the Strays." *YJ*, 8 October 1922, 8. For a discussion of the ways Jim Crow ex-

cluded blacks from public institutions and space and simultaneously "facilitated the creation and maintenance" of "unmonitored, unauthorized social sites," see Kelley, "'We Are Not What We Seem,'" 79–81.

17. See Flamming's *Bound for Freedom* and Gregory's *Southern Diaspora* for perhaps the best historical examinations of the Great Migration and California.

18. Fickle, "Management Looks at the 'Labor Problem,'" 63–67. The only other documented case of the migration of southern African American lumber workers to the West is the creation of McNary, Arizona, in 1923. See Weinker, "McNary," 282–85.

19. Bradley, *Robert Alexander Long*, 42–50. For a fascinating study of the difference biophysical nature made in the shape of the western forest industry, see Prudham, *Knock on Wood*.

20. Bradley, *Robert Alexander Long*, 37, 44.

21. Weed Chamber of Commerce, "Abner Weed," 1; Weed, "Weed," 31; Shoup, *Speed, Power, Production, and Profit*, 63, 65–70; *YJ*, 15 February 1918, 1; 1 February 1922, 1; Langford, "Black Minority," 6. Abner Weed sold his interest in the Weed Lumber Company to Long-Bell in 1905.

22. See, for example, Parker, "Motives in Economic Life," 213; McClelland, *R. A. Long's Planned City*, 212; and Robbins, *Hard Times in Paradise*, 57. Some still regard the wood products industry's labor force as mostly unskilled; for example, see Amsden, "'De-Skilling,'" 334.

23. Niklason, *Commercial Survey*, 301; Howard, *Negro in the Lumber Industry*, 10. In 1919, capital per wage earner was $3,826 in California and $2,717 in Louisiana. Bureau of the Census, *Fourteenth Census*, 466–67, table 74.

24. Howd, *Industrial Relations*, 46–47.

25. "Labor Unrest in the Lumber Industry," 796; Shoup, *Speed, Power, Production, and Profit*, 65; McClelland, *R. A. Long's Planned City*, 7; Bradley, *Robert Alexander Long*, 129–30; Parker, "California Casual," 118–19; Legge, "Sanitation of Logging Camps," 49–50; Silcox, "Forestry and Labor," 317; Kirkland, "Effects of Destructive Lumbering," 318.

26. Kirkland, "Effects of Destructive Lumbering," 318–19; McClelland, *R.A. Long's Planned City*, 40; Myrdal, *Negro Social Structure*, 1090–96; Greene and Woodson, *Negro Wage Earner*, 126–27; Todes, *Labor and Lumber*, 83–84; Weed Bicentennial Committee, *Weed*, 21; Langford, "Black Minority," 9; Wesley Vandercook, Chief Engineer, Long-Bell Lumber Co., quoted in McClelland, *R.A. Long's Planned City*, 6.

The history of the southern lumber industry furnishes two important exceptions to this generalization: the IWW "Lumber Wars" of Louisiana and east Texas in 1910–13, and the efforts of the Timber Workers in eastern Louisiana in 1919. Interestingly, the "Lumber Wars" took place in the region from which Long-Bell brought many black workers. Although it is safe to assume that none of those who were came to Weed were labor radicals, it is notable that many of those who did come would have been witness to the violent and successful suppression of efforts to organize across the color line. See Jensen, *Lumber and*

Labor, 71–89; Green, "Brotherhood of Timber Workers"; Roediger, *Towards the Abolition of Whiteness,* 127–80; and Norwood, "Bogalusa Burning."

27. Bradley, *Robert Alexander Long,* 124; Shoup, *Speed, Power, Production, and Profit,* 72; Weed, "Weed," 41–42; *SN,* 4 August 1921, 1. On the frequency with which this strategy was used at the time, see Spero and Harris, *Black Worker,* 155.

28. *SH,* 14 April 1921, 1.

29. The Long-Bell executive was "closely connected" to the Southern Lumber Operators' Association, an organization that frequently used violence to achieve "its single obsessive purpose—the elimination of labor organizations from the southern lumber region." See Bradley, *Robert Alexander Long,* 67–72; Fickle, "Management Looks at the 'Labor Problem,'" 62–63; Todes, *Labor and Lumber,* 149–50, 172; McClelland, *R. A. Long's Planned City,* 210; and Weed, "Weed," 30.

30. Statistics from National Bureau of Economic Research, Macrohistory Series, U.S. Index of Wholesale Prices Of Lumber.

31. *SH,* 5 May 1921, 1; Todes, *Labor and Lumber,* 31–33; *SH,* 20 March 1922, 4.

32. *SN,* 9 December 1920, 3; *SH,* 6 January 1921, 1.

33. *SH,* 7 April 1921, 1; 5 May 1921, 1.

34. *SH,* 2 January 1922, 1.

35. *YJ,* 1 February 1922, 6; 25 January 1922, 2.

36. *SB,* 1 March 1922, 8; *KFEH,* 24 February 1922, 1.

37. *OLP,* 3 March 1922, 1; *SB,* 2 March 1922, 14; *KFEH,* 6 March 1922, 1; *SN,* 2 March 1922, 6; *SH,* 2 March 1922, 1; *KFEH,* 7 March 1922, 1; *SB,* 7 March 1922, 1. The reported number of Weed strikers varied considerably. In the labor press, it was as high as twelve hundred; *SUR,* 6 March 1922, 1.

38. *SB,* 31 March 1922, 14; *KFEH,* 8 March 1922, 1; *SB,* 8 March 1922, 9; *SUR,* 16 March 1922, 1; *YJ,* 23 March 1922, 1.

39. *SN,* 23 March 1922, 7; *SH,* 30 March 1922, 3; 13 April 1922, 5; *SUR,* 25 March 1922, 1; *KFEH,* 7 April 1922, 1; *SB,* 30 March 1922, 10; *YJ,* 22 March 1922, 2; 5 April 1922, 3; 19 April 1922, 7; *KFEH,* 20 April 1922, 1; 22 April 1922, 1; 28 April 1922, 1; *SH,* 27 April 1922, 1; *YJ,* 3 May 1922, 4.

40. *SB,* 10 March 1922, 24; 29 March 1922, 9; *KFEH,* 5 April 1922, 1; 7 March 1922, 1; 28 March 1922, 2; *YJ,* 3 May 1922, 4; *SB,* 7 March 1922, 12. Without the benefit of a company town structure, and faced with the Board of Conciliation's decision in the union's favor (rejected by employers), operators were not able to resolve the strike in Klamath Falls as quickly as in Weed, and it continued into midsummer (*OLP,* 23 June 1922, 3).

41. *OLP,* 7 April 1922, 1; Harry W. Call, "Lumber Trust Has Driven Wages Down to Minimum," *SUR,* 7 March 1922, 2; *OLP,* 10 March 1922, 1.

42. Weed Bicentennial Committee, *Weed,* 21; Langford, "Black Minority," 9; McClelland, *R. A. Long's Planned City,* 6, 12, 40.

43. To label this system "Jim Crow" is perhaps inappropriate in light of the specifically southern origins and practices that constituted that mode of domi-

nation. The everyday "separateness" experienced by blacks in Weed, however, would probably have appeared very similar to the contemporary observer.

44. McClelland, *R. A. Long's Planned City*, 7.

45. Saxton, *Indispensable Enemy*, 7–8, 271; Almaguer, *Racial Faultlines*, 201–3.

46. Bradley, *Robert Alexander Long*, 67–68.

47. *OLP*, 21 April 1922, 1; *SB*, 16 May 1922, 10.

48. *YJ*, 11 April 1923, 7.

49. Saxton, *Rise and Fall of the White Republic*; Roediger, *Wages of Whiteness*.

50. Sam Catalano, conversation with author, Weed, Calif., August 2001. Aware of Eric Arnesen's attack on the whiteness literature, I like to think that this chapter goes some small way toward addressing those aspects of his polemic that are well founded. See Arnesen, "Whiteness and the Historians' Imagination."

51. McClelland, *R. A. Long's Planned City*, 40; Robbins, *Hard Times in Paradise*, 57; Parker, "Motives in Economic Life," 213; Parker, "California Casual," 118; Kirkland, "Effects of Destructive Lumbering," 319–20.

52. Howd, *Industrial Relations*, 51–52.

53. Roediger, *Towards the Abolition of Whiteness*, 137.

54. Du Bois, *Black Reconstruction*, 700. Arnesen's convincing critique of the ways in which the whiteness literature has leaned uncritically on this passage from Du Bois is apposite here. Reading elsewhere, Arnesen points out that Du Bois also says (in Arnesen's paraphrase), "[W]hat capital offered, white organized labor knowingly accepted. . . . Here, the wages of whiteness came in the form of . . . well, conventional wages and access to jobs." Point well taken; the "psychological wage" is rarely, if ever, sufficient on its own; it virtually always demands a "material" complement, as Gramsci, writing at the same time as Du Bois, frequently said (see chapter 6). Moreover, as Arnesen remarks, it is often assumed that the "psychological" portion of the "public and psychological wage" is primarily a mode of compensation for the presumably otherwise inevitable unity of the working class. That this unity is by no means inevitable is another key contribution. The limits of Arnesen's critique become visible, however, in his claim that this dramatic irony is somehow unbeknownst to whiteness scholars like David Roediger or George Lipsitz. Arnesen's apparently antitheoretical bent leads him to forget that the larger historical question in the whiteness literature is not what he glosses as "why did white workers refuse to make common cause with their black counterparts?" It is, rather, "what forms do the articulation of race and class take in the United States?" These questions are not the same. The whiteness literature is no more mired in teleological naïveté than is labor history in general, and the best of it is well aware that "common cause" is not a "natural" proletarian equilibrium that has somehow been disturbed. But acknowledging the fact that there is no reason to hold our breath until class trumps race, or until workers get it together and act in their "objective interests," is no substitute for an engagement with the question of the forms in which racisms and class politics have interacted. Labor history's traditionally empiricist, undertheorized answers

to that question have not gotten us very far, especially if the ultimate goal is to construct what will be a history of a relatively emancipatory future. The whiteness literature's willingness to stick its neck out, to suggest creative explanations for dynamics like the "pleasure" or "status" of whiteness, seems to me one of its signal merits. Castigating creative theoretical risk taking seems entirely counterproductive, a reactionary act of disciplinary policing. See Arnesen, "Whiteness," 9–13; Roediger, *Wages of Whiteness*; Lipsitz, *Possessive Investment in Whiteness*.

55. Indeed, although it took many years, job segregation in Weed was ultimately largely overcome by local African American workers.

56. Langford, "Black Minority," 19, quoted in McClelland, *R. A. Long's Planned City*, 212.

57. For a similar conception of the genesis and reproduction of white supremacy both at the point of production and within the broader social sphere, see Almaguer, *Racial Faultlines*.

58. *SN*, 21 April 1921, 1; 20 July 1922, 1; *YJ*, 8 October 1922, 8; *SH*, 17 November 1921, 5.

59. *YJ*, 13 December 1922, Suppl., 2; 9 May 1923, 2; 23 May 1923, 2; *SH*, 16 February 1922, 1; 16 February 1922, 1; *YJ*, 15 February 1922, 6.

60. *YJ*, 23 May 1923, 2; 28 February 1923, 2; 13 June 1923, 4; 11 April 1923, 7; 7 March 1923, 7; 13 December 1922, 2.

61. *SN*, 12 April 1917, 8; 16 March 1922, 1; 1 March 1923, 4. Minstrelsy proves a fascinating window on the cultural politics of the white working class in the late nineteenth and early twentieth centuries and mediates an extraordinarily complex relationship between black and white Americans, a complexity I forgo here. For seminal accounts, see Saxton, *Rise and Fall of the White Republic*, 165–82; Roediger, *Wages of Whiteness*, 115–31; and Lott's brilliant *Love and Theft*.

62. *SN*, 15 December 1921, 2; quoted in Langford, "Black Minority," 15; *YJ*, 24 September 1924, 5; *SDN*, 18 September 1924, 1; *SN*, 4 September 1924, 1. See Lay, *Invisible Empire in the West*.

63. *SH*, 6 March 1922, 1.

64. *YJ*, 15 March 1922, 2.

65. *YJ*, 7 March 1923, 7. Although they constituted a much smaller part of the local population, Mexican workers were also targeted.

66. Roediger, *Towards the Abolition of Whiteness*, 135, 152, emphasis in original.

67. Saxton, *Rise and Fall of the White Republic*, 6–8; Holt, "Marking," 4–5.

68. Marshall, *Elements of Economics of Industry*, 140.

69. Moynihan, *Negro Family*; Becker, *Economics of Discrimination*; Sowell, *Race and Economics*; Herrnstein and Murray, *Bell Curve*. See also Orlando Patterson's opinion piece "A Poverty of the Mind" in the *New York Times* of 26 March 2006.

70. Milkman, *Gender at Work*, 59–60.

71. For example, Greene and Woodson, *Negro Wage Earner*, 125.

72. Spero and Harris, *Black Worker*, 169–71. Such accounts are numerous. See, for example, Feldman, *Racial Factors*, 41–42.

73. Marshall, *Negro and Organized Labor*, 145.

74. Starobin, *Industrial Slavery in the Old South*; Spero and Harris, *Black Worker*, 149, 160, 169.

75. Spero and Harris, *Black Worker*, 56. For compelling analyses of this process, see Saxton, *Rise and Fall of the White Republic*; Roediger, *Wages of Whiteness*; Almaguer, *Racial Faultlines*.

76. Spero and Harris, *Black Worker*, 158. See also Storper and Walker, *Capitalist Imperative*.

77. Baron, "Demand for Black Labor," 33–40.

78. These claims became very useful for southern politicians and businessmen, especially during the New Deal. They succeeded in having regional wage differences built into the industrial codes of the National Recovery Administration in 1933–34, tried unsuccessfully to obtain the same concessions in the 1938 Fair Labor Standards Act (but did obtain agricultural exemption), and structured the Agricultural Adjustment Administration so as to dispossess African American farmers, consequently subsidizing the costs of urban/industrial labor in the post–World War II era. Craft-union complicity in these and other maneuvers exacerbated the problems. For a detailed contemporary account of the practices of the 1920s, see Feldman, *Racial Factors*, 11–77.

79. Greene, "Economic Conditions of Negroes in the South," 266.

80. Greene and Woodson, *Negro Wage Earner*, 125; Feldman, *Racial Factors*, 34; Spero and Harris, *Black Worker*, 155.

81. Blackburn, *Making of New World Slavery*, 12.

82. Ibid., 22; Feldman, *Racial Factors*, 53–55. The eagerness for virtually any job in the North (and, to a lesser extent, the West) is amply demonstrated by the thousands of letters of inquiry black workers sent employers and labor recruiters in the 1910s. See Scott, "Letters of Negro Migrants."

83. Dublin, "Life, Death and the Negro," 44.

84. On workers' confidence, see Scott, "Letters of Negro Migrants"; on sectoral or factory dominance, see Greene and Woodson, *Negro Wage Earner*, 316–36.

85. Ellison, *Shadow and Act*, 303–17; Spero and Harris, *Black Worker*, 63. Garvey encouraged African Americans to keep their wage demands one step lower than whites' until they could move out of wage dependence (Spero and Harris, *Black Worker*, 135–36).

86. Dobb, *Wages*, 140–41, 144.

87. Milkman, *Gender at Work*.

88. Shoup, *Speed, Power, Production, and Profit*, 83.

89. *YJ*, 12 July 1922, 5.

90. Shoup, *Speed, Power, Production, and Profit*, 66.

91. Linville, "Union," 81.

92. Schwantes, "Concept of the Wageworkers' Frontier."

Chapter Five

1. Foner, *Reconstruction*, 104; Mandle, *Not Slave, Not Free*, 14–15; Mandle, *Roots of Black Poverty*, 44–47.

2. Slichter, "Revision of the Taft-Hartley Act," 168.

3. The same can be said of the stereotype of small owner-operators in analogous industries like farming and truck driving.

4. In addition, a discussion of the IFAWA demands a reexamination of the dominant assumptions about the context of union organization and the range of organizational forms considered in the literature on common-property natural resource management. In an earlier version of this chapter, I show that both prove to be excessively narrow. I also suggest that common-property fisheries management efforts reflected the geographic specificity of that class consciousness. For a fuller consideration, see Mann, "Class Consciousness and Common Property." Moreover, as I argue in what follows, a geographically dispersed trade unionism among "worker-producers" calls attention to class consciousness—both "cultural" and "strategic"—among smallholders.

5. Marglin, *Growth*, 64.

6. Mann and Dickinson, "Obstacles to the Development of a Capitalist Agriculture," 468; de Janvry, *Agrarian Question*, 187.

7. This conception of the dialectic is perhaps most closely associated with Theodor Adorno. See his *Negative Dialectics* and Fredric Jameson's brilliant exegetical work in *Late Marxism*.

8. *IFAWA Views the News*, December 1942, 10.

9. Federated Fishermen's Council, Minutes of Executive Committee, IFAWA Papers, Bancroft.

10. The United Fishermen's Union (UFU) was created by the Salmon Purse Seiners' Union (of Puget Sound), the Deep Sea and Purse Seine Fishermen's Union of California, and the Herring Fishermen's Union. The non-UFU unions were the Copper River and Prince William Sound Fishermen's Union, the CRFPU, and the Alaska Fishermen's Union (*IFAWA Views the News*, December 1942, 10).

11. Stevens and Knight, *Homer Stevens*, 84; Randall, "Labor Agreements," 526. Beachmen were those working anywhere but in the canneries or on the boats. Although gender is not a focus of this chapter and deserves a more complete investigation, it should be mentioned that the "industrial" nature of the union did bring women cannery workers into the membership, but neither like the numbers in rival unions nor to the extent that the IFAWA hoped. See Ruiz, *Cannery Women, Cannery Lives*, and Davis, "Sardine Oil on Troubled Waters."

12. For example, union locals could discriminate in the allocation of resources so that residents were primary beneficiaries of local contract agreements. See subsection 2(i) of Contract #6 between the Alaska Salmon Industries and the Alaska Fishermen's Union, IFAWA Papers, Bancroft: "Misrepresentation: Non-resident fisherman posing as resident shall be reported to the Territorial Revenue Dept., and no company shall be permitted to hire such man as a fisherman." In

addition, subsections 17(c) and (d) afford Alaskan residents earlier payment at the season's end.

13. Proceedings of the First Annual Convention of the International Fishermen and Allied Workers of America (CIO), IFAWA Papers, ILWU, 3; *IFAWA News*, December 1942; Fish and Wildlife Service, *Fishery Statistics of the United States, 1942*, 149–50, 154, 201.

14. *IFAW*, July 1944, 3.

15. Calif. CIO–IFAWA, *Fisheries of California*, 20; Federal Trade Commission, *Report of the Federal Trade Commission on Distribution Methods and Costs*, 56.

16. Fish and Wildlife Service, *Fishery Statistics of the United States, 1949*, 186–87, 238.

17. *IFAWA Views the News*, 1 August 1941, 1.

18. *IFAWA News*, July/August 1943, 1. The ceilings for pilchard sardine were instituted at a later date.

19. *IFAW*, May 1944, 6; Jeff Kibre, "Price Stabilization—Key to Unity, Postwar Growth," *IFAW*, July 1944, 1–2.

20. *IFAW*, June 1944, 2; Kimeldorf, "World War II."

21. Senate Committee on Interstate and Foreign Commerce, *Fisheries Legislation: Hearings before the Senate Committee on Interstate and Foreign Commerce*, 84th Cong., 2nd sess., 10 October–5 December 1955, 302, table 2.

22. Minutes of the Coastwise Salmon Conference, IFAWA Papers, Bancroft, 3.

23. In its opposition to OPA and its increased organizational capacity following the termination of price controls, the IFAWA stands in stark contrast to virtually all other unions, as well as to CIO national policy. Labor organizations almost universally supported OPA and fought hard to save it in the months immediately following V-J day. This seemingly "conservative" stance, especially in combination with the fact that the IFAWA was expelled from the CIO for its "leftist" politics, further complicates the structure of fishers' working-class identity. On the politics of OPA, see Leff, "Politics of Sacrifice"; Jacobs, "'How about Some Meat?'"; Lichtenstein, "Class Politics"; and chapter 3 above.

24. Minutes of the Coastwise Bottom Fish Conference, 30 October 1946, IFAWA Papers, Bancroft, 2. During the war, the federal government bought 80 percent of Pacific salmon and sardine (Minutes of the Northwest Cannery Workers Conference, IFAWA Papers, Bancroft, 2).

25. Minutes of the Coastwise Conference on Bottom Fish, 14 March 1947, IFAWA Papers, Bancroft, 5–6; *Columbia River Packers Association, Inc. v. Hinton et al.*, 315 U.S. 143 (1942); *IFAWA Views the News*, September 1942; *IFAW*, May 1944, 5. Neither of these concerns was merely anticipatory. The California sardine fishery "failed" in the years immediately following the war, and in 1946 San Pedro fishers were convicted of collusion under the Clayton Act. See Pinsky and Ball, *California Sardine Fishery*, i–ii, and Proceedings Report of the Cordova Conference, both in IFAWA Papers, Bancroft.

26. Conservation concerns and the antitrust attack will be addressed in more

detail below. Among other things, the Taft-Hartley Act required all union leaders to sign affidavits that they were in no way affiliated with, or in support of, communism and the Communist Party.

27. Summary of Minutes of Conference of Northwest IFAWA Council, IFAWA Papers, Bancroft, 4.

28. Ibid.

29. *IFAW*, March 1949, 7. There were some whose opposition to the merger was sufficiently strong to leave the IFAWA. For example, some of the Alaska leadership formed the Alaska Independent Fisheries Federation one month after the decision to merge (Summary of Minutes of Conference of Northwest IFAWA Council, 4).

30. CIO decision, cited in Slichter, "Revision of the Taft-Hartley Act," 168.

31. Rosswurm, *CIO's Left-Led Unions*. The means through which the ILWU survived a similarly incessant red-baiting for decades before and after the CIO trials is a fascinating story. See, for example, Wellman, *Union Makes Us Strong*.

32. IFAWA Local 36, "Around Fishermen's Wharf," IFAWA Papers, ILWU.

33. Minutes of the Coastwise Fisheries Conference, IFAWA Papers, Bancroft.

34. Stevens and Knight, *Homer Stevens*, 84; *Local 36 of International Fishermen and Allied Workers of America et al. v. United States*, in Ben Margolis, attorney, to Jeff Kibre, secretary, IFAWA, 6 October 1949, IFAWA Papers, ILWU.

35. Federal Trade Commission, *Annual Reports*.

36. Stevens and Knight, *Homer Stevens*, 86.

37. Jeff Kibre, Washington representative of the ILWU, to Senator Frederick Payne, 17 July 1958, in Senate Committee on Interstate and Foreign Commerce, *Fisheries Legislation: Hearing before the Committee on Interstate and Foreign Commerce*, 85th Cong., 2nd sess., 15–17 July 1958, 276.

38. Crutchfield, "Collective Bargaining in the Pacific Coast Fisheries," 548; Vrana, conversation with author.

39. In addition, it is possible that the IFAWA also had difficulty maintaining autonomy and focus within the ILWU. On the surface, the ILWU's organizational goals did not conflict with the those of the IFAWA, but it is also reasonable to expect that the interests of the wider ILWU membership would overshadow those of fishers and fisheries workers.

40. For a detailed differentiation of these statuses, see Randall, "Labor Agreements," 516–25.

41. Federal Trade Commission, *Report of the Federal Trade Commission on Distribution Methods and Costs*, 1; Fish and Wildlife Service, *Fishery Statistics, 1942*, 149–50, 201, and annually to *Fishery Statistics, 1957*, 250, 342.

42. Fish and Wildlife Service, *Fishery Statistics, 1942*, 154, 201, and annually to *Fishery Statistics, 1957*, 256, 342.

43. Senate Subcommittee on Merchant Marine and Fisheries, *Fisheries Legislation: Hearings before the Senate Committee on Commerce*, 113–15.

44. Federal Trade Commission, *Report of the Federal Trade Commission on Distribution Methods and Costs*, 34.

45. McEvoy, *Fisherman's Problem*, 95–100, 172–73.

46. See, for example, Peterson, "Fisherman and a Whaler," 47; Ghio and Ghio, "Fishermen by Trade," 45.

47. Calif. CIO–IFAWA, *Fisheries of California*, 19.

48. The effort to find a "fit" is exemplified by work like Erik Olin Wright's massive *Class Counts: Comparative Studies in Class Analysis*. This is not to say that Wright's efforts to reposition class in social science are unwelcome but that the theoretical and methodological means through which he and his fellow "analytical Marxists" go about doing so involves a rejection not only of Marx's own method and theory but of much that I would argue is most important about the Marxian tradition, i.e., the dialectic and its possibilities. In the end, all that remains is a loose commitment to a "market socialism" that, although perhaps "radical," is arguably pretty darn far from most things Marxian. An elegant attempt to deal with the problem theoretically can be found in Miriam Wells's still pertinent "What Is a Worker?"

49. De Janvry, *Agrarian Question*, 187.

50. For a review of this literature, see Mann, *Agrarian Capitalism in Theory and Practice*.

51. In accordance with common practice in the industrial relations literature, a union is here defined as "an organization of employees that has the function of pursuing their work-related interests by dealing with their employer on their behalf." Wheeler, *Industrial Conflict*, 5.

52. Ibid., 214.

53. It is slightly tempting to suggest that union organization is de facto representative of (emergent) working-class consciousness, but my historicist commitments get in the way of making the claim. For those who do try to make the case, and do so fairly convincingly, see (among others) Adamic, *Dynamite*, and Harvey, *Urban Experience*, 115–24. There is a related century-old debate on the reasons for the apparently inadequate organizational capacities of "peasants" and simple commodity producers throughout the world. See Marx, *Eighteenth Brumaire*; Lenin, *Development of Capitalism in Russia*; and, for more recent works, Wolf, *Peasant Wars of the Twentieth Century*, and Paige, *Agrarian Revolutions*.

54. Joe Jurich and Martin Hegeberg, "Forward with IFAWA," *IFAW*, July 1944, 3.

55. See, for example, Wells, "What Is a Worker?," and Davis, "Capitalist Agricultural Development."

56. Such a federation—the Pacific Coast Federation of Fishermen's Associations—now represents many Pacific coast small-boat fishers.

57. By "multigear," I mean that the IFAWA represented fishers from all major fishing techniques: trolling, longlining, seining, trawling, and gillnetting. Fishermen mostly use only one type of gear, and there can be considerable animosity among conflicting gear users.

58. Emirbayer and Goodwin, "Network Analysis, Culture, and the Problem of Agency," 1438.

59. Ibid., emphasis in original.

60. See McAdam, McCarthy, and Zald, *Comparative Perspectives on Social Movements*.

61. Some influential work in geography suggests that space should always play this critical part in analyses of capitalist societies' class structures. See Harvey, *Urban Experience*; Storper and Walker, *Capitalist Imperative*.

62. This is a case of what in the field of political ecology is often called the "constantly shifting dialectic" between society and the environment. The high quality of much of this work aside, however, I point this out mostly because the dialectic is so important to me in these pages, and the dialectic as political ecology has it is definitely not my dialectic. In fact, I would argue that it is not a dialectic at all in any meaningful sense of the concept but merely another way of saying "mutual constitution." It bears emphasis that this claim in no way contradicts my full agreement with political ecology's fundamental arguments that society and environment constantly reshape and constitute each other and that the line between them is a cultural artifact. It is just that what political ecology suggests is dialectical in these movements is dialectical only in the most bland, uninteresting meaning of the term (i.e., thesis-antithesis-synthesis). For a most helpful entry point into (and sensitive critique of) the field of political ecology, see McCarthy, "First World Political Ecology."

63. Harvey, *Urban Experience*, 112.

64. Ibid., 111.

65. "There is today an ever-present temptation to suppose that class is a thing. This was not Marx's meaning, in his own historical writing, yet the error vitiates much latter-day 'Marxist' writing" (Thompson, *Making of the English Working Class*, 9). "In the context of the capitalist mode of production . . . class has a more specific meaning that relates to the basic social relationships pertaining in capitalist society" (Harvey, *Urban Experience*, 111).

66. Thompson, *Making of the English Working Class*, 8–9.

67. McCay and Acheson, "Human Ecology and the Commons," 8, 34.

68. *IFAW*, July 1944, 3.

69. *IFAWA Views the News*, September 1942, 2.

70. Minutes of the Northwest Cannery Workers Conference, IFAWA Papers, Bancroft; 2. Minutes of the Coastwise Conference on Bottom Fish, 14 March 1947, 7.

71. For instance, the 1902 Alaska Fishermen's Union (AFU) strike at Nushagak River was part of the legendary past that IFAWA leadership frequently cited. The AFU threatened a tie-up (a fishers' strike, during which all boats stay in port) if the price per fish was not raised from two to three cents, and it was successful (*IFAWA News*, December 1942, 10).

72. Minutes of the Coastwise Conference on Bottom Fish, 14 March 1947, 1.

73. Columbia River Fishermen's Protective Union, "Constitution and By-laws."

74. *Fair Labor Standards Act*, 29 U.S.C. §213(a)(5).

75. Senator Frederick Payne, in Senate Committee on Interstate and Foreign Commerce, *Fisheries Legislation: Hearing before the Committee on Interstate and Foreign Commerce*, 1958, 101.

76. George Johansen to Senator Warren Magnuson, 9 July 1958, in Senate Committee on Interstate and Foreign Commerce, *Fisheries Legislation: Hearing before the Committee on Interstate and Foreign Commerce*, 1958, 276.

77. *IFAW*, June 1945.

78. *IFAW*, May 1945, 6.

79. Minutes of the Coastwise Conference on Bottom Fish, 14 March 1947, 5.

80. *IFAW*, January 1945, 5.

81. Calif. CIO–IFAWA, *Fisheries of California*, 26.

82. Ibid., 21; testimony of Victor Turpin, in Senate Committee on Interstate and Foreign Commerce, *Fisheries Legislation: Hearing before the Committee on Interstate and Foreign Commerce*, 1958, 99.

83. For example, Contract #6 between the Alaska Salmon Industries and the Alaska Fishermen's Union, Section 14(a), IFAWA Papers, Bancroft.

84. For example, Contract #30 between the Alaska Salmon Industries and the Alaska Fishermen's Union, Section 12, IFAWA Papers, Bancroft.

85. Contract #6 (see n. 83 above), Sections 8, 13, 15, and 25; Contract #30 (see previous note), Section 6.

86. This credit relationship was very widespread (Department of Agriculture, Farmer's Cooperative Service, "Legal Series No. 1") and still holds in many fisheries today.

87. IFAWA Local 34, "Forward and Not Back," 1, IFAWA Papers, ILWU.

88. IFAWA members were not the only small producers to recognize this. Between the late 1940s and 1960s, farmers and fishers on both sides of the country tried to restructure their cooperatives as unions in light of their de facto status as "employees." See Department of Agriculture, Farmer's Cooperative Service, "Legal Series No. 1" and "Legal Series No. 12."

89. Columbia River Fishermen's Protective Union, "Constitution and By-laws."

90. Minutes of the Coastwise Bottomfish Conference, 30 October 1946, 2; Minutes of the Coastwise Conference on Bottomfish, 14–15 March 1947, 2, both in IFAWA Papers, Bancroft.

91. Notably, David Harvey has produced a great deal of work arguing that this is true of all capitalism. For example, see Harvey, *Urban Experience*.

92. See, for example, McWilliams, *California*, or Stegner, *Joe Hill*.

93. Laclau, *Emancipation(s)*, chap. 2.

94. *Columbia River Packers Association, Inc. v. Hinton et al.*, 34 F.Supp. 970 (1939). The first time the Ninth Circuit heard the case, it found in the IFAWA's favor (*Columbia River Packers Association, Inc. v. Hinton et al.*, 117 F.2d 310 [1941]). The Supreme Court reversed this decision for reconsideration (*Columbia River Packers Association*, 315 U.S. 143), and it was finally decided by the

Ninth Circuit in October 1942 (*Hinton et al. v. Columbia River Packers Association, Inc.*, 131 F.2d 88).

95. *Columbia River Packers Association*, 315 U.S. at 145, 147.

96. *Hinton et al.*, 131 F.2d at 89.

97. *Local 36 of International Fishermen and Allied Workers of America et al. v. United States*, 177 F.2d 325 (1949).

98. Randall, "Labor Agreements," 522–25.

99. Calif. CIO–IFAWA, *Fisheries of California*, 30.

100. Stevens and Knight, *Homer Stevens*, 84–85; Calif. CIO–IFAWA, *Fisheries of California*, 35.

101. *Local 36 of International Fishermen and Allied Workers of America et al.*, 177 F.2d at 337.

102. Ibid., 329.

103. Calif. CIO–IFAWA, *Fisheries of California*, 30. The specificity, choice, and embodied skill in this labor contrast sharply with Marx's vision of the capitalist labor process and the sale of labor-power. The IFAWA never accused the dealers of forcing fishermen to fish; the "traditional" fishermen's identity that helped constitute fishing communities would mitigate against this claim.

104. Columbia River Fishermen's Protective Union, "Constitution and By-laws."

105. Calif. CIO–IFAWA, *Fisheries of California*, 35–36.

106. Senate Committee on Interstate and Foreign Commerce, *Pacific Coast and Alaska Fisheries: Hearings before Committee on Interstate and Foreign Commerce*, 50, 52.

107. *United States v. Local 36 of International Fishermen and Allied Workers of America*, 70 F.Supp. 784 (1947).

108. Ibid., 783. The inclusion of "Negroes" in this list is very interesting. Although (to my knowledge) there were no African American members of the IFAWA, the assumption that black Americans would be sympathetic to white unionists' cause deserves further examination, especially after Marcus Garvey. Garvey argued that black workers had—at least in the short term—an ally in white capitalists, whose profit orientation would lead them to destroy the racial exclusion practiced by most white unions. He encouraged black workers to actively undercut white wages until they had sufficient power in the workforce to press for better wages. See the limited remarks in chapter 4 on African American opposition to organization by white unions.

109. Historians have long debated the extent to which organized labor acquiesced to the "national interest" during World War II. It is evident that unions made considerable gains during the war years—particularly in membership—in spite of, or perhaps because of, their vocal commitment to industrial peace. This issue is considered in a little more detail in chapter 3.

110. *IFAWA Views the News*, 1 August 1941. On the secretary of the navy's take over of U.S. oil refineries, see chapter 3.

111. There are occasional comments in the IFAWA's correspondence refer-

ring to similar efforts to disable agricultural cooperatives (see, for example, Proceedings Report of the Cordova Conference, IFAWA Papers, Bancroft).

112. Kimeldorf, "World War II," 248–50; Schrecker, *Many Are the Crimes*.

113. *Local 36 of International Fishermen and Allied Workers of America*, 177 F.2d at 340.

114. Quoted in Department of Agriculture, Farmer's Cooperative Service, "Legal Series No. 1," 4–5.

115. McCay, "Culture of the Commoners," 196. McCay also hints that in enforcing open access the state often enabled what is known as the "tragedy of the commons."

116. De Janvry, *Agrarian Question*, 187.

117. Ibid.

Chapter Six

1. I borrow the phrase "without guarantees" from Stuart Hall's justly famous essay "The Problem of Ideology: Marxism without Guarantees."

2. Sraffa was not only a friend and political supporter of Gramsci. He also provided vital intellectual resources to Gramsci while he was imprisoned, through letters and by giving him an open account at a bookstore. He helped secure the clandestine passage of Gramsci's notebooks out of fascist Italy after his death in April 1937. On the intimate relationship between Sraffa and Gramsci, see Boothman, "General Introduction," xvii–xx, xxxv–xxxviii; Fiori, *Antonio Gramsci*, 261; Sen, "Sraffa, Wittgenstein, and Gramsci." There is an extensive literature on the Sraffa-Gramsci friendship that unfortunately remains untranslated from the Italian and on which I am therefore sadly unable to comment.

3. Gramsci, *Prison Notebooks*, 161.

4. Influential examples include Anderson, "Antinomies of Antonio Gramsci," and Althusser, *Lenin and Philosophy*, 127–86.

5. Gramsci, *Prison Notebooks*, 310, 303.

6. Ibid., 311.

7. Przeworski, *Capitalism and Social Democracy*, 67.

8. Ibid., 136; Gramsci, *Prison Notebooks*, 285.

9. Przeworski, *Capitalism and Social Democracy*, 148–50.

10. Ibid., 92–97. Przeworski's universalizing rational choice commitments are no longer merely afterthought: see his *States and Markets*, a highly formalized argument for a constrained optimization principal-agent approach to political economy.

11. I refer to the fact that for Przeworski race is an ahistorical, individual trait, not a historically particular product of the politics of culture that are crucial to this discussion: "It may be that blacks and whites do not cooperate as workers because it is rational for capitalists to divide and rule, but it still remains that they do not cooperate because they are black and white. Segmented labor markets imply different structures of choice for people with different individual endowments, and segmented labor markets breed disunity among those who

become workers" (*Capitalism and Social Democracy*, 97). For him, then, either race is a (presumably social) "endowment," which in fact undermines a call for individualism in the study of labor market outcomes, or being black or white is an individual biological characteristic (as opposed to a culturally inscribed and historical category), which would suggest that there is no politics of culture. This is refutable.

12. Ibid., 149.

13. Gramsci, *Prison Notebooks*, 182.

14. Przeworski, *Capitalism and Social Democracy*, 83 n. 31.

15. Przeworski's recognition that a historically accurate understanding of the wage acknowledges that it might contain some of the profit, just as Sraffa suggested, is exemplary, and it again binds Gramsci and Sraffa.

16. Gramsci, *Prison Notebooks*, 327.

17. Przeworski, *Capitalism and Social Democracy*, 147.

18. For example, McWilliams, *California*, 128–30. On "conflict consciousness," see Giddens, *Class Structure*, 202.

19. For example, Walker, "California's Golden Road," 180.

20. William S. Hallagan, "Labor Contracting in Turn-of-the-Century California Agriculture"; Cross, *History of the Labor Movement in California*; Schwantes, "Concept of the Wageworkers' Frontier"; Saxton, *Indispensable Enemy*, 6–7, 167.

21. Walker, "California's Golden Road."

22. Przeworski, *Capitalism and Social Democracy*, 3.

23. Bourdieu, *Distinction*, chap. 7; Okun, *Equality and Efficiency*, 49; Bénabou and Ok, "Social Mobility and the Demand for Redistribution"; Sennett and Cobb, *Hidden Injuries of Class*, 258.

24. Giddens, *Class Structure*, 202.

25. A very readable example is Frank's *What's the Matter with Kansas?*

26. Laclau and Mouffe, *Hegemony and Socialist Strategy*; Reddy, *Money and Liberty in Modern Europe*.

27. Laclau and Mouffe, *Hegemony and Socialist Strategy*, 83–84.

28. Hirschman, *The Passions and the Interests*, 32. My account, at its most general, is broadly consistent with Laclau and Mouffe's elaboration of interests in their acid response ("Post-Marxism without Apologies") to Norman Geras's no-holds-barred attack on *Hegemony and Socialist Strategy*. There, they argue: "*There are* interests, but these are precarious historical products which are always subjected to processes of dissolution and redefinition. What there are not, however, are *objective* interests, in the sense in which they are postulated in the 'false consciousness' approach" (97, emphasis in original). I concur but try to historicize the content *and* the concept of interests; in other words I wonder why the historical fact of capitalism as mode of production, and the foundational cleavage of class, necessarily must recede from view here.

29. (a) Laclau and Mouffe, *Hegemony and Socialist Strategy*; (b) Hall, "Cannery Row"; (c) Derrida, *Negotiations*, 169.

30. Deleuze and Guattari, *Anti-Oedipus*, 348–49, 378–79; cf. Laclau, *Politics and Ideology in Marxist Theory*, 160.

31. Indeed, Laclau and Mouffe found a large part of their argument for "post"-Marxism on the claim that we are "post"-class; see *Hegemony and Socialist Strategy*, 85–87; Laclau and Mouffe, "Post-Marxism without Apologies."

32. Thompson, *Making of the English Working Class*, 8.

33. Jameson, *Postmodernism*, 345.

34. Althusser, *Lenin and Philosophy*; Judith Butler, *Psychic Life of Power*, 107.

35. Lukács, *History and Class Consciousness*, 186, emphasis in original.

36. Marx, *Grundrisse*, 83.

37. Not just Marx and Hegel, certainly, but also many others working the Marxian vein, among them Rosa Luxemburg, Georg Lukács, Antonio Gramsci, Theodor Adorno, Lucien Goldmann, and Fredric Jameson.

38. On the dialectic as descriptive, see Taylor, *Hegel*, 129.

39. Lukács, *History and Class Consciousness*, 204, 206.

Conclusion

1. Willis, *Learning to Labor*, 138–39 n. 4.

2. Postone, *Time, Labor, and Social Domination*, 6.

3. Adorno, *Minima Moralia*, 120. The entry from which these words are drawn (#77, *Auction*) is far more subtle than I can register here. It renders the ironic combination of anger and surrender in Adorno's hopeful pessimism as well as anything else I have read.

4. Quoted in Jameson, *Late Marxism*, 78. (This is Jameson's own rendering of a passage worded differently in the only, and much maligned, English translation of Adorno's *Negative Dialectics*, 212.) For a brilliant and fascinating development of these thoughts, read Adorno's withering critique of the "vague and brutal commandment of clarity" in "Skoteinos, or How to Read Hegel," in *Hegel*, esp. 96–110.

5. Marx, *Grundrisse*, 85.

6. Bhaduri and Robinson, "Accumulation and Exploitation," 83, 89.

7. Reddy, *Money and Liberty in Modern Europe*, 32.

8. AFL-CIO, Legislation Department, "Raising the Minimum Wage," 10; AFL-CIO, Department of Economic Research, "America Needs a Raise."

9. For example, the Principles of Environmental Justice adopted by the First Peoples of Color Environmental Leadership Summit in 1991 contain no reference to inequitable distribution of the income from natural resource or other "environmental services." See <www.ejnet.org/ej/principles.html> (last accessed 2 January 2007).

10. For a compelling attempt to begin such a conversation, see Romm's "Coincidental Order of Environmental Injustice."

11. Marx, *Capital*, 1:769.

12. Hall, "Problem of Ideology," 38–39.

13. Adorno, *Can One Live after Auschwitz?*, 103.

Bibliography

Archival Sources

Berkeley, California
   University of California
      Bancroft Library, Papers of the International Fishermen and Allied
         Workers Union
         Alaska Salmon Industries–Alaska Fishermen's Union Contract #6,
            Bristol Bay General Agreement, 11 June 1949
         Alaska Salmon Industries–Alaska Fishermen's Union Contract #30,
            1949
         Bottom Fisheries Conference, Astoria, Oreg., 15 September 1948
         Federated Fishermen's Council, Minutes of Executive Committee,
            Seattle, Wash., 31 January 1938
         Minutes of the Coastwise Bottomfish Conference, Seattle, Wash., 30
            October 1946
         Minutes of the Coastwise Conference on Bottomfish, Seattle, Wash.,
            14–15 March 1947
         Minutes of the Coastwise Fisheries Conference, Seattle, Wash., 9 April
            1952
         Minutes of the Coastwise Salmon Conference, Eureka, Calif., 22
            August 1946
         Minutes of the Conference on Bottomfish, Astoria, Oreg., 22 March
            1949
         Minutes of the Northwest Cannery Workers Conference, Seattle,
            Wash., 7 December 1946
         Paul Pinsky and Wayne Ball, *The California Sardine Fishery: Review
            of the Biological, Statistical and Environmental Information about the
            California Sardine* (San Pedro, Calif., 1948)
         Proceedings Report of the Cordova Conference, Cordova, Alaska,
            25–27 October 1947
         Summary of Minutes of Conference of Northwest IFAWA Council,
            Seattle, Wash., 27 May 1950
         Lee Tulin, "Digest of California Criminal Syndicalism Cases,"
            unpublished manuscript, University of Michigan, 1926

Doe Library
Columbia River Fishermen's Protective Union, "Constitution and
Bylaws of the Columbia River Fishermen's Protective Union,"
preamble (Astoria, Oreg., n.d.)

National War Labor Board, "Wage Report to the President on the
Wartime Relationship of Wages to the Cost of Living," mimeo, 22
February 1945

U.S. Department of Labor, Bureau of Labor Statistics, "Cost of
Living Adjustment Clauses (Escalator Clauses)," mimeo, 1948

U.S. Department of Labor, Bureau of Labor Statistics, "Indexes of
Primary Market Prices for Petroleum and Products 1935–45,
Inclusive," mimeo, 1950

U.S. Department of Labor, Bureau of Labor Statistics, "Primary
Market Prices and Indexes for Petroleum and Products," mimeo,
1950

U.S. Department of Labor, Bureau of Labor Statistics, "Workers'
Experiences during the First Phase of Reconversion," mimeo, 1946

U.S. Department of Labor, Oil Panel, "Oil Panel Report and
Recommendations to the Secretary of Labor," mimeo, 1946
Boulder, Colorado
University of Colorado, Norlin Library Archives, Records of Local #1-128,
Oil Workers International Union

Series 1, box 21

Folder 3: Minutes, District Council #1, OWIU-CIO, Bakersfield
Calif., 3 July 1943

Folder 4: Minutes, District Council #1, OWIU-CIO, Bakersfield
Calif., 6–7 October 1944

Folder 5: Minutes, District Council #1, OWIU-CIO, Bakersfield
Calif., 5–6 January 1945, 4–5 May 1945, 6–7 July 1945

Folder 6: Minutes, District Council #1, OWIU-CIO, Bakersfield
Calif., 1–2 February 1946

Folder 9: Minutes, District Council #1, OWIU-CIO, Bakersfield
Calif., 25–26 March 1949

Series 2, box 43

Folder 14: NWLB Case No. 111-15635 (10-D-936)

Folder 18: Shell Chemical Wage Schedule

Folder 20: Minutes of Shell Wage Conference, 19 March 1945

Series 2, box 59

Folder 19: Union Oil Co. Negotiations, Request by Los Angeles
Refinery Paint Shop

Folder 43: Committee Report: Employment of Women at L.A.
Refinery, Union Oil Unit, 28 October 1942

Folder 45: Telegram, O. A. Knight to C. E. Fredericks, 5 October
1945; Union Oil Co.—OWIU Negotiations, 12 November 1945

Series 4, box 1
>Folder 19: Minutes, Local 128 Meetings of 12 June 1944, 27
November 1944
>Folder 20: Resolutions by Local 128 for Delegation to International
Convention, 14 September 1945, 16 September 1946, 1 October
1945
>Folder 22: Minutes, Weekly Meeting, 29 September 1947
Series 4, box 3
>Folder 65: Minutes, Shell Adjustment Committee, 12 December 1942;
Minutes, Continental Unit Meeting, 20 November 1946
Series 4, box 10
>Folder 67: Minutes, Shell Chemical Unit Meeting, 11 February
1944
Ithaca, New York
>Cornell University, Kheel Center for Labor-Management Documentation
and Archives, Collection 5092, box 1
>Union's Brief and Statements, In the Matter of: Ashland Oil and Refining
Co. et al. and Oil Workers International Union, CIO, 17 December
1945
San Francisco, California
>International Longshore and Warehouse Union Library, Collected Papers of
the International Fishermen and Allied Workers Union
>IFAWA Local 34, "Forward and Not Back: A Fighting Program for
California Fishermen" (San Francisco, n.d.)
>IFAWA Local 36, "Around Fishermen's Wharf" (San Pedro Calif., 6 June
1950)
>Ben Margolis, attorney, letter to Jeff Kibre, secretary, IFAWA, 6 October
1949
>Proceedings of the First Annual Convention of the International
Fishermen and Allied Workers of America (CIO), Bellingham
Wash., 4–8 December 1939

Court Cases

Columbia River Packers Association, Inc. v. Hinton et al., 34 F.Supp. 970
(1939)
Columbia River Packers Association, Inc. v. Hinton et al., 117 F.2d 310 (1941)
Columbia River Packers Association, Inc. v. Hinton et al., 315 U.S. 143 (1942)
Hinton et al. v. Columbia River Packers Association, Inc., 131 F.2d 88 (1942)
Local 36 of International Fishermen and Allied Workers of America et al. v. United
States, 177 F.2d 325 (1949)
United States v. Local 36 of International Fishermen and Allied Workers of America,
70 F.Supp. 784 (1947)

Periodicals

California Labor Market Bulletin (published by the California Department of
Industrial Relations, Division of Labor Statistics and Law Enforcement)
210–57 (Monthly 1942–46)

IFAWA News (Seattle, Wash.), 1942–43

IFAWA Views the News (Seattle, Wash.), 1941–42

International Fisherman and Allied Worker (San Francisco, Calif.), 1944–48

International Oil Worker (Denver, Colo.), 1945–48

Klamath Falls Evening Herald (Klamath Falls, Oreg.), 1922

Labor Herald (published by California CIO, San Francisco, Calif.), 1945

Los Angeles Times, 1945–48

The Militant (New York City), 1946

Mount Shasta Herald & Sisson Headlight (Sisson, Calif.), 1922–23

The Nation, 1945–46

National Petroleum News (published by American Petroleum Institute), 1945

New York Times, 1946

Oregon Labor Press (Portland, Oreg.), 1922

Sacramento Bee (Sacramento, Calif.), 1922

Seattle Union Record, 1922

Siskiyou Daily News (Yreka, Calif.), 1924

Siskiyou News (renamed *Siskiyou Daily News* in 1924; Yreka, Calif.), 1917–24

Sisson Headlight (renamed *Mount Shasta Herald & Sisson Headlight* in 1922;
Sisson, Calif.), 1921–22

Yreka Journal (Yreka, Calif.), 1918–24

Secondary Sources

Adamic, Louis. *Dynamite: The Story of Class Violence in America*. New York:
Viking Press, 1934.

Adorno, Theodor. *Can One Live after Auschwitz? A Philosophical Reader*. Edited
by Rolf Tiedemann. Stanford, Calif.: Stanford University Press, 2003.

———. *Hegel: Three Studies*. Translated by Shierry Weber Nicholsen.
Cambridge, Mass.: MIT Press, 1999.

———. *Minima Moralia*. Translated by E. F. N. Jephcott. London: Verso,
1974.

———. *Negative Dialectics*. Translated by E. B. Ashton. London: Continuum,
1973.

AFL-CIO, Department of Economic Research. "America Needs a Raise."
Cornell University School of Industrial and Labor Relations Associations
and Institutes, Paper 1, February 1996. <http://digitalcommons.ilr.cornell.
edu/institutes/1>.

———, Legislation Department. "Raising the Minimum Wage: Talking Points
and Background." May 2006.

Aglietta, Michel. *A Theory of Capitalist Regulation: The US Experience*. Translated
by David Fernbach. London: NLB, 1979.

Akerlof, George A. "Gift-Exchange and Efficiency-Wage Theory: Four Views."
    American Economic Review 74, no. 2 (1984): 79–83.
———. "Labor Contracts as Partial Gift Exchange." *Quarterly Journal of
    Economics* 97, no. 4 (1982): 543–69.
Alchian, Armen A., and Harold Demsetz. "Production, Information Costs,
    and Economic Organization." *American Economic Review* 62, no. 5 (1972):
    777–95.
Allmendinger, Blake. *Imagining the African American West.* Lincoln: University
    of Nebraska Press, 2005.
Almaguer, Tomás. *Racial Faultlines: The Historical Origins of White Supremacy in
    California.* Berkeley: University of California Press, 2004.
Althusser, Louis. *For Marx.* Translated by Ben Brewster. New York: Verso,
    1969.
———. *Lenin and Philosophy and Other Essays.* Translated by Ben Brewster.
    New York: Monthly Review Press, 1971.
Althusser, Louis, and Étienne Balibar. *Reading Capital.* Translated by Ben
    Brewster. New York: Verso, 1970.
Amsden, Alice H. "'De-Skilling,' Skilled Commodities, and the NICs'
    Emerging Competitive Advantage." *American Economic Review* 73, no. 2
    (1983): 333–37.
Anderson, Perry. "The Antinomies of Antonio Gramsci." *New Left Review* 100
    (1976/77): 5–78.
Arnesen, Eric. "Whiteness and the Historians' Imagination." *International Labor
    and Working Class History* 60 (2001): 3–32.
Aronowitz, Stanley. *False Promises: The Shaping of American Working Class
    Consciousness.* Durham, N.C.: Duke University Press, 1992.
Asad, Talal. "Ethnographic Representation, Statistics, and Modern Power." In
    From the Margins: Historical Anthropology and Its Futures, edited by Brian K.
    Axel, 66–91. Durham, N.C.: Duke University Press, 2002.
Attali, Jacques. *Noise: The Political Economy of Music.* Translated by Brian
    Massumi. Minneapolis: University of Minnesota Press, 1985.
Auerbach, Paul, Meghnad Desai, and Ali Shamsavari. "The Transition from
    Actually Existing Capitalism." *New Left Review* 170 (1988): 61–78.
Bain, Joe S. *War and Postwar Developments in the Southern California Petroleum
    Industry.* Los Angeles: Haynes Foundation, 1944.
Banaji, Jairus. "From the Commodity to Capital: Hegel's Dialectic in Marx's
    Capital." In *Value: The Representation of Labour in Capitalism,* edited by
    Diane Elson, 14–45. Atlantic Highlands, N.J.: Humanities Press, 1979.
Baron, Harold M. "The Demand for Black Labor: Historical Notes on the
    Political Economy of Racism." In *Workers' Struggles, Past and Present: A
    Radical America Reader,* edited by James Green, 33–40. Philadelphia: Temple
    University Press, 1983.
Barrera, Mario. *Race and Class in the Southwest: A Theory of Racial Inequality.*
    Notre Dame, Ind.: University of Notre Dame Press, 1979.

Becker, Gary S. *The Economics of Discrimination.* 2nd ed. Chicago: University of Chicago Press, 1971.

Bénabou, Roland, and Efe A. Ok. "Social Mobility and the Demand for Redistribution: The POUM Hypothesis." *Quarterly Journal of Economics* 116, no. 2 (2001): 447–87.

Bernstein, Edward. *Ferdinand Lassalle as a Social Reformer.* Translated by Eleanor Marx Aveling. London: Swan Sonnenschein and Sons, 1893.

Bewley, Truman. *Why Wages Don't Fall during a Recession.* Cambridge, Mass.: Harvard University Press, 1999.

Bhaduri, Amit, and Joan Robinson. "Accumulation and Exploitation: An Analysis in the Tradition of Marx, Sraffa and Kalecki." In *Piero Sraffa: Critical Assessments,* edited by John C. Wood, 2:79–95. New York: Routledge, 1995.

Biernacki, Richard. *The Fabrication of Labor: Germany and Britain, 1640–1914.* Berkeley: University of California Press, 1995.

Blackburn, Robin. *The Making of New World Slavery: From the Baroque to the Modern, 1492–1800.* New York: Verso, 1997.

Blauner, Robert. *Racial Oppression in America.* New York: Harper and Row, 1972.

Bonacich, Edna. "Advanced Capitalism and Black/White Relations in the United States: A Split Labor Market Interpretation." *American Sociological Review* 41, no. 1 (1976): 34–51.

Boothman, Derek. "General Introduction." In *Further Selections from the Prison Notebooks,* edited and translated by Derek Boothman, xiii–lxxxvii. Minneapolis: University of Minnesota Press, 1995.

Bourdieu, Pierre. *Distinction: A Social Critique of the Judgement of Taste.* Translated by Richard Nice. Cambridge, Mass.: Harvard University Press, 1984.

Bowles, Samuel. "Endogenous Preference Formation: The Cultural Consequences of Markets and Other Economic Institutions." *Journal of Economic Literature* 36, no. 1 (1998): 75–111.

———. "The Production Process in a Competitive Economy: Walrasian, Neo-Hobbesian, and Marxian Models." *American Economic Review* 75, no. 1 (1985): 16–36.

Bowles, Samuel, and Herbert Gintis. "The Revenge of Homo Economicus: Contested Exchange and the Revival of Political Economy." *Journal of Economic Perspectives* 7, no. 1 (1993): 83–102.

———. "Walrasian Economics in Retrospect." *Quarterly Journal of Economics* 115, no. 4 (2000): 1411–39.

Boyte, Harry C. "The Pragmatic Ends of Popular Politics." In *Habermas and the Public Sphere,* edited by Craig Calhoun, 340–55. Cambridge, Mass.: MIT Press, 1992.

Bradley, Lenore K. *Robert Alexander Long: Lumberman of the Gilded Age.* Durham, N.C.: Forest Historical Society, 1989.

Bradley, Philip D., ed. *The Public Stake in Union Power.* Charlottesville: University of Virginia Press, 1959.

Bratt, Charles. "Profiles: Los Angeles." *Journal of Educational Sociology* 19, no. 3 (1945): 179–86.

Braverman, Harry. *Labor and Monopoly Capital: The Degradation of Work in the Twentieth Century.* New York: Monthly Review Press, 1974.

Brenner, Robert, and Mark Glick. "The Regulation Approach: Theory and History." *New Left Review* 188 (1991): 45–119.

Brody, David. *Workers in Industrial America: Essays on the 20th Century Struggle.* New York: Oxford University Press, 1980.

Brown, Clair. "An Institutional Model of Wives' Work Decisions." *Industrial Relations* 24, no. 2 (1985): 182–204.

———. "Unemployment Theory and Policy, 1946–1980." *Industrial Relations* 22, no. 2 (1983): 164–85.

Buhle, Paul, and Nicole Shulman, eds. *Wobblies! A Graphic History of the Industrial Workers of the World.* New York: Verso, 2005.

Burawoy, Michael. *Manufacturing Consent: Changes in the Labor Process under Monopoly Capitalism.* Chicago: University of Chicago Press, 1979.

Butler, Judith. *The Psychic Life of Power: Theories in Subjection.* Stanford, Calif.: Stanford University Press, 1997.

California Department of Industrial Relations, Division of Labor Statistics and Research. *Labor in California, 1945–1946.* San Francisco: California State Printing Office, 1947.

California State Reconstruction and Reemployment Commission. *Report and Recommendations for the Year Ending December 31, 1945.* Sacramento: State Reconstruction and Reemployment Commission, 1946.

———. *Third Report to the Governor and the Legislature.* Sacramento: State Reconstruction and Reemployment Commission, 1947.

Cassady, Ralph, Jr., and Wylie L. Jones. *The Nature of Competition in Gasoline Distribution at the Retail Level: A Study of the Los Angeles Market Area.* Berkeley: University of California Press, 1951.

Coase, Ronald. "The Nature of the Firm." *Economica* 4, no. 16 (1937): 386–405.

Cohen, G. A. *Karl Marx's Theory of History: A Defence.* Princeton, N.J.: Princeton University Press, 1978.

———. *Self-Ownership, Freedom, and Equality.* Cambridge: Cambridge University Press, 1995.

Cohen, Sheila. "A Labour Process to Nowhere." *New Left Review* 165 (1987): 34–50.

Colletti, Lucio. *Marxism and Hegel.* Translated by Lawrence Garner. London: New Left Books, 1973.

Collinson, David, and Jeff Hearn. "'Men' at 'Work': Multiple Masculinities/ Multiple Workplaces." In *Understanding Masculinities: Social Relations and Cultural Arenas,* edited by Máirtín Mac An Ghaill, 61–76. Buckingham, England: Open University Press, 1996.

Comer, Krista. *Landscapes of the New West: Gender and Geography in Contemporary Women's Writing.* Chapel Hill: University of North Carolina Press, 1999.

Commons, John, and Associates, eds. *History of Labor in the United States.* New York: Macmillan, 1918.

Congress of Industrial Organizations, California Council. *The Taft-Hartley Plot Unfolds.* San Francisco: Research Department, California CIO, 1948.

Congress of Industrial Organizations, California Council, Research Department, and International Fishermen and Allied Workers of America. *The Fisheries of California: The Industry, The Men, Their Union.* San Francisco: International Fishermen and Allied Workers of America, 1947.

Cooper, Frederick, Thomas C. Holt, and Rebecca J. Scott. *Beyond Slavery: Explorations of Race, Labor, and Citizenship in Postemancipation Societies.* Chapel Hill: University of North Carolina Press, 2000.

Corlett, William. *Class Action: Reading Labor, Theory, and Value.* Ithaca, N.Y.: Cornell University Press, 1998.

Cox, Oliver C. *Caste, Class and Race.* New York: Monthly Review Press, 1959.

Cross, Ira B. *History of the Labor Movement in California.* Berkeley: University of California Press, 1935.

Crutchfield, James A. "Collective Bargaining in the Pacific Coast Fisheries: The Economic Issues." *Industrial and Labor Relations Review* 8, no. 4 (1955): 541–56.

David, Paul A., and Gavin Wright. "Increasing Returns and the Genesis of American Resource Abundance." *Industrial and Corporate Change* 6 (1997): 203–45.

Davis, John E. "Capitalist Agricultural Development and the Exploitation of the Propertied Laborer." In *The Rural Sociology of Advanced Societies*, edited by Fred Buttel and H. Newby, 133–53. Montclair, N.J.: Allanheld, Osmun, 1980.

Davis, Kate. "Sardine Oil on Troubled Waters: The Boom and Bust of California's Sardine Industry, 1905–1955." Ph.D. diss., University of California, Berkeley, 2001.

Davis, Mike. "'Fordism' in Crisis: A Review of Michel Aglietta's *Régulation et crises: L'expérience des États Unis.*" *Review, A Journal of the Fernand Braudel Center* 2, no. 2 (1978): 207–69.

———. *Prisoners of the American Dream: Politics and Economy in the History of the US Working Class.* New York: Verso, 1986.

———. "Sunshine and the Open Shop: Ford and Darwin in 1920s Los Angeles." *Antipode* 29, no. 4 (1997): 356–82.

de Janvry, Alain. *The Agrarian Question and Reformism in Latin America.* Baltimore: Johns Hopkins University Press, 1981.

Deleuze, Gilles, and Félix Guattari. *Anti-Oedipus: Capitalism and Schizophrenia.* Translated by Robert Hurley, Mark Seem, and Helen Lane. Minneapolis: University of Minnesota Press, 1983.

della Volpe, Galvano. *Logic as a Positive Science.* Translated by Jon Rothschild. London: New Left Books, 1980.

Derrida, Jacques. *Negotiations: Interventions and Interviews, 1971–2001.* Edited and translated by Elizabeth Rottenberg. Stanford, Calif.: Stanford University Press, 2002.

Deutsch, Sarah. *No Separate Refuge: Culture, Class, and Gender on an Anglo-Hispanic Frontier in the American Southwest, 1880–1940.* New York: Oxford University Press, 1987.

di Leonardo, Micaela. *Exotics at Home: Anthropologies, Others, American Modernity.* Chicago: University of Chicago Press, 1998.

Dobb, Maurice. *Theories of Value and Distribution since Adam Smith.* Cambridge: Cambridge University Press, 1973.

———. *Wages.* Rev. ed. Cambridge: Cambridge University Press, 1956.

Doeringer, Peter, and Michael Piore. *Internal Labor Markets and Manpower Analysis.* Lexington, Mass.: D. C. Heath, 1971.

Dore, Ronald. *Taking Japan Seriously.* London: Athlone Press, 1987.

Douglas, Paul H. *Real Wages in the United States, 1890–1926.* New York: Houghton Mifflin, 1930.

Douglass, Frederick. *Life and Times of Frederick Douglass: His Early Life as a Slave, His Escape from Bondage, and His Complete History.* London: Collier-Macmillan, 1962.

Dublin, Louis I. "Life, Death and the Negro." *American Mercury,* September 1927, 44.

Dubofsky, Melvyn. *We Shall Be All: A History of the Industrial Workers of the World.* Chicago: Quadrangle Books, 1969.

Du Bois, W. E. B. *Black Reconstruction in America, 1860–1880.* New York: Atheneum, 1969.

———. "Shasta and Siskiyou." *Crisis* 26, no. 1 (1923): 9–10.

Dunlop, John T. "A Review of Wage-Price Policy." *Review of Economic Statistics* 29, no. 3 (1947): 154–60.

Edwards, Richard. *Contested Terrain: The Transformation of the Workplace in the Twentieth Century.* New York: Basic Books, 1979.

Ehrenreich, Barbara. "The Decline of Patriarchy." In *Constructing Masculinity,* edited by Maurice Berger, Brian Wallis, and Simon Watson, 284–90. London: Routledge, 1995.

Ellison, Ralph. *Shadow and Act.* New York: Random House, 1964.

Elson, Diane. "The Value Theory of Labour." In *Value: The Representation of Labour in Capitalism,* edited by Diane Elson, 115–80. Atlantic Highlands, N.J.: Humanities Press, 1979.

Emirbayer, Mustafa, and Jeff Goodwin. "Network Analysis, Culture, and the Problem of Agency." *American Journal of Sociology* 99, no. 6 (1994): 1411–54.

Fanon, Frantz. *The Wretched of the Earth.* New York: Grove Press, 1963.

Feldman, Herman. *Racial Factors in American Industry.* New York: Harper and Brothers, 1931.

Fickle, James E. "Management Looks at the 'Labor Problem': The Southern Pine Industry during World War I and the Postwar Era." *Journal of Southern History* 40, no. 1 (1974): 61–76.

Fiori, Giuseppe. *Antonio Gramsci: Life of a Revolutionary.* Translated by Tom Nairn. New York: Schocken Books, 1970.

Fisher, Lloyd H. "The Harvest Labor Market in California." *Quarterly Journal of Economics* 65, no. 4 (1951): 463–91.

Flamming, Douglas. *Bound for Freedom: Black Los Angeles in Jim Crow America.* Berkeley: University of California Press, 2005.

Foner, Eric. *Reconstruction: America's Unfinished Revolution, 1863–1877.* New York: Harper and Row, 1988.

———. *The Story of American Freedom.* New York: Norton, 1998.

Foner, Philip S. *The Industrial Workers of the World, 1905–1917.* Vol. 4 (1968) of *History of the Labor Movement in the United States.* New York: International Publishers, 1947–94.

Frank, Thomas. *What's the Matter with Kansas? How Conservatives Won the Heart of America.* New York: Owl Books, 2004.

Garegnani, Pierangelo. "Sraffa's Revival of Marxist Economic Theory." *New Left Review* 112 (1978): 71–80.

Gerstle, Gary. *Working-Class Americanism: The Politics of Labor in a Textile City, 1914–1960.* New York: Cambridge University Press, 1989.

———. "The Working Class Goes to War." *Mid-America* 75, no. 3 (1993): 303–22.

Ghio, Tony, and Dominic Ghio. "Fishermen by Trade: Sixty Years in San Francisco Bay." Regional Oral History Office, University of California, Berkeley, 1990.

Giddens, Anthony. *The Class Structure of the Advanced Societies.* New York: Harper and Row, 1973.

Gilman, Madelon G. "The City of Weed." *Siskiyou Pioneer* 7, no. 3 (2000): 35–36.

Gilroy, Paul. *Against Race: Imagining Political Culture beyond the Color Line.* Cambridge, Mass.: Harvard University Press, Belknap Press, 2000.

Glaberman, Martin. *Wartime Strikes: The Struggle against the No-Strike Pledge in the UAW during World War II.* Detroit: Bewick, 1980.

Glickman, Lawrence B. *A Living Wage: American Workers and the Making of Consumer Society.* Ithaca, N.Y.: Cornell University Press, 1997.

Goldin, Claudia, and Robert A. Margo. "The Great Compression: The Wage Structure in the United States at Mid-Century." *Quarterly Journal of Economics* 107, no. 1 (1992): 1–34.

Gordon, David M., Richard Edwards, and Michael Reich. *Segmented Work, Divided Workers: The Historical Transformation of Labor in the United States.* New York: Cambridge University Press, 1982.

Gordon, Margaret S. *Employment Expansion and Population Growth: The*

California Experience, 1900–1950. Berkeley: University of California Press, 1954.

Gorz, André. *Farewell to the Working Class: An Essay on Post-Industrial Socialism.* Translated by Michael Sonenscher. London: Pluto Press, 1982.

Gramsci, Antonio. *Further Selections from the Prison Notebooks.* Edited and translated by Derek Boothman. Minneapolis: University of Minnesota Press, 1995.

———. *Selections from the Prison Notebooks.* Edited and translated by Quintin Hoare and Geoffrey Nowell Smith. New York: International Publishers, 1971.

Green, George N. "Labor in the Western Oil Industry." *Journal of the West* 25, no. 2 (1986): 14–19.

Green, James R. "The Brotherhood of Timber Workers, 1910–1913: A Radical Response to Industrial Capitalism in the Southern U.S.A." *Past and Present* 60 (1973): 161–200.

Greene, Lorenzo J. "Economic Conditions of Negroes in the South, 1930, as Seen by an Associate of Dr. Carter G. Woodson." *Journal of Negro History* 64, no. 3 (1979): 265–73.

Greene, Lorenzo J., and Carter G. Woodson. *The Negro Wage Earner.* Washington: Association for the Study of Negro Life and History, 1930.

Gregory, James N. *The Southern Diaspora: How the Great Migrations of Black and White Southerners Transformed America.* Chapel Hill: University of North Carolina Press, 2005.

Griliches, Zvi. "Capital-Skill Complementarity." *Review of Economics and Statistics* 51, no. 4 (1969): 465–68.

Hall, Covington. *Labor Struggles in the Deep South and Other Writings.* Chicago: Charles H. Kerr, 1999.

Hall, John R. "Cannery Row: Class, Community, and the Social Construction of History." In *Reworking Class,* edited by John R. Hall, 243–86. Ithaca, N.Y.: Cornell University Press, 1997.

Hall, Stuart. "Marx's Notes on Method: A 'Reading' of the '1857 Introduction.'" *Working Papers in Cultural Studies* 6 (1974): 132–70.

———. "The Problem of Ideology: Marxism without Guarantees." In *Stuart Hall: Critical Dialogues in Cultural Studies,* edited by David Morley and Kuan-Hsing Chen, 25–46. London: Routledge, 1996.

———. "Race, Articulation, and Societies Structured in Dominance." In *Sociological Theories: Race and Colonialism,* edited by UNESCO, 305–45. Paris: UNESCO, 1980.

Hall, Stuart, et al. *Policing the Crisis: Mugging, the State, and Law and Order.* London: Macmillan, 1978.

Hallagan, William S. "Labor Contracting in Turn-of-the-Century California Agriculture." *Journal of Economic History* 40, no. 4 (1980): 757–76.

Halle, David. *America's Working Man: Work, Home, and Politics among Blue-Collar Property Owners*. Chicago: University of Chicago Press, 1984.

Harvey, David. *The Limits to Capital*. New York: Verso, 1999.

———. *The Urban Experience*. Baltimore: Johns Hopkins University Press, 1989.

Haywood, William. *Big Bill Haywood's Book*. New York: International Publishers, 1929.

Hegel, G. W. F. *Elements of the Philosophy of Right*. Translated by H. B. Nesbit. Cambridge: Cambridge University Press, 1991.

———. *Hegel's Logic, Being Part One of the Encyclopædia of the Philosophical Sciences*. Translated by W. Wallace. Oxford: Oxford University Press, 1975.

———. *The Phenomenology of Mind*. Translated by J. B. Baillie. New York: Harper and Row, 1967.

———. *Science of Logic*. Translated by A. V. Miller. Amherst, N.Y.: Humanity Books, 1969.

Herod, Andrew. "From a Geography of Labor to a Labor Geography: Labor's Spatial Fix and the Geography of Capitalism." *Antipode* 29, no. 1 (1997): 1–31.

Herrnstein, Richard J., and Charles Murray. *The Bell Curve: Intelligence and Class Structure in American Life*. New York: Free Press, 1994.

Hicks, John R. *The Theory of Wages*. London: Macmillan, 1932.

———. *The Theory of Wages*. 2nd ed. London: Macmillan, 1963.

Hirschman, Albert O. *The Passions and the Interests: Political Arguments for Capitalism before Its Triumph*. Princeton, N.J.: Princeton University Press, 1977.

Hise, Greg. "'Nature's Workshop': Industry and Urban Expansion in Southern California, 1900–1950." *Journal of Historical Geography* 27, no. 1 (2001): 74–92.

Hoch, Myron. "The Oil Strike of 1945." *Southern Economic Journal* 15, no. 2 (1948): 117–33.

Holt, Thomas C. "Marking: Race, Race-Making, and the Writing of History." *American Historical Review* 100, no. 1 (1995): 1–20.

———. *The Problem of Race in the 21st Century*. Cambridge, Mass.: Harvard University Press, 2000.

Howard, John C. *The Negro in the Lumber Industry*. Philadelphia: University of Pennsylvania Press, 1970.

Howd, Cloice R. *Industrial Relations in the West Coast Lumber Industry*. Washington: Government Printing Office, 1924.

International Union of Operating Engineers. "Resolution No. 4." *International Engineer* 86, no. 1 (1944): 60–61.

Jacobs, Meg. "'Democracy's Third Estate': New Deal Politics and the Construction of a 'Consuming Public.'" *International Labor and Working Class History* 55 (1999): 27–51.

———. "'How about Some Meat?' The Office of Price Administration, Consumption Politics, and State Building from the Bottom Up, 1941–1946." *Journal of American History* 84, no. 3 (1997): 910–41.

Jacoby, Sanford M. "The Development of Internal Labor Markets in American Manufacturing Firms." In *Internal Labor Markets*, edited by Paul Osterman, 22–69. Cambridge, Mass.: MIT Press, 1984.

———. *Modern Manors: Welfare Capitalism since the New Deal.* Princeton, N.J.: Princeton University Press, 1997.

James, C. L. R. *The Black Jacobins: Toussaint L'Ouverture and the San Domingo Revolution.* New York: Vintage, 1989.

Jameson, Fredric. Introduction to *Noise: The Political Economy of Music*, by Jacques Attali. Translated by Brian Massumi. Minneapolis: University of Minnesota Press, 1985.

———. *Late Marxism: Adorno, or, The Persistence of the Dialectic.* New York: Verso, 1990.

———. *Marxism and Form: Twentieth-Century Dialectical Theories of Literature.* Princeton, N.J.: Princeton University Press, 1971.

———. *The Political Unconscious: Narrative as a Socially Symbolic Act.* Ithaca, N.Y.: Cornell University Press, 1981.

———. *Postmodernism, or, The Cultural Logic of Late Capitalism.* Durham, N.C.: Duke University Press, 1990.

Jay, Martin. *Marxism and Totality: The Adventures of a Concept from Lukács to Habermas.* Berkeley: University of California Press, 1984.

Jensen, Vernon L. *Lumber and Labor.* New York: Farrar and Rinehart, 1945.

Jevons, W. S. *Theory of Political Economy.* New York: A. M. Kelly, 1965.

Kalecki, Michał. "Class Struggle and the Distribution of National Income." *Kyklos* 24, no. 1 (1971): 1–9.

———. "Money and Real Wages." In *Collected Works of Michał Kalecki*, vol. 2, *Capitalism: Economic Dynamics*, edited by Jerzy Osiatynski, translated by C. A. Kisiel, 21–50. Oxford: Clarendon Press, 1991.

Karatani, Kojin. *Transcritique: On Kant and Marx.* Translated by Sabu Kohso. Cambridge: MIT Press, 2003.

Kefalas, Maria. *Working-Class Heroes: Protecting Home, Community, and Nation in a Chicago Neighborhood.* Berkeley: University of California Press, 2003.

Kelley, Robin D. G. "'We Are Not What We Seem': Rethinking Black Working-Class Opposition in the Jim Crow South." *Journal of American History* 80, no. 1 (1993): 75–112.

Kerr, Clark. *Labor Markets and Wage Determination: The Balkanization of Labor Markets and Other Essays.* Berkeley: University of California Press, 1977.

Kessler-Harris, Alice. *In Pursuit of Equity: Women, Men, and the Quest for Economic Citizenship in 20th-Century America.* New York: Oxford University Press, 2001.

———. *A Woman's Wage: Historical Meanings and Social Consequences.* Lexington: University Press of Kentucky, 1990.

Keynes, John Maynard. *The Applied Theory of Money.* Vol. 2 of *A Treatise on Money.* New York: AMS Press, 1976.

———. *The General Theory of Employment, Interest, and Money.* New York: Harcourt, Brace and World, 1976.

Kidner, Frank, and Philip Neff. *An Economic Survey of the Los Angeles Area.* Los Angeles: Haynes Foundation, 1945.

———. *Los Angeles—The Economic Outlook.* Los Angeles: Haynes Foundation, 1946.

———. *A Statistical Appendix to an Economic Survey of the Los Angeles Area.* Los Angeles: Haynes Foundation, 1945.

Kimeldorf, Howard. "World War II and the Deradicalization of American Labor: The ILWU as a Deviant Case." *Labor History* 33, no. 2 (1992): 248–78.

Kirkland, Burt. "Effects of Destructive Lumbering on Labor." *Journal of Forestry* 18 (1920): 318.

Klein, Kerwin Lee. *Frontiers of the Historical Imagination: Narrating the European Conquest of Native America, 1890–1980.* Berkeley: University of California Press, 1999.

"Labor Unrest in the Lumber Industry." *Journal of Forestry* 15 (1917): 796.

Laclau, Ernesto. *Emancipation(s).* New York: Verso, 1997.

———. *On Populist Reason.* New York: Verso, 2005.

———. *Politics and Ideology in Marxist Theory.* London: Verso, 1977.

Laclau, Ernesto, and Chantal Mouffe. *Hegemony and Socialist Strategy: Toward a Radical Democratic Politics.* New York: Verso, 1985.

———. "Post-Marxism without Apologies." *New Left Review* 166 (1987): 79–106.

Lambert, Paul F., and Kenny A. Franks, eds. *Voices from the Oil Fields.* Norman: University of Oklahoma Press, 1984.

Lamont, Michèle. *The Dignity of Working Men: Morality and the Boundaries of Race, Class, and Immigration.* New York: Russell Sage Foundation; Cambridge, Mass.: Harvard University Press, 2000.

Langford, James. "The Black Minority of Weed—Its History, Institutions, and Politics." M.A. thesis, California State University, Chico, 1984.

Lapides, Kenneth. *Marx's Wage Theory in Historical Perspective: Its Origins, Development and Interpretation.* London: Praeger, 1998.

Lay, Shawn, ed. *The Invisible Empire in the West: Toward a New Historical Appraisal of the Ku Klux Klan of the 1920s.* Urbana: University of Illinois Press, 1992.

Leff, Mark. "The Politics of Sacrifice on the American Home Front in World War II." *Journal of American History* 77, no. 4 (1991): 1296–1318.

Legge, R. T. "Sanitation of Logging Camps." *California Forestry* 1, no. 7 (1917): 49–50.

Leier, Mark. *Where the Fraser River Flows: The IWW in British Columbia.* Vancouver, British Columbia: New Star Books, 1990.

Lenin, Vladimir I. *The Development of Capitalism in Russia.* Moscow: Foreign Languages Publishing House, 1960.

Levenstein, Harvey A. *Communism, Anti-Communism, and the CIO.* Westport, Conn.: Greenwood Press, 1981.

Levinson, Harold M. "Collective Bargaining and Income Distribution." *American Economic Review* 44, no. 2 (1954): 308–16.

Lichtenstein, Nelson. "Class Politics and the State during World War Two." *International Labor and Working Class History* 58 (2000): 261–74.

———. *Labor's War at Home: The CIO in World War II.* New York: Cambridge University Press, 1982.

———. "The Making of the Postwar Working Class: Cultural Pluralism and Social Structure in World War II." *The Historian* 51, no. 1 (1988): 42–63.

Linville, Alford. "Unions—Strikes—Aftermath." *Siskiyou Pioneer* 7, no. 3 (2000): 77–85.

Lipset, Seymour Martin. "Radicalism in North America: A Comparative View of the Party Systems in Canada and the United States." *Transactions of the Royal Society of Canada* 4, no. 14 (1976): 19–55.

Lipset, Seymour Martin, and Reinhard Bendix. *Social Mobility in Industrial Society.* Berkeley: University of California Press, 1959.

Lipsitz, George. *The Possessive Investment in Whiteness: How White People Profit from Identity Politics.* Philadelphia: Temple University Press, 1998.

———. *Rainbow at Midnight: Labor and Culture in the 1940s.* Urbana: University of Illinois Press, 1981.

Lott, Eric. *Love and Theft: Blackface Minstrelsy and the American Working Class.* New York: Oxford University Press, 1993.

Lukács, Georg. *History and Class Consciousness: Studies in Marxist Dialectics.* Translated by Rodney Livingstone. Cambridge, Mass.: MIT Press, 1971.

Lynch, Gerald. *Roughnecks, Drillers and Tool Pushers: Thirty-Three Years in the Oil Fields.* Austin: University of Texas Press, 1987.

Mandle, Jay R. *Not Slave, Not Free: The African American Experience since the Civil War.* Durham, N.C.: Duke University Press, 1992.

———. *The Roots of Black Poverty: The Southern Plantation Economy after the Civil War.* Durham, N.C.: Duke University Press, 1978.

Mann, Geoff. "Class Consciousness and Common Property: The International Fishermen and Allied Workers of America." *International Labor and Working Class History* 61 (2002): 141–60.

———. "'Discrimination Costs You Dough': Innocent Identity and the Anti-Politics of Race." *Political Power and Social Theory* 16 (2003): 103–38.

———. "Interests and the Political Terrain of Time." *Rethinking Marxism* 18, no. 4 (2006): 565–72.

———. "Reflections on Scott Prudham's *Knock on Wood*: Is Labor-*Power* a Fictitious Commodity?" *Antipode* 38, no. 5 (2006): 1066–69.

———. "The Social Production of Skill." In *Beyond Resistance: The Future of Freedom,* edited by Robert Fletcher. Hauppage, N.Y.: Nova Science, 2006.

Mann, Susan A. *Agrarian Capitalism in Theory and Practice*. Chapel Hill: University of North Carolina Press, 1990.

Mann, Susan A., and James M. Dickinson. "Obstacles to the Development of a Capitalist Agriculture." *Journal of Peasant Studies* 5, no. 4 (1978): 466–81.

Marglin, Stephen A. *Growth, Distribution and Prices*. Cambridge, Mass.: Harvard University Press, 1984.

Marshall, Alfred. *Elements of Economics of Industry*. London: Macmillan, 1892.

Marshall, Ray. *The Negro and Organized Labor*. New York: J. Wiley and Sons, 1965.

Marx, Karl. *Capital*. Vol. 1. Translated by Ben Fowkes. Vintage: New York, 1977.

———. *Capital*. Vol. 3. London: Penguin, 1981.

———. *Contribution to the Critique of Political Economy*. Moscow: Progress Publishers, 1970.

———. *The Critique of the Gotha Programme*. In *The Marx-Engels Reader*, 2nd ed., edited by Robert Tucker, 525–41. New York: W. W. Norton, 1978.

———. *The Eighteenth Brumaire of Louis Bonaparte*. New York: International Publishers, 1935.

———. *Grundrisse*. Translated by Martin Nicolaus. New York: Vintage, 1973.

———. *Le Capital*, livre I, sections I à IV. Translated by J. Roy. Paris: Flammarion, 1985.

———. *Theories of Surplus-Value*. London: Lawrence and Wishart, 1972.

———. *Value, Price, and Profit*. New York: International Publishers, 1935.

———. *Wage-Labour and Capital*. New York: International Publishers, 1933.

———. "Wages." In *The Collected Works of Karl Marx and Friedrich Engels*, 6:415–37. New York: International Publishers, 1976.

Marx, Karl, and Friedrich Engels. *The Communist Manifesto*. Translated by Samuel Moore. London: Pelican, 1967.

———. *Selected Correspondence, 1846–1895*. Translated by Dona Torr. New York: International Publishers, 1936.

Matthews, John L. "The 'Roughneck' Oil Worker." *International Engineer*, March 1949, 16–17, 22.

Mattick, Paul, Jr. "Marx's Dialectic." In *Marx's Method in Capital*, edited by Fred Moseley, 115–34. Atlantic Highlands, N.J.: Humanities Press.

May, Elaine Tyler. "Rosie the Riveter Gets Married." *Mid-America* 75, no. 3 (1993): 269–82.

McAdam, Douglas, John D. McCarthy, and Mayer Zald, eds. *Comparative Perspectives on Social Movements: Political Opportunities, Mobilizing Structures, and Cultural Framings*. Cambridge: Cambridge University Press, 1996.

McCarthy, James. "First World Political Ecology: Lessons from the Wise Use Movement." *Environment and Planning A* 34, no. 7 (2002): 1281–1302.

McCay, Bonnie J. "The Culture of the Commoners: Historical Observations on New and Old World Fisheries." In *The Question of the Commons: The Culture and Ecology of Communal Resources*, edited by Bonnie J. McCay and James M. Acheson, 195–216. Tucson: University of Arizona Press, 1987.

McCay, Bonnie J., and James M. Acheson. "Human Ecology and the Commons." In *The Question of the Commons: The Culture and Ecology of Communal Resources*, edited by Bonnie J. McCay and James M. Acheson, 1–34. 1987. Reprint, Tucson: University of Arizona Press, 1990.

McClary, Susan. *Feminine Endings: Music, Gender, Sexuality*. Minneapolis: University of Minnesota Press, 1991.

McClelland, John, Jr. *R. A. Long's Planned City: The Story of Longview*. Longview, Wash.: Longview Publishing Co., 1976.

McEvoy, Arthur. *The Fisherman's Problem: Ecology and Law in the California Fisheries*. New York: Cambridge University Press, 1986.

McWilliams, Carey. *California: The Great Exception*. Berkeley: University of California Press, 1949.

Meek, Ronald. "Mr Sraffa's Rehabilitation of Classical Economics." *Scottish Journal of Political Economy* 8 (1961): 119–36.

Menger, Carl. *Principles of Economics*. Translated by James Dingwall and Bert Hoselitz. New York: New York University Press, 1984.

Milkman, Ruth. *Gender at Work: The Dynamics of Job Segregation by Sex during World War II*. Urbana: University of Illinois Press, 1987.

Milton, David. *The Politics of U.S. Labor: From the Great Depression to the New Deal*. New York: Monthly Review Press, 1982.

Mitchell, Don. *The Lie of the Land: Migrant Workers and the California Landscape*. Minneapolis: University of Minnesota Press, 1996.

Moore, Donald, Anand Pandian, and Jake Kosek. "The Cultural Politics of Race and Nature: Terrains of Power and Practice." In *Race, Nature, and the Politics of Difference*, edited by Donald Moore, Anand Pandian, and Jake Kosek, 1–70. Durham, N.C.: Duke University Press, 2003.

Mosse, George L. *The Image of Man: The Creation of Modern Masculinity*. Oxford: Oxford University Press, 1996.

Moynihan, Daniel. *The Negro Family: A Case for National Action*. Washington: Government Printing Office, 1965.

Mulligan, Casey B. "Pecuniary Incentives to Work in the United States during World War II." *Journal of Political Economy* 106, no. 5 (1998): 1033–77.

Murray, Philip. *The CIO Case for Substantial Pay Increases*. Washington: Congress of Industrial Organizations, 1945.

———. *The CIO Reemployment Plan*. Washington: Congress of Industrial Organizations, Department of Research and Education, 1947.

Myrdal, Gunnar. *Negro Social Structure*. Vol. 2 of *An American Dilemma: The Negro Problem and American Democracy*. New York: McGraw-Hill, 1964.

National Bureau of Economic Research. Macrohistory Series, U.S. Index of Wholesale Prices Of Lumber. <www.nber.org/databases/macrohistory/data/04/m04164a.db> (Autumn 2006).

———. Macrohistory Series 08084c, Unemployment. <www.nber.org/databases/macrohistory/data/08/m08084b.db> (Autumn 2006).

Negri, Antonio. *Marx beyond Marx: Lessons on the Grundrisse*. Translated by Harry Cleaver, Michael Ryan, and Maurizio Viano. Brooklyn, N.Y.: Autonomedia, 1991.

———. *Time for Revolution.* Translated by Matteo Mandarini. London: Continuum, 2003.

Nelson, Dana D. *National Manhood: Capitalist Citizenship and the Imagined Fraternity of White Men.* Durham, N.C.: Duke University Press, 1998.

Nicolaus, Martin. Foreword to *Grundrisse*, by Karl Marx, translated by Martin Nicolaus. New York: Vintage, 1973.

Niklason, C. R. *Commercial Survey of the Pacific Southwest.* U.S. Department of Commerce, Domestic Commerce Series No. 37. Washington: Government Printing Office, 1930.

Norwood, Stephen H. "Bogalusa Burning: The War against Biracial Unionism in the Deep South, 1919." *Journal of Southern History* 63, no. 3 (1997): 591–628.

O'Connor, Harvey. *History of Oil Workers International Union—CIO.* Denver: Oil Workers International Union, 1950.

Offe, Claus. *Disorganized Capitalism: Contemporary Transformation of Work and Politics.* Cambridge, Mass.: MIT Press, 1985.

Oil Workers International Union. *Facts about the Wage Dispute in the Oil Industry.* Fort Worth, Tex.: OWIU-CIO, 1945.

———. *Proceedings, Seventeenth National Convention of the Oil Workers International Union.* Denver, Colo.: OWIU, 1946.

———. *Proceedings of the Ninth National Convention, Oil Workers International Union.* Houston: OWIU, 1938.

Okun, Arthur. *Equality and Efficiency: The Big Tradeoff.* Washington: Brookings Institution, 1975.

Ollman, Bertell. *Dance of the Dialectic: Steps in Marx's Method.* Urbana: University of Illinois Press, 2003.

Olson, Mancur. *The Logic of Collective Action.* Cambridge, Mass.: Harvard University Press, 1965.

Omi, Michael, and Howard Winant. *Racial Formation in the United States: From the 1960s to the 1980s.* London: Routledge and Kegan Paul, 1986.

Pacific Historical Review 32, no. 2 (1970). Special Issue on Oil.

Paige, Jeffrey. *Agrarian Revolutions: Social Movements and Export Agriculture in the Underdeveloped World.* New York: Free Press, 1975.

Parker, Carleton. "The California Casual and His Revolt." *Quarterly Journal of Economics* 30, no. 1 (1915): 110–26.

———. "Motives in Economic Life." *American Economic Review* 8, no. 1 (1918): 212–31.

Patterson, Orlando. "A Poverty of the Mind." *New York Times*, 26 March 2006, sec. 4, 1.

Peck, Gunther. *Reinventing Free Labor: Padrones and Immigrant Workers in the North American West, 1880–1930.* Cambridge: Cambridge University Press, 1999.

Perry, Louis B., and Richard S. Perry. *A History of the Los Angeles Labor Movement, 1911–1941.* Berkeley: University of California Press, 1963.

Peterson, Pratt. "A Fisherman and a Whaler: Recollections of the Richmond Whaling Station, 1958–72." Regional Oral History Office, University of California, Berkeley, 1990.

Piore, Michael J. "Fragments of a 'Sociological' Theory of Wages." *American Economic Review* 63, no. 2 (1973): 377–84.

———. "Unemployment and Inflation: An Alternative View." In *Unemployment and Inflation: Institutionalist and Structuralist Views*, edited by Michael J. Piore, 5–16. White Plains, N.Y.: M. E. Sharpe, 1979.

Polanyi, Karl. *The Great Transformation.* Boston: Beacon Press, 1965.

Postone, Moishe. *Time, Labor, and Social Domination.* Cambridge: Cambridge University Press, 1993.

Poulantzas, Nicos. *Fascisme et dictature.* Paris: Seuil/Maspero, 1974.

Preve, Costanzo. "Louis Althusser: La lutte contre le sens commun dans le mouvement communiste 'historique' au xxᵉ siècle." In *Politique et philosophie dans l'oeuvre de Louis Althusser*, edited by Sylvain Lazarus, 125–36. Paris: Presses Universitaires de France, 1993.

Prudham, W. Scott. *Knock on Wood: Nature as Commodity in Douglas-Fir Country.* London: Routledge, 2005.

Przeworski, Adam. *Capitalism and Social Democracy.* New York: Cambridge University Press, 1985.

———. *States and Markets: A Primer in Political Economy.* Cambridge: Cambridge University Press, 2003.

Radosh, Ronald. *American Labor and United States Foreign Policy.* New York: Vintage, 1969.

Randall, Roger L. "Labor Agreements in the West Coast Fishing Industry: Restraint of Trade of Basis of Industrial Stability?" *Industrial and Labor Relations Review* 3, no. 4 (1950): 514–41.

Reddy, William. *Money and Liberty in Modern Europe: A Critique of Historical Understanding.* Cambridge: Cambridge University Press, 1987.

Reed, Adolph, Jr. "Unraveling the Relation of Race and Class in American Politics." *Political Power and Social Theory* 15 (2002): 265–74.

Reich, Michael. *Racial Inequality: A Political Economic Analysis.* Cambridge, Mass.: Harvard University Press, 1981.

Rex, John. *Race Relations in Sociological Theory.* New York: Schocken Books, 1970.

Ricardo, David. *On the Principles of Political Economy and Taxation.* Vol. 1 of *The Works and Correspondence of David Ricardo.* Edited by Piero Sraffa. Cambridge: Cambridge University Press, 1951.

Robbins, William G. *Colony and Empire: The Capitalist Transformation of the American West.* Lawrence: University Press of Kansas, 1994.

———. *Hard Times in Paradise: Coos Bay, Oregon, 1850–1996.* Seattle: University of Washington Press, 1988.

Robinson, Joan. *The Accumulation of Capital.* 2nd ed. London: Macmillan, 1966.

———. *An Essay on Marxian Economics.* 2nd ed. London: Macmillan, 1966.

———. *Essays in the Theory of Economic Growth.* London: Macmillan, 1962.

Roediger, David. *Towards the Abolition of Whiteness.* New York: Verso, 1994.

———. *The Wages of Whiteness: Race and the Making of the American Working Class.* New York: Verso, 1991.

Roediger, David, and Philip Foner. *Our Own Time: A History of American Labor and the Working Day.* New York: Greenwood Press, 1989.

Roemer, John. *A General Theory of Exploitation and Class.* Cambridge, Mass.: Harvard University Press, 1982.

Romm, Jeff. "The Coincidental Order of Environmental Injustice." In *Justice and Natural Resources,* edited by K. M. Mutz, G. C. Bryner, and D. S. Kenney, 117–37. Washington: Island Press, 2002.

Rosdolsky, Roman. *The Making of Marx's "Capital."* Translated by Pete Burgess. London: Pluto Press, 1977.

Rose, Sonya O. "Class Formation and the Quintessential Worker." In *Reworking Class,* edited by John R. Hall, 133–66. Ithaca, N.Y.: Cornell University Press, 1997.

Ross, Arthur M. *Trade Union Wage Policy.* Berkeley: University of California Press, 1948.

Rosswurm, Steve, ed. *The CIO's Left-Led Unions.* New Brunswick, N.J.: Rutgers University Press, 1992.

Rothbaum, Melvin. *The Government of the Oil, Chemical and Atomic Workers Union.* New York: John Wiley and Sons, 1962.

Rothman, Hal K. *Devil's Bargains: Tourism in the Twentieth-Century American West.* Lawrence: University of Kansas Press, 1998.

Rothschild, Kurt W. *The Theory of Wages.* Oxford: Basil Blackwell, 1956.

Rowthorn, Bob. *Capitalism, Conflict and Inflation.* London: Lawrence and Wishart, 1980.

Ruiz, Vicki. *Cannery Women, Cannery Lives: Mexican Women, Unionization, and the California Food Processing Industry.* Albuquerque: University of New Mexico Press, 1987.

Samuelson, Paul A. "Sraffa's Other Leg." *Economic Journal* 101, no. 406 (1991): 570–74.

———. "Wages and Interest: A Modern Dissection of Marxian Economic Models." *American Economic Review* 47, no. 6 (1957): 884–912.

Saxton, Alexander. *The Indispensable Enemy: Labor and the Anti-Chinese Movement in California.* Berkeley: University of California, 1971.

———. *The Rise and Fall of the White Republic: Class Politics and Mass Culture in Nineteenth Century America.* New York: Verso, 1990.

Schrecker, Ellen. *Many Are the Crimes: McCarthyism in America.* Boston: Little, Brown, 1998.

Schultze, Charles L. *Recent Inflation in the United States.* Washington: Government Printing Office, 1959.

Schwantes, Carlos A. "The Concept of the Wageworkers' Frontier: A Framework for Future Research." *Western Historical Quarterly* 18, no. 1 (1987): 39–55.

Scott, Allen J., and Doreen J. Mattingly. "The Aircraft and Parts Industry in Southern California: Continuity and Changed from the Inter-War Years to the 1990s." *Economic Geography* 65, no. 1 (1989): 48–71.

Scott, Emmett J. "Letters of Negro Migrants of 1916–1918." *Journal of Negro History* 4, no. 3 (1919): 290–340.

Scott, Mel. *Metropolitan Los Angeles: One Community*. Los Angeles: Haynes Foundation, 1949.

Seidman, Joel. *American Labor from Defense to Reconversion*. Chicago: University of Chicago Press, 1953.

Sellars, Nigel A. *Oil, Wheat & Wobblies: The Industrial Workers of the World in Oklahoma, 1905–1930*. Norman: University of Oklahoma Press, 1998.

Sen, Amartya. "Sraffa, Wittgenstein, and Gramsci." *Journal of Economic Literature* 41, no. 4 (2003): 1240–55.

Sennett, Richard, and Jonathon Cobb. *The Hidden Injuries of Class*. London: Faber and Faber, 1993.

Shapiro, Carl, and Joseph E. Stiglitz. "Equilibrium Unemployment as a Worker Discipline Device." *American Economic Review* 74, no. 3 (1984): 433–44.

Shoup, Lawrence H. *Speed, Power, Production, and Profit: Railroad Logging in Northeastern Siskiyou County, 1900–1956*. Yreka, Calif.: Siskiyou County Historical Society, 1987.

Silcox, F. A. "Forestry and Labor." *Journal of Forestry* 18 (1920): 317.

Simmel, Georg. *The Philosophy of Money*. Translated by Tom Bottomore and David Frisby. London: Routledge and Kegan Paul, 1978.

Singh, Nikhil Pal. *Black Is a Country: Race and the Unfinished Struggle for Democracy*. Cambridge, Mass.: Harvard University Press, 2004.

Slichter, Sumner. "Revision of the Taft-Hartley Act." *Quarterly Journal of Economics* 67, no. 2 (1953): 149–80.

Smith, Adam. *The Wealth of Nations*. New York: Modern Library, 2000.

Soja, Edward, Rebecca Morales, and Goetz Wolff. "Urban Restructuring: An Analysis of Social and Spatial Change in Los Angeles." *Economic Geography* 59, no. 2 (1983): 195–230.

Solow, Robert M. *The Labor Market as a Social Institution*. Oxford: Basil Blackwell, 1990.

Solow, Robert M., and Joseph E. Stiglitz. "Output, Employment, and Wages in the Short Run." *Quarterly Journal of Economics* 82, no. 4 (1968): 537–60.

Sowell, Thomas. *Race and Economics*. New York: D. McKay and Co., 1975.

Spivak, Gayatri Chakravorty. *A Critique of Postcolonial Reason: Toward a History of the Vanishing Present*. Cambridge, Mass.: Harvard University Press, 1999.

Spero, Sterling D., and Abram L. Harris. *The Black Worker*. New York: Atheneum, 1972.

Spurgeon, Sara. *Exploding the Western: Myths of Empire on the Postmodern Frontier*. College Station: Texas A&M University Press, 2005.

Sraffa, Piero. *Production of Commodities by Means of Commodities: Prelude to a Critique of Economic Theory*. Cambridge: Cambridge University Press, 1960.

Starobin, Robert S. *Industrial Slavery in the Old South*. New York: Oxford University Press, 1970.

Stegner, Wallace. *Joe Hill: A Biographical Novel*. Garden City, N.Y.: Doubleday, 1969.

Stevens, Homer, and Rolf Knight. *Homer Stevens: A Life in Fishing*. Madeira Park, B.C.: Harbour, 1992.

Stiglitz, Joseph E., and Stefan Grossman. "On the Impossibility of Informationally Efficient Markets." *American Economic Review* 70, no. 3 (1980): 266–93.

Stimson, Grace H. *Rise of the Labor Movement in Los Angeles*. Berkeley: University of California Press, 1955.

Stoler, Ann Laura. "Racial Histories and Their Regimes of Truth." *Political Power and Social Theory* 11 (1997): 183–206.

Storper, Michael, and Richard Walker. *The Capitalist Imperative: Territory, Technology, and Industrial Growth*. Oxford: Basil Blackwell, 1989.

Strathern, Marilyn. *The Gender of the Gift*. Berkeley: University of California Press, 1988.

Taylor, Charles. *Hegel*. Cambridge: Cambridge University Press, 1975.

Taylor, Paul. *Mexican Labor in the United States*. Berkeley: University of California Press, 1930.

Thomas, Robert J. *Citizenship, Gender, and Work: Social Organization of Industrial Agriculture*. Berkeley: University of California Press, 1985.

Thompson, E. P. *The Making of the English Working Class*. London: Penguin, 1963.

Tickell, Adam, and Jamie Peck. "Social Regulation after Fordism: Regulation Theory, Neo-Liberalism and the Global-Local Nexus." *Economy and Society* 24, no. 3 (1995): 357–86.

Todes, Charlotte. *Labor and Lumber*. New York: International Publishers, 1931.

U.S. Bureau of the Census. *Fourteenth Census of the United States*. Vol. 10, *Manufacturing, 1919*. Washington: Government Printing Office, 1923.

U.S. Congress. Senate. Committee on Interstate and Foreign Commerce. *Fisheries Legislation: Hearing before the Committee on Interstate and Foreign Commerce*. 85th Cong., 2nd sess., 15–17 July 1958. Washington: Government Printing Office, 1959.

———. Committee on Interstate and Foreign Commerce. *Fisheries Legislation: Hearings before the Senate Committee on Interstate and Foreign Commerce*. 84th Cong., 2nd sess., 10 October–5 December 1955. Washington: Government Printing Office, 1956.

———. Committee on Interstate and Foreign Commerce. *Pacific Coast* and Alaska Fisheries: Hearings before Committee on Interstate and Foreign Commerce. 84th Cong., 2nd sess., 10 October–5 December 1955. Washington: Government Printing Office, 1956.

———. Subcommittee on Merchant Marine and Fisheries. *Fisheries Legislation: Hearings before the Senate Committee on Commerce.* 88th Cong., 1st sess., 8, 24, 25, 27 May 1963. Washington: Government Printing Office, 1964.

U.S. Department of Agriculture, Farmer's Cooperative Service. "Summary of Legal Cases, Legal Series No. 1." Washington, April 1957.

———. "Summary of Legal Cases, Legal Series No. 12." Washington, April 1960.

U.S. Department of Labor, Bureau of Labor Statistics. *Employment Outlook in Petroleum Production and Refining.* Washington: Government Printing Office, 1950.

———. *Occupational Wage Survey: Los Angeles, California.* Bull. 1094. Washington: Government Printing Office, 1952.

———. "Wages and Hours of Labor in Petroleum Refineries." *Monthly Labor Review* 41, no. 5 (1935): 1308–12.

———. *Wages and Hours of Labor in the Lumber Industry in the United States: 1925.* Washington: Government Printing Office, 1926.

———. *Wage Structure: Petroleum Production and Refining.* Report 83, Series 2. Washington: Government Printing Office, 1952.

———. *Wage Structure: Petroleum Refining, 1948.* Report 71, Series 2. Washington: Government Printing Office, 1948.

———. "Work Stoppages Caused by Labor-Management Disputes in 1945." Bull. 8781, 1946.

U.S. Federal Trade Commission. *Annual Reports.* Washington: Government Printing Office, 1954–58.

———. *Report of the Federal Trade Commission on Distribution Methods and Costs, Part IX: Cost of Production and Distribution of Fish on the Pacific Coast.* Washington: Government Printing Office, 1946.

U.S. Fish and Wildlife Service. *Fishery Statistics of the United States, 1942–1957.* Washington: Government Printing Office, 1946–59.

Viehe, Fred W. "Black Gold Suburbs: The Influence of the Extractive Industry on the Suburbanization of Los Angeles, 1890–1930." *Journal of Urban History* 8, no. 1 (1981): 3–26.

Walker, Richard A. "California's Golden Road to Riches: Natural Resources and Regional Capitalism, 1848–1940." *Annals of the Association of American Geographers* 91, no. 1 (2001): 167–99.

Walras, Léon. *Elements of Pure Economics, or, The Theory of Social Wealth.* Translated by William Jaffé. London: Royal Economic Society, 1954.

Ware, Caroline F., and Gardiner Means. *The Modern Economy in Action.* New York: Harcourt, Brace and Co., 1936.

Weber, Devra. *Dark Sweat, White Gold: California Farmworkers, Cotton, and the New Deal.* Berkeley: University of California Press, 1994.

Weed, Abner E., Jr. "Weed: The Evolution of a Company Town." M.A. thesis, California State University, Chico, 1974.

Weed Bicentennial Committee. *Weed . . . The Way It Was.* Weed, Calif.: Weed Bicentennial Committee, 1976.

Weed Chamber of Commerce. "Abner Weed." *Siskiyou Pioneer* 7, no. 3 (2000): 1–2.

Weinker, Curtis W. "McNary: A Predominantly Black Company Town in Arizona." *Negro History Bulletin* 37, no. 5 (1974): 282–85.

Weintraub, Hyman. "The IWW in California." M.A. thesis, University of California, Los Angeles, 1947.

Weiss, Andrew. *Efficiency Wages: Models of Unemployment, Layoffs, and Wage Dispersion.* Princeton, N.J.: Princeton University Press, 1990.

Wellman, David. *The Union Makes Us Strong: Radical Unionism on the San Francisco Waterfront.* Cambridge: Cambridge University Press, 1997.

Wells, Miriam. *Strawberry Fields: Politics, Class and Work in California Agriculture.* Ithaca, N.Y.: Cornell University Press, 1996.

———. "What Is a Worker? The Role of Sharecroppers in Contemporary Class Structure." *Politics and Society* 13 (1984): 295–320.

Wheeler, Hoyt N. *Industrial Conflict: An Integrative Theory.* Columbia: University of South Carolina Press, 1985.

White, Richard. *Organic Machine: The Remaking of the Columbia River.* New York: Hill and Wang, 1995.

Willis, Paul. *Learning to Labor: How Working Class Kids Get Working Class Jobs.* New York: Columbia University Press, 1977.

Wolf, Eric. *Peasant Wars of the Twentieth Century.* New York: Harper and Row, 1969.

Wright, Erik Olin. *Class Counts: Comparative Studies in Class Analysis.* Cambridge: Cambridge University Press, 1996.

———. *Classes.* New York: Verso, 1985.

Wright, Gavin. "American Agriculture and the Labor Market: Whatever Happened to Proletarianization?" *Agricultural History* 62, no. 3 (1988): 182–209.

———. "Labor History and Labor Economics." In *The Future of Economic History,* edited by Alexander Field, 313–41. Boston: Kluwer Nijhoff, 1987.

———. *Old South, New South: Revolutions in the Southern Economy since the Civil War.* Baton Rouge: Louisiana State University Press, 1996.

Young, Iris Marion. *Justice and the Politics of Difference.* Princeton, N.J.: Princeton University Press, 1990.

Index

Breadwinner ideology, 4, 63–68, 72–73, 76–77. *See also* Gender; Masculinity; Women

Bridges, Harry (president, International Longshoreman's and Warehouseman's Union), 121

Brotherhood of Carpenters and Joiners, 101

Bunyan, Paul, 15, 113

Burawoy, Michael, 44, 186 (n. 78)

Butler, Judith, 156, 178 (n. 40)

Calculation, 21–22, 34, 146

California, 4, 11–12, 51–113 passim

California State Reconstruction and Reemployment Commission (CSRRC), 75

Canada, 116, 119, 174–75 (n. 3)

Cannery workers, 119, 128, 131, 201 (n. 11)

Capitalism, 1–210

Chinese workers, 97–98, 149

Church, 74, 87, 89

Citizenship, 141, 150, 153, 155, 167–70; economic, 52, 55, 63–68, 72, 187–88 (n. 1); and labor, 176 (n. 18); industrial, 193 (n. 79)

Civil War (United States), 184 (n. 56)

Class, 23, 31, 41, 152, 166–70; relation to race, 5–10; centrality of, 10; ambiguity of, 11, 115–18, 123, 204 (n. 48); politics of, 76–79, 137–41, 153–54; class consciousness, 117, 123, 126, 130, 134, 137–38, 156, 188 (n. 7), 201 (n. 4), 204 (n. 53); class analysis, 127–30, 134, 154; class war, 139; theory of, 153–57, 205 (n. 65); class-in-itself vs. class-for-itself, 154; and interpellation, 156; class primacy, 175–76 (n. 12); historical-geographic specificity of, 201 (n. 4), 204 (n. 53); class structure, 205 (n. 61); and post-

Marxism, 210 (n. 31). *See also* Race: race-class relation

Clayton Act, 134, 136, 202 (n. 25)

Coase, Ronald, 183 (n. 47)

Cohen, G. A., 31, 45

Cold War, 188 (n. 8)

Collective bargaining, 41, 183–84 (n. 52), 201 (n. 12); regulationists on, 38; and Fordism, 62; and contractual mechanisms, 68–75; and unionism, 119–20, 124, 137. *See also* Unionization; Wage: negotiation of; Working day

Colton, Calvin (U.S. economist), xv

Columbia River Fishermen's Protective Union (CRFPU), 118–19, 128–29, 132, 136

Columbia River Packers Association, 134–35

Common property, 128–29, 131, 140, 201 (n. 4), 208 (n. 115)

Commons, John, 183 (n. 47)

Communism, 61, 74, 140, 203 (nn. 26, 31); and anticommunism, 78, 120–21. *See also* Congress of Industrial Organizations: trial of communists in; Taft-Hartley Act

Congress of Industrial Organizations (CIO), 59, 71–72, 74–75, 78, 119, 202 (n. 23); trial of communists in, 121, 133, 203 (nn. 30, 31). *See also* International Fishermen and Allied Workers of America; International Longshoreman's and Warehouseman's Union; Oil Workers International Union; United Automobile Workers

Connally Amendment, 139

Contracts. *See* Collective bargaining

Cooperatives, 125–27, 206 (n. 88), 208 (n. 111). *See also* Petty commodity production

Corlett, William, 177 (n. 36)

Fordism, 37–38, 53, 72, 183 (n. 45), 188 (n. 8). *See also* Gramsci, Antonio; Regulation school

Fort Bragg (Calif.), 129

Freedom, 1–2, 18, 115–16, 140, 150, 152, 170

Friedman, Milton, 29

Future, politics of, 152, 157–61

Garvey, Marcus, 109, 200 (n. 85), 207 (n. 108)

Gender, 23, 40, 51–81 passim, 85, 149–50, 153–55, 191 (n. 58); and interpellation, 156; and social hierarchy, 166–67; and citizenship, 187–88 (n. 1); in cannery work, 201 (n. 11). *See also* Breadwinner ideology; Masculinity; Women

General Motors, 77

Geras, Norman, 209 (n. 28)

Gerstle, Gary, 188 (n. 8)

Giddens, Anthony, 150–51

Gilroy, Paul, 9

Glaberman, Martin, 188 (n. 8)

Goldmann, Lucien, 210 (n. 37)

Gompers, Samuel (president, American Federation of Labor), 98

Gorz, André, 175 (n. 5)

Government, 130, 139–41; federal, 116, 120, 128–29, 134; state, 116, 128; purchasing of fish by, 120, 202 (n. 24); and World War II propaganda, 192 (n. 64). *See also* California State Reconstruction and Reemployment Commission; Federal Trade Commission; U.S. Department of Labor; U.S. Forest Service

Gramsci, Antonio, xiv–xv, 21, 38, 50, 140, 148, 150, 182 (n. 42), 210 (n. 37); on "Fordism," 37, 44, 144; on ideology, 45; and "war of position," 123; on hegemony, 143–47, 164, 198 (n. 54); Sraffa's

relation to, 143–47, 208 (n. 2); *Prison Notebooks*, 144; as critical theorist, 163

Great Accord. *See* Fordism

Great Migration, 89–90, 106, 196 (n. 17), 200 (n. 82). *See also* African Americans: migrants from southern United States

Greene, Lorenzo, 107

Hall, Stuart, 8–9, 16, 45, 78, 150, 155, 208 (n. 1)

Harris, Abram, 107

Harvey, David, 10, 42, 127; *Limits to Capital*, 184–85 (n. 63), 187 (n. 103)

Hegel, G. W. F., 15, 21, 81, 178 (n. 42); and dialectic, 13, 16, 26–28, 158–59, 177 (n. 32), 210 (n. 37); and measure, 26–28; and history, 118; and Marx, 177 (n. 35); *Logic*, 179 (nn. 9, 13), 180 (n. 14)

Hegemony, xv, 92, 140–41, 149, 160. *See also* Gramsci, Antonio; Ideology; Przeworski, Adam

Herod, Andrew, 54–55

Hicks, John, 34–35, 181 (nn. 23, 24)

Hirschman, Albert, 153

History, 10, 158; historicism, xv, 18, 32, 158, 204 (n. 53). *See also* Dialectic

Holt, Thomas, 9

Homo economicus, 30

Housing, 74, 87–88, 95, 103

Ideology, 157; regulationists on, 38; neo-Marxians on, 44; and capitalism, 73, 123, 141, 150; practical, 78; race and, 105; and history, 112; fishers', 129; and war effort, 192 (n. 64). *See also* Hegemony

Indeterminacy, 26, 28–50, 118, 150,

Labor: reserve army of, 31, 47, 187
(n. 94); division of, 65, 81, 84;
labor contractors, 86, 88, 97, 103,
200 (n. 82); mobility of, 98, 100,
103, 106–7, 132, 184 (n. 43);
seasonality of, 131–32
Labor market, 7, 29, 33, 36, 41, 47,
69, 132, 165–66; segmented,
39–40, 85, 105, 109–10, 195 (n. 3),
208 (n. 11); institutionalist theory
of, 39–41, 45, 148, 184 (nn. 53,
56); regional, 85, 149, 191 (n. 58)
Labor movement, 53; and deradicalization, 54; and spatial fix,
54; in World War II, 56–58; and
post–World War II reconversion,
58, 68, 70
Labor process, 69, 77, 81, 84–85,
88–89, 98, 106, 110, 186 (n. 78);
Marx on, 207 (n. 103)
Laclau, Ernesto, 153–54, 209 (n. 28),
210 (n. 31)
Laissez-faire, 130, 140–41
Langford, James, 195 (n. 1)
Lassalle, Ferdinand, 185 (n. 64)
Lenin, V. I., 177 (n. 35)
Levenstein, Harvey, 78
Liberalism, xiv, 7, 37, 118, 141, 152,
169, 178 (n. 40)
Lichtenstein, Nelson, 55, 188 (n. 8)
Lipsitz, George, 188 (n. 8), 198
(n. 54)
Liquor, 101–2
Little Steel formula, 67, 69, 192
(n. 75). *See also* National War
Labor Board
Long, Robert A., 90, 92–94. *See also*
Long-Bell Lumber Company
Long-Bell Lumber Company, 82–113.
See also Long, Robert A.; Weed
Lumber Company
Longview (Wash.), 97, 195 (n. 7)
Longville (La.), 87, 89, 97
Los Angeles (Calif.), 4, 15, 52–79

passim, 113; importance of oil in,
56, 61, 190 (n. 41); war industries
in, 56–57, 191 (n. 58); organized
labor in, 58, 69, 72–75, 129, 166,
189 (n. 12); postwar era in, 58–59,
149; port of, 122–23, 133. *See also*
Oil Workers International Union
Los Angeles Times, 56, 61, 74
Lukács, Georg, 15, 17, 45, 158–59,
210 (n. 37)
Lumber industry. *See* Timber
industry
Luxemburg, Rosa, 10, 157, 160, 163,
170, 185 (n. 64), 210 (n. 37)

Malthus, Thomas, 180 (n. 17)
Marginalism, 180 (n. 16), 181 (n. 24).
See also Economics; Wage theory:
neoclassical
Marglin, Stephen, 22, 37, 42
Market clearing, 29–35, 47
Market socialism, 204 (n. 48)
Marshall, Alfred, 46, 104–5, 182
(n. 34)
Marshall, Ray, 105
Marx, Karl, xii–xiii, 1, 29, 33–34,
171, 191 (n. 53), 210 (n. 37);
Capital, 1–2, 16, 169; on dialectic,
15, 18; *Contribution to the
Critique of Political Economy*,
16; *Manifesto of the Communist
Party*, 16; *Grundrisse*, 16, 158;
and "economic determinism,"
16, 187 (n. 92); theory of history,
16–17, 28, 31, 48, 110, 118–19,
158, 177 (n. 36); on commodity,
23, 137; value theory, 25, 136,
179 (nn. 8, 13); and Ricardo,
41–43, 180 (n. 16), 185 (n. 70); on
labor-power, 43–44, 186 (n. 73),
207 (n. 103); on class, 127–28,
205 (n. 65); on free labor, 140;
as critical theorist, 160, 163; and
Hegel, 177 (n. 35), 179 (n. 13),

116–18, 123–24, 132, 137–38, 201
(nn. 3, 4), 204 (nn. 48, 53)
Piece rates, 137
Piore, Michael, 184 (n. 53)
Polanyi, Karl, 165, 178–79 (n. 5), 180
(n. 21)
Political ecology, 117–18, 123, 127–28,
139–41; dialectic in, 205 (n. 62)
Populism, xii, 37, 149, 191 (n. 54)
Positivism, 6
Postone, Moishe, 16, 164, 177 (n. 35),
179 (n. 8)
Poulantzas, Nicos, 76
Price, 129, 136, 149; price mechanism,
36, 93, 183 (n. 47); politics of, 53,
71–72; price structure, 120, 126;
price discrimination, 131–32, 137;
price fixing, 134–37
Price controls. *See* Office of Price
Administration
Prince William Sound (Alaska), 133
Prisoners' dilemma, 181 (n. 28)
Profits, 36, 149; excess, 192 (n. 75)
Prohibition, 101
Property, 12, 149. *See also* Common
property
Prudham, Scott, 179 (n. 5)
Przeworski, Adam, 37, 78, 144–47,
149–50, 156, 208 (nn. 10, 11), 209
(n. 15)
Puget Sound (Wash.), 129, 133
Purchasing power, 57, 62–63, 72–73,
191 (n. 54); Marx on, 182 (n. 39);
and Truman administration, 190
(n. 38)

Quantity and quality. *See* Measure,
politics of

Race, 23, 40, 81–113 passim, 153;
race-class relation, 6–10, 149,
153, 155–56, 175–76 (n. 12); and
region, 96, 104; and job quality, 97,
100, 105; race hierarchy, 99, 108,

150, 166–70; and interpellation,
156; as biological, 208–9 (n. 11).
See also African Americans;
Racism; Whiteness; White
supremacy
Racism, 5, 87, 97, 101–2, 104–7, 109,
166
Regulation school, 37–38, 62, 71,
182–83 (n. 44), 183 (n. 45)
Reich, Michael, 8–9, 40, 44
Resource capitalism, 11, 167
Reuther, Walter (president, United
Automobile Workers), 62
Ricardo, David, 29, 33, 41–43, 47–48.
See also Wage theory: classical
Robinson, Joan, 36, 166, 182 (n. 35)
Roediger, David, xv, 99–100, 104, 198
(n. 54)
Roemer, John, 45–46, 186 (n. 82)
Romm, Jeff, 210 (n. 10)
Rosdolsky, Roman, 157, 175 (n. 5),
180 (n. 14), 183 (n. 45), 189
(n. 26)
Ross, Arthur, 51–52
Rothschild, Kurt, 22
Rowthorn, Bob, 45

Sacramento River Fishermen's Union,
121
Samuelson, Paul, 41–42, 48, 185
(n. 64)
San Francisco (Calif.), 87, 121–22,
133
San Pedro (Calif.), 121, 129, 202
(n. 25)
Saxton, Alexander, 9, 11, 99
Schwantes, Carlos, 12
Schwellenbach, L. B. (secretary of
labor, 1945–49), 59
Seasonality. *See* Labor: seasonality of
Seattle (Wash.), 122, 131, 133
Segregation, 89, 97–99. *See also*
Housing; Jim Crow; Racism
Shares system, 135–36

129, 132–34, 148, 201 (n. 4), 204
(nn. 51, 53), 206 (n. 88)
Union Oil Company, 61, 63, 70
United Automobile Workers (UAW),
59, 62, 77
United Fishermen's Union (UFU),
119
U.S. Department of Labor, 59, 91, 95,
98, 197 (n. 40)
U.S. Forest Service, 112
U.S. Steel, 140
Utility, 34, 51–52, 143, 147, 152, 160

Value, 2, 23, 26–28, 43; exchange
value and use value, 24, 28, 51,
155; surplus, 44, 49, 148–49, 184
(n. 56); labor theory of, 48, 179
(n. 8); politics of, 139, 155, 167;
immanent theory of, 160. *See also*
Interests; Measure, politics of
Vigilantism, 102
V-J Day (Victory in Japan, 14 August
1945), 4, 56, 58, 202 (n. 23). *See
also* World War II

Wage: determination of, 3, 22–50,
100, 113, 139, 147, 149, 165, 181
(n. 22); cultural politics of, 6–7,
10, 41, 46, 84–85, 115, 139, 143,
163; definition of, 7, 115–16,
150; and nonwage benefits, 21,
160; negotiation of, 24, 35, 51–79
passim, 150; models of, 30–31,
181 (n. 28); wage rate vs. wage
share, 32, 42–43, 146, 148–49;
wage inequality, 35, 69–70, 193
(n. 81); wage rigidity, 35–36,
38–39; subsistence, 42–43, 46, 49,
148, 185 (n. 64); as golden chain,
43, 148, 169–70; wage legitimation,
44–45, 144–48; racial differentials
in, 82, 97, 175 (n. 4), 180–81
(n. 22); regional differentials in, 88,
90, 195 (n. 12), 200 (n. 78); wage-
price, 136–38; wage differentials,
146, 193 (nn. 79, 84)
Wages fund, 182 (n. 34), 185 (n. 69)
Wage theory: economic, 4, 22–23, 28,
34; sociological, 23; Keynesian,
29, 31–41, 165, 180 (n. 20), 181
(n. 31), 182 (nn. 34, 35, 37), 183
(n. 45); classical, 29, 33, 41–43,
49, 185 (n. 70); institutional,
29, 33–41, 139, 148, 151, 165;
neoclassical, 29–41, 44–45, 48, 139,
144, 147–48, 165, 183 (nn. 47, 49,
52); and efficiency, 32, 84, 146;
Marxian, 41–44, 48, 148, 151, 183
(n. 45), 184 (n. 63); as critical, 43,
165–66; and neo-Marxian theory,
45–47; Sraffian, 47–50, 145–47,
150, 165–66; pre-Ricardian, 180
(n. 16). *See also* Institutionalism;
Keynes, John Maynard; Labor
market; Marxism; Wage
Wagner Act, 120
Walker, Richard, 11–12
Walras, Léon, 181 (n. 24)
Ware, Caroline, 191 (n. 54)
War Powers Act, 59
Weed, Abner, 87, 90
Weed (Calif.), 82–113 passim, 148,
166, 195 (nn. 7, 16), 197 (n. 40),
198 (n. 43)
Weed Lumber Company, 86–87, 90,
94–95
Wells, Miriam, 9, 11, 204 (n. 48)
White, J. M. (manager, Weed Lumber
Company), 95, 97
Whiteness, xi, xiii, 5, 7, 13–19, 96, 99,
104, 106, 154, 176–77 (n. 30), 199
(n. 61); studies of, 198–99 (n. 54)
White supremacy, 101–2, 109, 113,
189 (n. 8), 199 (n. 57)
Willis, Paul, 45, 163
Wittgenstein, Ludwig, 48
Wobblies. *See* Industrial Workers of
the World